Best of Friends

Alan Thornhill

This was given to me by
Father José

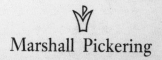

Marshall Pickering

Front cover photographs: top row: *Bishop Peter Ball and 'The Three Mile Man',* bottom row: *Muriel Smith, actress, and Malcolm Muggeridge.*

Back cover photograph: the author enjoying a walk with Malcolm Muggeridge.

Marshall Morgan and Scott
Marshall Pickering
3 Beggarwood Lane, Basingstoke, Hants RG23 7LP, UK

Copyright © 1986 By Alan Thornhill

First published in 1986 by Marshall Morgan and Scott
Publications Ltd
Part of the Marshall Pickering Holdings Group
A subsidiary of the Zondervan Corporation

British Library Cataloguing in Publication Data
Thornhill, Alan
 Best of Friends
 1. Friendship 2. Christian Life
 I. Title
 248.4   BV4647.F7

 ISBN 0–551–01395–8

Phototypeset in Linotron Ehrhardt
by Input Typesetting Ltd, London
Printed in Great Britain by
Guernsey Press Ltd, Channel Islands, UK

Contents

1: Theme and Variations   1
2: Three Muggeridges   10
3: The Family   28
4: Mrs Charles   40
5: Bunny and the Boss   50
6: Encounter with Frank Buchman   58
7: Cruttwell   75
8: Sumi   87
9: B H Streeter   103
10: Another Stage   122
11: Artur   137
12: Muriel Smith   154
13: Bishops   167
14: Three Mile Man   183
15: Peter and the Dragon   191
16: Bishop Peter   202
17: The Eternal Friendship   212

Acknowledgements

The creation of this book has been for me a rich experience of friendship.

My special thanks are due to Kenneth Belden, a friend from Oxford days, whose constant, detailed care for both book and author has made it all possible.

Gratitude also to John Bright-Holmes, Joan Kendall, Richard and Patricia Ducé, Hugh Elliott, Joanna Sciortino, Nancy Walters, Ruth Warrington, and above all Hugh Nowell, who have been most generous in their help.

Alan Thornhill
1986

The extract from G H Wilson's book *The History of Windlesham House School* is reproduced by kind permission of The Governors of the Malden Trust, Windlesham House School.

The quotation from the poem 'Hell Gate' by A E Housman is reproduced by kind permission of the Society of Authors and of Jonathan Cape Ltd.

Material appearing in Chapter 14: Three Mile Man originally appeared in *Three Mile Man* by Alan Thornhill and is reproduced by permission of Collins Publishers.

1

Theme and Variations

It was a dark December afternoon, and St Mary's Road stretched like a long tunnel ahead. Down at the grander end of the street the tall grey walls of Victorian houses loomed on either side. These had once been the homes of the carriage folk, back in the days when Peckham was a desirable suburb on the edge of South London. Now some of these houses contained the worst slums in the area. At the other end the houses were smaller and all alike, more than a hundred of them.

As I stood there looking up the road, I felt like a lonely spy in enemy territory. Although it was nearly Christmas, there were no visible signs of Christmas cheer behind the muslin curtains. The aspidistras did not beckon. There were few passers-by at that hour in the afternoon. My grey clerical suit (five guineas from Wippells) seemed stiff and heavy. The unfamiliar collar grated under my chin. This was the climactic moment of a long and expensive education; prep school, Repton, Oxford, then a year abroad and theological college. Yesterday I had kneeled in the chancel of Southwark Cathedral, all awe and burnished gold, to receive from the Bishop God's commission to be a parson: 'Take thou authority to read the Gospel . . . and to preach the same.'

My trunk, still unpacked, was heavy with books. There were piles of notes, lectures from some of the best minds in Oxford; talks on pastoral psychology from Professor L W Grensted. ('We will divide people into three categories; the sane, the insane, and ourselves.') Practical tips from visiting vicars. ('Remember, girls will laugh at you for one of two reasons—either because you are good-looking or because you aren't.') All very wise and witty, but what help were they now? Here was the moment of truth.

My vicar believed the best way to teach a curate was to throw him in at the deep end. 'Go out into St Mary's Road, introduce yourself, tell people who you are and that you have just come to work at St Mary's Church.'

But which house to choose? How to begin? I prayed and chose a door. I knocked boldly. I tried a second time. The door was on a chain and it opened a few inches. A rough voice snarled through the crack. 'Yes? What do you want?'

'I am the new curate at St Mary's Church down there. I just wanted to say "how-do-you-do?" '

The door remained on its chain. 'Oh? And how long have you been here?'

'Three days.'

'And how long have you been a clergyman?'

'Just since yesterday.'

'Do you know these parts at all?'

'No, I have never been here before.'

The chain came off the door. It opened and there stood a large and formidable lady, her arms folded fiercely across her ample bosom, as she looked me up and down.

'How old are you?'

'Twenty-three.'

Then with a sigh, 'Poor young man. It makes me feel queer all over.'

Then with a sudden smile. 'Have a glass of sherry, dear.'

I went in. The joy was unspeakable. I had found my first friend in the parish.

Friendship begins, grows and flourishes in mutual discovery. My wife, who is an American, is by temperament and training more apt to show her feelings than I, who am the product of an English public school and the tradition of the 'stiff upper-lip'. When, during our occasionally stormy engagement, something went wrong, either between us or with someone else, she could explode like a box of rockets. My instinct would be to try and calm her down, pour oil on troubled waters, reduce things to their proper proportions, turn mountains into molehills. A few days later I might appear on the scene unusually silent, glum and moody.

'What's the matter?' Barbara would ask.

'Nothing.'

'You don't look very happy.'

'I'm fine. Leave me alone.'

After a few more attempts at conversation, Barbara said as she gently kissed my forehead, 'I wish there was a little television set in there, where I could turn a few knobs and get a picture of what's happening.'

'Well, perhaps I've been feeling a trifle upset about that incident the other day.'

'What incident?'

She had forgotten all about it. I of course had been seething with a mounting turbulence only painfully beginning to come to the surface, if, indeed, it ever came to the surface at all. It would take a lot of patience and insight on her part, and honesty on mine, before we could begin to get our reactions 'in sync', and eventually to enjoy the difference between us.

I owe to my wife, more than to anyone else, the discovery that difference can be the very spice of friendship. Barbara van Dyke grew up in the hectic jazz and Prohibition era in the United States. Her father worked on Wall Street. He helped to promote and publicize Thomas J Watson, founder of IBM, pioneers of the computer age. By the age of seventeen Barbara had her own sports car, with a string of boy friends in tow at dances at Princeton and Dartmouth, or in less exalted places. Soon she was trying her hand at dirt track racing and learning to fly, or occasionally standing in for Harriet as vocalist in Ozzie Nelson's band. There were visits to speakeasies ('Knock three times and ask for Charlie') mostly for the fun of not getting caught. You could always make gin in the bath-tub. My boyhood in a country rectory was a happy but fairly protected one. Compulsory cold morning dips are my vivid bath-tub memories. Books rather than bootleggers were my milieu.

But then Barbara's father died in his early fifties. At the

same time came the Wall Street crash. In Detroit there were thirty-eight suicides in a single weekend. Roosevelt became President and closed the banks. The future was precarious for Barbara's widowed mother and younger brother. The bottom had dropped out of a self-centred life and for the first time Barbara found herself thinking of someone other than herself. When, several years later, I first set eyes on her, she was a caring, faith-filled person, still breezy, spontaneous and unexpected, and to me immensely attractive. We met from time to time, neither of us dreaming of marriage. But I realised that whenever she was around, almost sub-consciously, I would say to myself, 'Good! Life's looking up.'

It was not until after the war, under an English sky, that my deep feelings for Barbara hit me like a thunderbolt. Actually it was Victory Day in London, and after an emotional, exuberant series of parades and celebrations, we both found ourselves in the same party, weary but hilarious, watching the fireworks from Westminster Bridge. It was late, but somebody said, 'I hear that the King and Queen are coming out once more on the balcony at Buckingham Palace.'

Everyone was ready for bed. It was Barbara who said, 'My feet are killing me. I can hardly stand; but I'd like to go to Buckingham Palace again.'

'I'll come with you,' I said, and thought to myself, 'What a girl!'

In that vast, cheering throng, we suddenly felt alone. The King and Queen came out. On a surprisingly unecclesiastical impulse, I tossed Barbara high in the air to give her a better view. I knew who was the Queen in my victory celebration.

For her, after I had proposed, it was a more complicated decision. They say in baseball, 'Three strikes and you're out.' There were quite a few strikes against me. First, I was an Englishman. Barbara was, and often still is, as American as her favourite Fifth Avenue store, Lord and Taylor. After years living in England as my wife, she can still say, 'We always do it this way.' 'Who's we?' I will ask.

Strike two: I am a clergyman. She is a convinced down-to-earth Christian, but even now has not quite come to terms with my round collar.

4

Third strike: I had been an Oxford don and possibly, therefore, a stuck-up intellectual. That was not all. I had become involved in the theatre as a playwright, and even occasionally as a character actor. That meant being temperamental for sure.

Four strikes at least, but fortunately, blessedly, not out. Since then, nearly forty years later, I can say that life with Barbara has not for one day been dull. It has been a continuous adventure. In all that matters most, we are one; our love, our faith, our calling, our delight in our daughter Susan, her husband Rob and our grandchildren. In other things we can be gloriously different and enjoy it.

Every man is an island. In most islands, however, there is, somewhere, a tiny beach, hidden maybe, where a landing may be possible. Even a shared dislike may be enough to begin with. That salty cleric, the Reverend Sydney Smith, remarked to a lady one day, 'Madam, I have been looking for a person who disliked gravy all my life. Let us swear eternal friendship.'

I had an experience of a similar type with a different kind of cleric. I was in Agra, and feeling overwhelmed, after long visits to the Taj Mahal, once by moonlight and again in the early dawn. The Roman Catholic Archbishop of Agra was a friend, and he invited me to join him at lunch with a group of priests from his Province. I found myself next to an aged priest whose look of ascetic holiness and profound wisdom made me feel horribly clumsy and earthy. All my efforts at conversation met with a trance-like series of 'Ahs' and 'Ums' that seemed to drown further exchanges in a kind of mystical marsh. Of course I overdid my wonder and awe over the Taj, a subject of which he was probably very tired. I fared no better with the Ecumenical Movement, or with such scant knowledge of Indian poetry, music and philosophy as I could muster. But as we were just about to rise from the table, I mentioned almost casually that I was glad to see that India had just defeated Australia at cricket in a recent Test match. Suddenly the somnolent old man at my side leapt into life. 'Yes,' he said excitedly, 'and now everything depends on the next match.'

5

The landing was made. Soon we were discussing the respective merits of Pataudi, Bedi, Bobby Simpson and the Chappells. We could scarcely be separated as we shared a common enthusiasm. Friendship was born. Before we parted we were even gently touching on the beauties of the Taj, not to mention Indian philosophy and the Ecumenical Movement.

As a friend, and more particularly as a priest, I have had the hard task of visiting people at some moment of great, almost unbearable sorrow and tragedy. Words seem irrelevant, almost a blasphemy. I remember going to a family where a brilliant, infectiously loving and lovable twenty-one year old son had been suddenly killed in a motor bike accident. I sensed of course the deep shock, plus a strong element of bitterness towards a Christian minister who seemed by the nature of his cloth to be a sort of accomplice in the vengeful act of a cruel God. 'Here we have no faith,' said the daughter of the house defiantly as she answered the door. There was nothing to say, nothing to do, except to be silent as, bit by bit, mother and daughter poured out their anguish. Until at long last silence, blessed silence, began to work its mysterious balm. I don't know how it happened. Slowly they began to talk of the young man's many gifts, above all his gift of friendship. What would mean most to his friends and companions in a funeral service conceived especially for them? Not many of them perhaps, would call themselves Christians. The traditional liturgy would not meet the case. But gradually there were compiled some of the things that had meant most—pieces of music, a few sensitive poems he had written, verses marked in an old Bible or hymn book. The service above all must reflect something of his gaiety and humour and his love of life. In the end we were planning and talking as friends. The funeral service, when it finally happened, was of course heavy with sorrow, but the chapel was crowded with young people and the whole thing was lightened by beauty and thankfulness and by a sense of the loving-kindness of God. Many people afterwards said how they had found there a fresh experience of the meaning of life and love and death.

The friendships described in this book are mostly of the long, lasting variety, enriched over the years, or occasionally won at last out of pain and conflict and finally ripened in love. There are, however, other friendships of a more transitory kind; brushes with a stranger too short to be dignified with the name of friendship, but which nevertheless light up one evening, one occasion, like some mysterious star or comet—and never appear again. Yet they leave a mark on your life that enriches it for ever.

I was a friend of the comedian Wee Georgie Wood, whose tiny stature belied his considerable stature as a man, and the occasional caustic candour of his mind.

He was at one time 'Chief Rat', the President of the Water Rats—the company of Variety artistes who undertake benevolent work in this country.

We were in Switzerland once when he told me he had been invited by the Charlie Chaplins to visit them at their home above Vevey. Would I drive him over? I did, and discreetly stayed in the car outside so as not to intrude.

After a while out came a butler. Would I join the family for supper? It was a magical evening. Charlie and George were both veterans of the old Music Hall days in Britain. Memories were teased, reminiscences began to bubble up. Soon Chaplin was on his feet recalling his first stage experiences, which were with a troupe of young boys, 'The Six Lancashire Lads', none of whom came from Lancashire. He re-enacted the first dance steps, and the little jingle they performed. He impersonated their manager, who prayed with them on all possible occasions and paid them two shillings a week—with sixpence extra if they had a solo line. Fairly soon Wee Georgie was beside him. Stories grew, laughter rocked the room. Theatrical digs! *'Quoth the raven,'* in the visitors' book, as a secret warning to those who might follow: 'Never more. Never more!' Gradually Charlie really got going and let out all the stops. Lightning sketch followed lightning sketch. It was a series of vintage Chaplin performances designed, not for the millions, but just for a handful of friends and family, and for the sheer enjoyment of life. As we said goodbye Oona, his ever-attentive and caring wife,

7

whispered, 'I haven't seen him so happy for years.' I never saw him again, but he seems a friend for ever.

'Our Father', I began formally in a confirmation class that I was taking for a group of teenage boarders at a school of ballet situated in our village.

'I hate my father,' was the instant rejoinder from a fourteen year old. 'I love my mother.'

'No,' contradicted another, 'I love my father. I hate my mother.'

'Sometimes I lie in bed,' chimed in another, 'and hear my dad and mum fighting in the next room. It scares me.'

'Last holidays my dad said to me, "If your mother and I decide to break up, which would you rather go with?" '

Then there followed a flood of tears. Others more fortunate had constructive things to offer. It was moving to hear one trying to help or comfort another. We did not get very far in the Lord's Prayer that night and yet perhaps we got further than with many a formal instruction. Suddenly we were not a class, we were friends. I certainly learnt more about modern family life and issues like divorce than I had from books on marriage problems or Church Synod debates.

One friendship with a young man was infinitely sad and yet at the same time rich and enjoyable. Mark had muscular dystrophy, one of the most mysterious and most terrible of all hereditary illnesses. His body was a little shell, his mind and spirit that of a growing man. My visits to him began as a duty. Very soon they developed into a delight. Mark had a genius for friendship. Young men with long hair and odd manners would spend hours with him, designing model planes or painting coloured soldiers, or maybe just talking. Girls would adopt him as a favourite boy friend. The old gardener across the road would drop in for regular visits. For myself, I shall remember forever the day, near the end of his life, when he took me round the garden, he in his electric wheelchair, and we were suddenly able to talk naturally about life and death, fear and faith. Mark's parents devised every imaginative idea to give him at least a glimpse of normal life, whether it be flying model aeroplanes from a wheelchair, or even arranging for him to take a flight in a real plane. They and his sister attended to his every need, at the end turning him over every two hours. Mark died at twenty-one, older than most dystrophy patients. His short life lives on in the memory of a host of friends, and in the active work of many others who give and sacrifice to enable vital research to be undertaken to end this terrible disease.

Here then is the theme: Friendship. The chapters that follow are the variations: Friends. If most of the sketches in this book deal with some aspect of spiritual discovery, that is where my life has lain. If several touch on the life and work of Moral Re-Armament, that is because, since the age of twenty-two, my life has been lived in a fellowship known by millions, yet still little understood, difficult to describe or explain, but vivid and adventurous, unique and unexpected, to those who have a chance to share in it.*

* The Oxford Group, initiated by Frank Buchman in the 1920's came to be called Moral Re-Armament after his call in 1938 for moral and spiritual re-armament, urging the need for active Christian commitment in face of the mounting threats of war from totalitarian ideologies. After the war, the conference centre at Caux, in Switzerland, established by Swiss initiative, became a focus of reconciliation, notably between France and Germany, as well as in European industry, with Japan, among some of the emerging countries of Africa and in many other fields. Several thousand take part in the Caux assemblies every year. Moral Re-Armament strives for both a deeper and more effective Christian experience and for the widest application of faith to the issues of society.

2

Three Muggeridges

'By the way,' said Malcolm Muggeridge, over a third or fourth cup of tea, 'my brother Douglas has come to live in your village. You won't see him around though—he devotes his entire time and energy to looking after his wife, who's very ill. He has to do everything for her and he's only got one arm. He's the eldest of us brothers, an extraordinary chap really. I suppose in his way he's becoming a kind of saint.'

It was not many days later that I discovered where Douglas Muggeridge and his wife lived in Rotherfield, not far from my home in Sussex, and knocked at the door of their simple bungalow. It was as Malcolm had said. Mrs Muggeridge was extremely ill and scarcely able to communicate. Douglas, at first appearance, was not quite my idea of a saint. He looked more like a kind of roguish Friar Tuck; solid, moving rapidly about the house smoking cheroots, talking away without ever letting his eyes go far from the bed where his wife lay. With his left arm no more than a short stump, he made me think irreverently of a one-armed bandit.

But Malcolm was right. Douglas was a completely dedicated man. He told me much later that for ten months he had never had more than one hour's unbroken sleep. His wife needed turning over or he had to get her out of bed. She was a large woman and heavy. Douglas was over eighty. He rigged up a kind of pulley device for lifting her, using his forehead instead of a second arm. He nursed her, washed her, cooked for her, attended to all the messy details. There was nothing else in his life; no distractions, no side issues, no divided loyalties. It was as if he had taken vows. And of course he had; the vows of matrimony, more than fifty years before. He was fulfilling them 'for better, for worse . . . in sickness and in health' and intended to go on doing so, if he could, 'till death us do part.'

Not long after I met him Mrs Muggeridge died. Douglas moved away for a time and I heard of him in Tunbridge Wells. I had a feeling he had fought a good fight, he had finished his course; soon, perhaps, he would follow his wife into a Beyond in which he found it very hard to believe.

A year or so later, reconstruction started in the old 'Sweet Shoppe' in the middle of our village. Imagine my surprise when I discovered that the new owner was none other than Douglas Muggeridge, embarking on an entirely new chapter in his long and eventful life. In a very short time 'the Colonel', as he became known, was adopted by the village and his picture gallery and bookshop became a feature of Rotherfield. For browsers like myself it was an idyll. My friend 'the one-armed bandit' was the kindest and most gracious host imaginable. There was no pressure to buy—as a card in the window assured the tentative visitor—you were free to poke around for as long as you cared to. When I ventured to make some modest purchase I often found I had to work hard to prevent him from offering some impossibly unprofitable reduction, or even from pressing it on me as a gift. The Colonel's shop was a kind of cultural and social centre for all sorts of people. The sharp little bell which tinkled in the back room whenever the front door was pushed open rang steadily through the day. Behind the courteous welcome and the casual exterior was a shrewd business mind. The Colonel had in his time run four or five different businesses. He made a success of each one and then got bored and sold it or almost gave it away to some younger person whom he had trained and helped to establish.

He lived alone above the shop, except for a large, lively dog. He mostly fended for himself, though he had a way of enlisting the help of neighbours and friends. I took to dropping in quite often as I passed. There was always a warm welcome. 'Sit down, old boy. Let me make you a cup of tea or browse around if you want to. It's good to see you.' He loved to talk.

When I have to preach an Armistice sermon I like, if I can, to find somebody who actually served in the First World War and ask them to tell me something at first hand about it. Knowing that Douglas had a distinguished career in both world wars, I turned to him.

'Don't glamorize the war, old boy,' he said. 'It was a ghastly experience. At the age of seventeen I killed a man. I shot him at point-blank range. If I hadn't got him he would have got me. I was wounded three times, but I always managed to get back into the front line. When I came out of it all I was an impossible, conceited, unbearable little squirt, flaunting my ribbons, with all the girls falling over themselves to find one of the few who had survived. The one thing that saved me,' he said, 'was a good middle class wife. She brought me down to earth with a bump.'

The last years of their marriage before his wife died must have been a difficult and painful time for them both. But, 'They were the happiest years of my life,' he said. 'I was wholly content to serve her.'

'You know,' he would say, 'I'm afraid I don't share Malcolm's faith. I truly wish I did. It would be wonderful to believe but I just can't. I never have. I can't see anything beyond this life.'

One day I ventured to say, 'Perhaps, Douglas, you might be in for a surprise.' That seemed to stick in his mind and more than once he said, 'You know that was a clever reply. I've been thinking about it quite a lot.'

Our relationship took a new and dramatic turn with the publication of a book called *Three Mile Man*. 'The Man' in question was Peter Warnett, who had helped us in our garden week by week for many years; a man who had absorbed the lore of the countryside since his boyhood, and who was a self-taught photographer. The book contained Peter's remarkable photographs of every living thing observed within three miles of Rotherfield Church, together with a text I had written. Malcolm wrote an introduction to the book and, indeed, it was through Malcolm that the book ever came into being at all (see Chapter 14).

When *Three Mile Man* was due to come out, an elegant and satisfying production, worth every bit of its price, the Colonel charged into the fray with all his energy and business acumen. He got brother Malcolm over on publishing day to join a signing session, and half the district seemed to come pouring in to meet the authors and buy their signed copies. The sales went on and on. Each time new consignments arrived from Collins the Colonel would organize a new book-signing occasion.

After two or three of these affairs, when yet another was proposed, I would say to Douglas, 'Look, for goodness sake, don't bother Malcolm any more. He's signed quite enough of our books. What about all the books of his own that he needs to sign? Don't ask him to come again this time.'

'Nonsense,' Douglas would reply. 'He can come. Do him good.' I realized that 'young Malcolm', of whom Douglas was secretly proud and whom he loved dearly, was still rather a callow youth who could do with some fraternal discipline!

I suppose it can't be easy to be the brother of so well-known a figure. Douglas's education had been cut short by the outbreak of the First World War. He had never had the advantage of university. He did not share Malcolm's vast literary knowledge or his prose style. There may have been the odd twinge of jealousy.

But Malcolm would come again and again, generally bringing his wife Kitty with him, and by the end he and Peter Warnett and I had signed nearly a thousand of our books sold in Douglas's shop. As we signed we talked, and Kitty would prepare a tea party or luncheon snack in the back room.

Once, Douglas, obviously for the umpteenth time, was elaborating on his sad lack of faith, on his wish that he could share Malcolm's belief that they might be united in some way in another world. Malcolm interrupted him sharply and said, 'Douglas, when you die, I will tell you exactly what will happen. You will go straight to the Pearly Gates; St Peter will come out and you will start up your usual moan and

13

groan about wishing you had faith, and not being able to have any, and so on and so on. And St Peter will say, "Come on in and shut up".'

At the age of eighty-seven Douglas did embark on that final journey. The family kindly asked me to have a part in the funeral service at Rotherfield Church. I read some magnificent verses from St Paul: 'Who shall separate me from the love of Christ?' Douglas, the son, spoke of his father as a great realist and, more secretly, a great romantic, and read from Rupert Brooke. Malcolm spoke movingly. We sang the 23rd Psalm and 'Fight the good fight'. As the service ended, the organ peeled out with Douglas's regimental march, *Colonel Bogey*.

This idea, when first proposed by his son, had filled me with a certain foreboding. I could not picture the tread of the bearers falling into the quick rhythm of that lively, occasionally ribald song. When it happened it was perfect. As his son wrote to me afterwards, 'I thought we saw him off in fine style. I shall never forget the moment when the coffin was raised to leave the church and up struck *Colonel Bogey*. It was for me a fitting climax to a long and noble life. As for the surprise you promised him, now he will know you were right and he was wrong.'

It was Graham Turner who drove me through a golden November countryside in 1971 to the village of Roberts-bridge, to meet Malcolm and Kitty for the first time.

Malcolm Muggeridge. My mind was full of contradictory reactions as we lurched down that pock-marked, shell-holed country lane (often described or filmed) towards the small, trim cottage that is the Muggeridge home. So annoying, some of those recent television appearances—Malcolm trying to hold the ring while voluble and self-important characters hogged the mike and expressed their opinions in ever more strident tones. Sometimes he seemed, for a change, to be forced on the defensive. *The Reason Why*, the series was called. It had left me merely frustrated, with a muddled impression of Malcolm's mannerisms as he played ringmaster to odd combinations of circus acts. I wondered rather uncharitably 'the reason why' he had done the programme at all. And then there were his sharp comments on the Royal Family, so dear to my sometimes sentimental royalist heart. And I disliked his pessimism and cynicism. He had interviewed a group of young people I knew well, in Moral Rearmament. It had been hard for both sides to find common ground and nothing very satisfactory came about. I rather sympathized with one of those young people, a petite and lively girl from the East End of London, fresh from a vivid religious experience, who had asked him somewhat plaintively: 'Tell me, Mr Muggeridge, why are you so cynical?'

But what about Malcolm's interviews with Mother Teresa in Calcutta? That programme really was 'something beautiful for God'.

My first impression of that visit is of laughter. We seemed to spend most of the first hour or so laughing. From the moment we arrived Kitty Muggeridge teased Graham about the 'latest trade returns' and enquired sympathetically how things were faring with the gross national product and the nervous condition of the pound. I discovered she often did this. Graham had only recently resigned from the BBC as their Economics Correspondent. He had constantly been on 'the box'. His chubby, almost cherubic face seemed to invest even the gloomiest of predicaments and predictions with a certain solidity and optimism. However bad things might be, you felt that there in a few days would be Graham, solidly expounding more complicated facts: not indeed so that I could understand them, but at least giving the impression that he did.

I have a note in my diary of some of the things talked about on that first visit to the little white house, its roof raised like an eyebrow over the front door, and 'the Ark', a new building being completed alongside, where guests might stay or Malcolm could work away from telephones and interruptions. Over a vegetarian lunch, with delicious vegetable soup, home-made whole-wheat bread, good cheese and yoghurt, we discussed the Bible, American television, Mother Teresa and the virulence, almost violence, of the opposition if one dares to oppose outright what Malcolm described as 'the cult of eroticism'. He had done this very thing as Rector of Edinburgh University, and this was one of the actions I had most admired before meeting him. When the students asked him, as their elected Rector and traditional champion, to require of the University authorities that contraceptive machines be available in the University and every kind of restriction on free and promiscuous sex be removed, Malcolm had resigned his office. And he had resigned it in a sermon to the students in St Giles' Cathedral, a sermon which seemed to me to be one of the warmest, wittiest, most moving addresses I had ever read.

Although he did not know too much at that time of Moral Rearmament, Malcolm was aware that some of the most hysterical opposition to it, encountered in all kinds of quite godly places, was largely due to the stand we took on certain matters of chastity. 'Stand up against eroticism and you've had it. You may as well face the facts. The concept of sexual purity sticks in the craw of the twentieth century.'

Other subjects discussed that day were the Kingdom of God, music, writing (of course) and a sad story told by Kitty of a young American who had just committed suicide. I seem to have talked quite a lot—about John Wesley, B H Streeter, and my first play, *The Forgotten Factor*.

We went for a walk over ploughed fields under an autumn sky. Graham and Malcolm strode ahead, Kitty and I followed and she talked lovingly of her husband, the amazing agility of his repartee, and his almost total inability to say 'no' to anybody who really needed or wanted his help.

As we left that evening I did not know whether we would meet again. There was no kind of commitment to the future. But one thing I knew for certain: somehow, in a few short hours, completely unexpectedly, I had been given friends. So many of the essential ingredients of friendship were there, above all, perhaps, the willingness to listen. I had expected Malcolm to hold forth at length, guru-like. He can do that at times, but he also listens. Of course, as a newspaperman, he is trained to do so but he also loves to do so as a friend. The fact that I had talked so much rather surprised me. So many learned people or brilliant intellectuals crush a person like me by the weight of their knowledge. Malcolm, on the other hand, with a vast knowledge of literature and, above all, of men and women whom he had known and met personally, somehow inspired me to be a little more intelligent, a little more witty, a bit more forthcoming than usual. The ability to draw out the best from the other person seems to me to be a mark of real friendship.

Another impression I retain of that day is the sheer love of words, the enjoyment of language well and accurately spoken. I had long admired Malcolm's style in writing. I found that it pervaded all his conversation, without a trace of self-consciousness or artifice. Somebody once asked him what he would like as his epitaph. After a pause he said, 'I think it would be "He used words well".'

I told him once that in a recent illness my doctor had said he felt I had at last 'bottomed out'. A look of slight pain came over Malcolm's face. 'What terrible things we do,' he said, 'to this lovely language of ours.'

My meetings with Malcolm were not frequent. Imagine my shock and amazement then, when I picked up the telephone one day, a few years after that first lunch, and heard his voice at the other end casually remark, 'I think you and I ought to write a play together.' The thought of being able to write with a man of Malcolm's genius amazed me. The shock was all the greater when he went on to say, 'I think the subject of our play ought to be mercy-killing, euthanasia.'

'Hardly a theme for a jolly evening at the theatre,' I replied.

'Mark my words,' said Malcolm seriously, 'this represents the next great moral issue for our generation. In a year or two it will be one of the most bitterly debated subjects of our time.'

It was the shrewd old newspaperman talking again. 'Besides,' he would say as we discussed things later, face to face, 'don't you see, this is the subject that raises everything that really matters, the ultimate sovereignty in the world—God's will or man's will; the meaning of life; the purpose of our existence; the great divide between truth and falsehood.'

He had a true story to form the basis of our plot and as he outlined it my enthusiasm grew. But it was more than a year before we did anything about it. We would often laughingly talk about 'our play', or occasionally it might be 'our TV film', because we were very uncertain of any of the practicalities of creating something together.

Finally, I came to realize that if anything were ever to come of this idea, somebody was going to have to apply the seat of his pants to the seat of a chair, a well-filled pen to some empty sheets of paper and actually begin to write. Malcolm was immersed in books, articles, travels, everything from 'Any Questions' to a temporary lectureship in a Canadian university. I must be the one to begin.

And so, bit by bit, I hammered out a forty page draft of a possible play. I thought it might be called *Life Sentence* and it would concern an Oxford don (after all, having been one, I knew something about them) with a wife who was an accomplished pianist, suddenly struck down by polio. She finally goads and pushes and coaxes a wretched husband, who in theory believes in euthanasia, to do the deed and put her to death. How it all happened and still more what happened afterwards, the great drama of repentance and ultimate forgiveness, had yet to be worked out.

It was a rough draft and incomplete, but I took it over to Robertsbridge and read it to Malcolm and Kitty. They were full of praise and enthusiasm. 'I think you've got it, Alan,' he said. 'I think it's *your* play. You should take it and make it your own, and if you want you can add a little footnote to the effect that some of the ideas came from me.'

I said nothing. It was a bitter disappointment. The clock ticked on for several minutes. Complete silence. Then, at last, very slowly and very diffidently from Malcolm, 'Or, of course, if you really and truly would like a genuine collaboration, perhaps I might be able to suggest one or two ideas.' I said that was the only basis on which I would ever touch the play again.

From that moment ideas, contributions, streams of writing, mostly not in dramatic form and scribbled rapidly in longhand on sheets of yellow paper, poured out from Malcolm and were sent on to me. We would meet and talk many times, Malcolm contributing most of the basic ideas, much of the humour, more and more of the dramatic twists of the plot; I doing my best to turn it all into some kind of dramatic form that might fill a stage and hold an audience.

Seldom have I enjoyed work more. It all seemed to happen so naturally. Malcolm was the humblest, most compliant of collaborators, always ready to listen, generally open to change. To work with him steadily, week by week, at times day by day, was of course a very stimulating and challenging experience. You cannot be in constant contact with one of the keenest minds and sharpest pens of our time without feeling the pricks. And yet there was nothing in the least alarming or overbearing in him. In his writing he may consign people and whole enterprises to the rubbish heap or somewhere worse, with a scathing, even vitriolic stab of his pen; when it came to dealing with anyone in person he was, in my experience, kindness itself. 'The old maestro' as he sometimes laughingly called me, felt free to take the flood of suggestions, the yellow sheets of pure Muggeridge and build out of them scenes for the theatre. Not that Malcolm did not know a good deal about the theatre. He had written a play thirty years before that to my mind is sound theatrically as well as arresting in its thought and content; but he was modesty and humility itself when it came to working on his ideas and material.

There were, of course, certain things about which he felt keenly. One, from the very start, was that there should be in the play a character who would stand for pure goodness. Kitty, who listened a lot and did not say very much, gave form to that idea. She suggested that there should be in the home of our protagonist an *au pair* girl, a German, because it was in Germany that the idea of purifying the race by some form of legalized killing was first established and then finally put into practice in the holocaust. This girl should be from a simple peasant background, earthy, practical, realistic, but above all fundamentally and genuinely good.

Anyone who has written, or who knows the theatre, will be aware of how difficult it is to depict goodness without lapsing into sentimentality, piousness or sheer dullness. Real goodness, so attractive in life, can be so boring in art.

Here, in our play, wherever else we may have failed, I believe we succeeded. We owe that partly to our director, David Williams, a sensitive and experienced man, who took infinite trouble and auditioned a host of young women for the part. He finally came up with a comparatively unknown actress, Susan Colverd. She gave a quite extraordinary and moving picture of an unselfconscious, completely genuine woman of faith.

Few people who saw our play were not in some degree moved and inspired by the strength and humour of Anna. The whole experience affected Susan Colverd's life deeply. Years later she still writes to Malcolm and Kitty and describes them as her spiritual home.

I look back on mornings spent with Malcolm in hard creative work, followed by one of Kitty's simple lunches, and then afterwards the relaxation by a wood fire; our eyelids grow heavy and Kitty, Malcolm and I find ourselves drifting into sleep. 'Three jolly geriatrics', murmurs Kitty contentedly as we doze off.

In Malcolm's long marriage it is Kitty who is the great server. Quietly and unobtrusively she looks after most of the practical side of life in their home. Malcolm, dressed like a spaceman, used to look after the beehives, but Kitty does most of the real gardening as well as all the housework. They are, as vegetarians, very nearly self-supporting, and apart from flour and a few other essentials, could live successfully off their land with eggs and vegetables, fruit and honey.

With it all, Kitty has a first class mind. She published a fine translation of the meditations of the eighteenth century French mystic, Jean-Pierre de Caussade and has written discerningly about her aunt, Beatrice Webb. At home she listens mostly, but her contributions to discussions are usually profound, witty and occasionally salty. The details of her anecdotes are sometimes a little exaggerated as Malcolm will gently point out—'Darling, you know I hate to interrupt you'—but as they both know the underlying truth is always sound. 'He has risen without trace,' she said of David Frost. Once, she described to me a cartoon from *The New Yorker* ('Not quite respectable enough for *Punch* in my day as

Editor', adds Malcolm). The cartoon depicted an aged gentleman in bed with a luscious and very young lady. 'Pass me my teeth,' said the elderly lover, 'I want to bite you.' Comic, profoundly tragic and how much more effective a comment on sin than indignation or lamentation.

Whatever the subject or the circumstances, Kitty is there to serve, to contribute, to enliven, and above all to love. Mr and Mrs Michael Parkinson once interviewed Malcolm and Kitty on the radio and they talked about their sometimes stormy life together as man and wife. Finally, Kitty was asked very seriously 'What would you say is the real secret of your surviving so many difficulties in marriage and being able to keep going?' There was a pause. 'Love,' said Kitty. The programme ended. A stone dropped into a lake; the ripples went quietly out in all directions.

Like many people, I have been puzzled by the apparent contradictions in Malcolm's life; his intense dislike of television, his profound suspicion of the effect of the presence of a camera in distorting the truth. He has no television set and he had his aerials removed, 'an operation,' he would say, 'which I heartily recommend.' His virulent criticisms of the broadcasting media seemed to contrast oddly with his own frequent and brilliant appearances on the air. 'But,' and a wry grimace would cross his world-worn face, 'it's here to stay, so we'd better make the best use of it we can.'

His prognostications for the future were gloomy and pessimistic, but I have heard him describe himself as an optimist, and he would seldom neglect to help someone to back a cause, however forlorn, which might improve life in our time.

Once, when Malcolm's grandchildren from Canada were visiting, I watched Matthew, then an endearing six year old, playing and laughing on his grandfather's knee. Malcolm was at the same time proclaiming gloom and doom for every aspect of our civilization. At last I could not refrain from asking, 'What about Matthew in all this?' Tears came into the old man's eyes. Quietly he said, 'Matthew will be all right.' It was not wishful thinking or grandfatherly sentiment. It was part of his profound belief in and reverence for the wonder and sanctity of human life. He might despair of our society but he was utterly certain of God's care and love for every single individual, from the moment of a child's conception in the womb to the last breath of a person whom society might classify as subnormal. He could both share the joy of Mother Teresa holding a tiny, premature, half-starved baby and saying, 'Look, he's alive. I think he's going to live', and also ask, 'What sort of life will it be?'

'Matthew will be all right. We'll all be all right. The human race will pull through. It always has and it always will. God is God and every single one of us will be all right.' As Mother Julian of Norwich, herself no stranger to suffering, said, 'All shall be well, and all manner of thing shall be well.'

But I was often exasperated by the immediate pessimism. Some of it, I learned to admit, came from his newsman's realism in facing facts. I arrived at the house one day, exuberant over the defeat of Mrs Gandhi in the Indian elections after her setting up of a police state. I knew how Malcolm abhorred her Government's policy of enforced sterilization. I felt the ordinary people in India had risen against the might of the State and of the experts. Malcolm shared my joy but then he added, 'Mind you it won't last. This new lot, I've met some of them; they're a bunch of utter fuddy-duddies. They'll never work together for longer than a month or so. They won't get anything done. In a few years' time Mrs G will be back.' How cynical, I thought. How true, in fact.

One day, after some particularly gloomy warnings about the futility of attempts to alter the course of events in a positive direction, our daughter Susan dared to say to him, 'You are near the end of your life, Mr Muggeridge; I am not yet thirty. I mind about what happens now, immediately, to me and my children.' Malcolm was silenced. I knew how much he cared.

When Susan and her husband Rob were setting out with a group of young people in Moral Rearmamanet on a mission to South Africa and what was then Rhodesia, Malcolm gave much thought and encouragement to their venture. 'Of course, our Lord will never let any of you harbour one grain of apartheid in your own attitude to people of every kind of colour. But I don't think that means that it is your duty to teach everyone in that country how to manage their affairs or to point out right and left how misguided they are.' He gave them letters of introduction to some of his friends in southern Africa. When they came back months later and told him what they had seen and done, his old face lit up. 'That's wonderful,' he kept saying, 'that's marvellous.' Then later he turned to me and whispered, 'But it won't make any difference.'

I wonder. I suppose it is only in the long perspectives of history that judgments about results can ever be made. In the great warfare of good and evil, battles are lost and battles are won. The war continues. I believe that in what is now Zimbabwe, the quiet and faithful work of a comparatively few people, like Ian Smith's son Alec, the Rev Arthur Kandereke, and others, helped the politicians to bring a bloody war to an end and gave the chance for a new beginning.* Even Malcolm's beloved BBC described it as a miracle.

That chance could be wasted. But we need not deny the power of God at work in people's lives, whatever the future holds.

One place where Malcolm does detect gleams of hope is Russia. As a young man he went to Russia with Kitty, full of high hopes and great expectations, only to return utterly disillusioned. While most of the press and pundits praised from a safe distance, Malcolm took a train and saw the man-made famine for himself. When we made one of our visits to Robertsbridge Malcolm had just returned from recording some programmes in Russian for television on the lives of Tolstoy and Dostoyevsky. Gleefully he told us how, proud of their great literary heritage, the powers-that-be in Russia were propagating the Gospel of Christ. I later saw one of the programmes. There was Malcolm's familiar gait, head and shoulders thrust forward as he threaded his way down a busy street in Moscow, quoting some of the most profoundly Christian passages of Dostoyevsky's majestic prose. I could

* See *Now I Call Him Brother* by Alec Smith.

23

scarcely believe my eyes. And it had all been done with the active help of the government in a State dedicated to the death of God.

He told us that he had even made his hosts laugh. 'You must be very careful with me,' he said to them one day when they were being particularly pernickety. 'If you arrest me, do you realize what will happen? Crowds will throng the Russian Embassy in London, shouting, "Keep Muggeridge!" ' He detected a new softness, a new hunger in the Russian people and widespread disillusionment with Communism as an idea. Above all, he reveres those dissidents of the gulags and the psychiatric asylums who risk and even give their lives in what is bound, one day, to become an unconquerable force. Solzhenitsyn is probably Malcolm's greatest contemporary hero. He shares with him the belief that 'one word of truth outweighs the whole world.'

I suppose the truth about Malcolm is that he is a prophet. I cannot read the Old Testament prophets without being struck by the extraordinary combination of dire and terrible warnings and, sometimes, in the very same chapter, glorious visions for our existence on earth. Consistency is not the point. Time, in God's perspective, does not seem so important. 'A thousand years in Thy sight are but as yesterday.' The dark and the light are both real. One would mean nothing without the other.

If I have been able to give anything in a relationship from which I have received so much, I hope it may be that I have taken to see him a number of my friends, many of them young people. Malcolm has always welcomed them. He has an unerring eye and ear for what is real. His eyes light up at any genuine experience of faith put into practice, of unpretentious adventuring with God. 'You bring me such interesting people,' he said once.

I hope I may have helped him to see more clearly how, in addition to pricking the twentieth century bubble, he can be used by God in the lives of individual men and women. A bright young writer of the extreme Left published an article in the popular press not just condemning Malcolm but pouring vitriol and scorn upon him. It seemed to me that at the very end of the article there was a note of uncertainty, even longing, on the part of the writer himself. I pointed this out to Malcolm and suggested that he might be able to do something to help the young man. He wrote what was a letter of extraordinary grace and humility on the part of a senior man towards a very junior one. The response was amazing. All the bristles vanished. The young man opened up. He and Malcolm became friends and I think it is true to say that this particular person has never been the same again.

I remember a dialogue in the twin pulpits of a London church when Enoch Powell and Malcolm discussed their differences in public. There came a moment of this double sermon when, after a certain amount of intellectual sparring, deep reality began to break through. I felt Malcolm reaching out in genuine love and longing to help liberate a friend in need. There was almost a fresh breakthrough of faith. Almost, though not quite.

Sometimes I have suggested to Malcolm that this kind of thing was still perhaps his greatest role in life—to be used by God as his instrument, to bring healing to individual lives. And of course as the years go by, I have been struck again and again by the ever-deepening, ever-growing love and devotion to Christ that possesses his being: *Jesus Rediscovered*; *Jesus the Man Who Lives*.

Few people, accustomed to Malcolm in his various guises as a public performer, realize the austere, disciplined life of spiritual devotion that is his. For many years he and Kitty have read the Bible and said the offices of the Book of Common Prayer together. The celebration of their Golden Wedding Anniversary was a service of great simplicity in their own home with family and a few neighbours, conducted by his life-long friend, Dr Alec Vidler, in which I was privileged to have a part.

More recently Malcolm and Kitty have been received into the Roman Catholic Church. Malcolm, ever the arch individualist, the lone wolf, unbound by allegiance to institutions or organizations, has found a spiritual home. The prayers of Mother Teresa must account for much, though Malcolm has said that in a way she may have postponed the final decision, so anxious has he been not to betray her by taking this solemn step just to please her, or indeed to please anybody except Christ. There is no doubt that Pope John Paul II, with his wide embracing love combined with his unwavering stand on moral issues dear to Malcolm's heart, also had his effect. Ecclesiastical 'with it' compromise is little to his liking. But beyond all that, and deeper, there is the sense, beautifully described by Malcolm himself, of a home-coming where a special place at the table has been long laid and prepared, the final summons of a bell that has been sounding over the years.

For me as an Anglican priest, this step seems to have brought us closer. Malcolm has long loved the little church in Mark Cross where I officiate. He has come as worshipper, preacher, reader. He has said that if only he lived nearer he could feel at home in our simple prayer-book services. I asked him how he felt now about his and Kitty's regular reading of Matins and Evensong. He said that he had raised this very point with the Bishop who was helping them prepare for being received. 'Why don't the three of us say the Anglican Evensong together now?' was the reply. Malcolm is a believer in letting ecumenism happen wherever it is natural and needed. We are different regiments fighting the same battle. He is characteristically suspicious of ecumenical movements laying down regulations, highlighting differences and organizing unity.

As for Kitty, she joins Malcolm in this step, I would say not out of duty but out of love. After the stormy, endlessly renewed and enriched partnership over the years, they are, at a very deep level, one. It would be inconceivable for one to make this move without the other.

Critics may laugh at 'St Mug'. But as the 'Mug' continues to hold forth (and long may he do so, with his rich humour, satire and provocativeness and brilliant use of words) so the saint becomes more central, more his overriding preoccupation, ever leading him on to fresh discoveries.

'You may be in for a surprise,' I had said to his brother Douglas. Humbly I would like to say the same to my dear friend, Malcolm, who is still inclined to feel that there is not

26

much hope of reversing the trend that is leading our wayward world to another dark age. Despite the old journalist's scepticism, God may yet surprise us all. By working in the lives of individuals as he has worked, and is working, in Malcolm's, he may still bring our decadent, declining, apparently hopeless civilization a wonderful surprise.

3

The Family

'Mr and Mrs Jones are married. They are friends.'
From a childhood novel

This sentence was the opening of the first novel I ever wrote. It was called *The Seaweed Life*, and was inspired by the *Adventures of Masterman Ready* which my father read to me in bed in the early morning. I suppose I was six or seven. It was to be full of storm, shipwreck and rescue. Unfortunately, like its heroes, it foundered on the rocks. I had set myself an almost impossible task by choosing my chapter headings before I had established my plot. Not only that, but I had spaced my headings at random through the exercise book which was to contain my masterpiece. So the story had to be tailored to fit such titles as *A Strange Adventure* or *A Friend in Need*, and the length of each chapter had to fill exactly the space allotted. It was too much even for a child's ingenuity, but the first sentence was promising, and was, I think, an unconscious tribute to my parents. For they, like Mr and Mrs Jones, were friends; friends of one another, and also of their children.

My earliest and happiest memories of my mother are simply of talking. We seem to have talked endlessly. Not baby-talk, thank goodness, and not the rather coy and pseudo children's talk that you hear on some children's television programmes. We had what an old aunt of mine used to call 'reasonable conversation'. We recounted experiences, we expressed likes and dislikes and we told stories. We both talked, though sometimes I monopolized the conversation.

28

When my mother was preoccupied with accounts or writing, she would say, 'You can talk to me but I can't talk to you', and that, as far as I was concerned, was satisfactory.

One of the first and most important lessons learnt was to be articulate. She did not agree in the least with the adage that 'children should be seen and not heard.' She felt they should be seen and heard distinctly; not all the time of course, and not interrupting weightier matters. But she expected us at a very early age to be able to hold our own in a conversation, and above all to speak clearly and audibly. This was necessary in her family, which consisted of a bevy of aunts and cousins, most of whom possessed extremely loud voices and a very emphatic manner. Mother would have hated the monosyllabic mumble which passes for conversation in most places today. What you might have to say was unlikely to be brilliant but at least it should be heard.

We came to live in our Sussex village when I was seven and my sister three. Soon after that mother would rehearse us in articulate conversation with friends and neighbours. Putting us at one end of a passage she would advance upon us from the other, hand outstretched or worse still, cheek extended, uttering such opening gambits as, 'Alan! how you've grown!' (which for years I didn't). Or, 'Are you glad to be back for the holidays?' Or, to my little sister, 'Are you glad to have your brother home?' Or simply, with reference to her blond and my black hair, 'What a contrast!' Such remarks as these (and they were always produced just as my mother had foreseen) might well have deserved a smart retort, or at least a dignified silence, but we were expected to reply with something that was, if possible, intelligible, but at any rate audible. The result is that in all the thousands of sermons, addresses, talks, lectures or speeches that I have perpetrated in a lifetime, few may have been worth hearing, but I think every one of them has been heard, mostly without benefit of loudspeaker. 'It's very rude not to be heard,' she would say, and at how many occasions have I wished she might have taught others the same lesson, both on and off the stage.

Mother's side of our conversations consisted largely of

stories; not fairy stories, which I had little use for, and not really children's stories as such, but true stories, though I daresay some of them improved a bit in the telling. Looking back I am surprised how macabre some of them were. She realized that few children are in the least shocked or horrified by the things that grown-ups think must distress them. I never found either *Shock-headed Peter* or the Old Testament anything but delightful and fascinating. There's a well-known story of a grim and grisly picture of Christians being mauled by lions in the Colosseum. A little girl who saw it burst into tears. 'There's a poor lion,' she said, 'hasn't got a Christian.'

Mother's stories were all vivid and many of them funny. But some contained a solemn and terrible warning. There was Uncle So-and-So who pulled away his wife's chair for a joke just as she was sitting down, with the result that she injured her spine and died. There was old Cousin Ben who, when some fatal disaster had befallen one of his children on an outing, wired to his wife: 'Prepare for bad news,' thinking that this would cushion anxiety. It must have been the same cousin who rushed away from the Boat Race to wire his family, 'Cambridge leading at Barnes Bridge!' He was matched by a very pious relative who announced her plans as 'Coming DV Thursday. Anyway Friday.' She also slightly mistook a Bible reference in a most worthy passage to a bridal pair. Instead of telegraphing I John 4, verse 18, she sent just John 4, verse 18, with the result that the reference which was supposed to read, 'Perfect love casteth out fear', did in fact come out as 'Thou hast had five husbands and he whom thou now hast is not thy husband.'

A more serious and terrible story, and one which I always wanted her to repeat, concerned a family who kept a litter of sweet little lion cubs as pets. They were so tame and lovable that no one noticed they were growing until suddenly in a fit of temper one of them mauled and killed one of the children. This story suggested the dire result of harbouring cosy little sins too long, and often came to my aid in later life.

The next thing I owe to my mother was the fact that she taught me to read at the age of three. I was extremely small and slow to walk, with the result that I electrified a whole carriage-full of passengers one day when, lying on my mother's lap and looking (I daresay) like a baby in arms, I suddenly announced in clearest tones, reading from the wall opposite, the delightfully readable warning, 'Do not Spit.'

Mother not only taught us to read, but she read aloud to us, and kept this up almost as long as she lived. She read us anything and everything under the sun. Perhaps the things that have stuck best were the Bible stories, from the Old Testament as well as the New. Whether read or told, they were superbly dramatic and unforgettable. I was particularly taken at one time by the story of how Jacob was tricked by his prospective in-laws and got the less attractive sister, Leah instead of the promised Rachel. We had once a missionary exhibition in our village in which some enterprising people dressed up in biblical costume and demonstrated an Eastern wedding. When the great climax came and the bride was unveiled, the face of a fairly plain local spinster was discovered. In a voice of real horror and, alas, as audibly as ever, I was heard to say, 'Look, look. It's Leah!'

My mother was a Miss Brodie Hoare. She came from an enormous family of bankers, Quakers, social reformers and, I would add, gluttons for adventurous living. Anywhere you come across Buxtons, Barclays, Gurneys, or Hoares, the odds are they are relatives of mine and they will proudly trace their connection with Elizabeth Fry, the great prison reformer. Mother's father was a director of Lloyds Bank and Conservative MP for Hampstead. He was a shrewd man of affairs, though, like the rest of us, not always shrewd enough. He had a way of saying, 'Mark my words', and people usually did, with good effect. However, although he was killed in a motor accident when I was still fairly young, I can remember him saying more than once, 'Mark my words. This hair-brained scheme of altering the clocks in summer is utter lunacy. It would create chaos!' He was also heard to say, 'Mark my words. That pettifogging little lawyer Lloyd George will never amount to anything.'

Mother was one of six children. In their teenage days she was the family chronicler and there are books of her poems

31

and excellent water-colour sketches of their family doings. Nothing could be farther removed from the image of Victorian repression or stuffiness. We see the family playing ice hockey or tobogganing flat-out down Titsey Hill, one of the steepest and longest in Surrey. Now they are sailing in a wherry on the Broads, now experimenting with a primitive phonograph made by my uncle Alan, who was the scientist of the family. There is a picture of this uncle in a long skirt, carrying a gun, as he sneaked out during a pause in family theatricals to shoot a rabbit over the garden wall. From the journals you would hardly have realized that the boys were growing up to be bankers or cotton brokers, or that the girls were immersed in a whirl of activity—training the village choir, helping an overworked vicar in Battersea, setting up a knitting machine industry for villagers, having visitors to stay, calling on elderly aunts and cousins, playing the organ in church, giving magic lantern shows, and incidentally helping to run quite a considerable estate.

Mother brought into our family this spirit of enterprise and eagerness for the next thing. She had the right attitude towards permissiveness. At a very early age I can hear her say, 'Whatever you want to do I shall always try to say "yes" if I possibly can. But if I do have to say "no", then I mean "no" '. She often said 'yes' to the point of fool-hardiness. My sister and I, as young children, used to roam the countryside catching butterflies and carrying precariously in a pocket a 'killing bottle'—obtained without question for a shilling or so at the local chemist—containing, I should imagine, enough cyanide to destroy the whole village.

When I was eight I was allowed to take my sister, aged four, on long walking expeditions to a railway station some way up the line and come back by train entirely unescorted. On questions of honesty, however, mother was absolutely unbending. I once brought home from kindergarten a purse that I had somehow managed to acquire or 'swap' from a little Jewish boy called Francis. The speed with which we set out to Francis' home to return the purse took my breath away and has never been forgotten.

But the eagerness, the desire to move on, was always there.

'You've got to live life on your toes,' she would say, 'as you play tennis,' a game which she played extremely well. She was often impatient. How embarrassed I have been to hear her say to some quite distinguished guest who had lingered a little, 'Now I expect you will want to be getting on. We mustn't keep you.' On her death bed almost her last words, very insistent, were, 'Die! Die!' She couldn't bear not to be getting on with it.

Mother's home, Tenchleys, was the Mecca of my childhood. The long journey south on the 'Sunny South Express' which took us round London to East Croydon, where we changed into the much inferior train to Oxted, with a tunnel through the chalk hills that suddenly echoed with a mysterious and terrifying roar to give an extra edge to the excitement of arrival; the brougham at the station to meet us with Charles, the coachman, on the box and a pair of horses, Bryant and May, between the shafts—these, for a small boy, were the big thrills of the year.

Then there was the tumult of the welcome at the house. It seemed as if hundreds of people were dashing to the door to greet us—dozens of aunts! In fact there were only two but their enthusiasm and volubility gave them a multiple personality and their number was usually swollen by guests, plus a mass of outdoor and indoor staff who all rallied to the occasion. My grandmother waited in the background, tall, handsome in black satin with a lace cap or else a big hat with ostrich feathers if she were going out.

It was on the lawns of Tenchleys, with the huge horse-chestnut tree in the front and the marvellously climbable cedar at the back, where my sister Kitty first learnt to walk, where I played my first tennis, discovered how to ride a bicycle, and took part in cricket matches and gymkhanas, or watched my uncle Maurice put his ferrets down a rabbit warren. The inside of the house was just as exciting—the long corridor on the maids' floor which was big enough for an indoor cricket pitch; the smell of lavender in my grandmother's bedroom, where once an owl came down the chimney and perched on her dressing table, flapping its wings in a cloud of soot; the little billiard table in the upstairs hall; the upright piano where I learnt to play hymns and where the boys of the village came in to practise with my aunt for the church choir. There were family prayers in the library, with the intriguing spectacle (through my fingers) of the maids' posterior view as they knelt in their devotions. There was the glorious occasion when somebody shouted 'Aeroplane!' and everyone leapt to their feet in the middle of a prayer and rushed out to see an aeroplane stutter over the house. My aunt explained to me solemnly that it was permissible to interrupt prayers for an aeroplane, 'but not for the hounds'.

There seems to have been a great place in families of those days for maiden aunts and a bachelor uncle or two. My aunts Elsie and Catherine, the Misses Brodie Hoare, bathed us all in a rosy glow of energy, affection and enthusiasm. In those more spacious days they seemed to have endless time to do things. Whether it was a jigsaw in the morning, or a game of hide-and-seek indoors on a wet afternoon, or endless reading aloud in the evening, there they were, ready and available. They also had any amount of time just to talk, and still more to listen. They, plus the cook Rose and the head gardener, Mr Danser, were the recipients of all my confidences and they must have given up hours of their time to be with me and my sister and our various cousins and friends.

My grandmother remains always in my memory as a kind of still centre amid all the whirl of family life. I see her always the same stately figure in black, pouring tea or riding in the back of the Daimler and speaking through a fascinating tube to Charles in the driver's seat, telling him not to go more than fifteen miles an hour. Her intense kindness and generosity were constant, though they did not stop her from being gloriously outspoken at times. She would complain in vigorous terms about 'this perfectly disgusting tea', quite oblivious of the fact that she was a guest at somebody else's party and not the hostess at her own.

My bachelor uncle Maurice deserves a paragraph or two of his own because he may have influenced my life as much as any of the family. It is to him I owe my introduction to the theatre. He was supposed to be a dull boy at school and, rather than send him to university, his father found him a job as a junior clerk in the local Lloyds Bank. There he was known to keep ferrets in the safe ready for a quick getaway to a shoot after office hours. He had a distinguished service in the First World War, going through the Somme, Passchendaele and the rest, miraculously, without a scratch. Only at the very end, due to shell shock, he climbed in his sleep out of an upstairs window of a French farm and broke his thigh.

After the war he returned to Lloyds Bank in London and rose to the position of Assistant Treasurer and, I believe, was a considerable power in the City. This did not at all prevent him from enjoying life to the full and passing on some of his enjoyment to me. It was when I was about ten years old that he invited me, Eton jacket, stiff collar and all, to stay with him in his bachelor flat and enjoy a night 'on the town'. I can feel now the thrill as my uncle Maurice shouted to the taxi driver, 'Simpson's in the Strand', and we whirled away into the golden, rainy blur of London. After dinner we walked across the Strand to the pantomime at the old Lyceum Theatre. My weight was not enough to hold down the very stiff springs of the tip-up seat, so I spent the whole evening folded up in my stall like a letter trying to escape from an envelope. But never for one minute did that interrupt or spoil the marvel and magic of my first real experience of the theatre.

The night out with my uncle became an institution and was repeated year after year, later joined by my sister Kitty. My knowledge and my critical faculties grew but never did that sense of wonder disappear, and it is with me still.

After the show uncle Maurice and I would walk home to his flat and he would begin to expound for me his philosophy of life. 'Wonderful place London,' he would say as we dodged the buses, 'Everyone working hard all day and everyone having a rattling good time at night!' Later, cigar in hand and a whisky at his side, he would tender some avuncular advice. 'If I had my time over again I wouldn't smoke and I wouldn't drink. I strongly advise you to do the same.'

Later, when I had decided to be ordained, he offered me a job for a year or two in the Bank so that I would learn how the 'other fellow lives'. I wish I had taken him up on it.

Perhaps I fulfilled his idea in another way when I let the theatre, to which he had introduced me, take me by the throat and become one of the factors in my life. You learn a little how the other fellow lives if you work in the theatre.

My father was much more reserved than my mother and I never knew very much about his side of the family. He was the youngest of a large family and he was over fifty years old when I was born, so there were no living grandparents on his side that I can remember. His family were originally Derbyshire farmers. I have seen the neat whitewashed farm where they lived for generations. Father's grandfather left all that and came to London to find his fortune and found it with his son in the form of an elegant shop which they established in Bond Street. Here among high class leather goods and expensive toilet articles, Edward VII, as Prince of Wales, and his friends would drop in to buy and perhaps drink a cup of coffee with my grandfather. When my uncles succeeded to the business they unfortunately ran it into the ground as quickly as it had been built up. House and shop have disappeared.

Another uncle distinguished himself, however, as chief engineer of the London and North Western Railway, and we never travelled down south without my father saying with pride: 'Just feel it. The smoothest, most comfortable line in the world.'

Father's mother was a good singer and much attracted to Italian opera. They had an Italian couple as butler and cook and my father had a vivid memory of visiting the kitchen one day and being dandled on the knee of a fiery little man with a big beard. He was Garibaldi, come to London to enlist support and visit old friends.

Father as a youth was sociable and fun-loving. He went to Merchant Taylors' School and won cups for running. At Oxford he rowed, was in the University trial Eights, and as Captain of Hertford Boats made a lot of bumps and won his oar, which became an increasing problem as we moved from larger to smaller homes. At Hertford he and his friends enjoyed life. When a worthy but pious undergraduate tried to start a Temperance Society in college, father and most of

36

the rowing club packed the opening meeting and elected the biggest drunk as President.

I came across a diary which father kept in those days. It was full of parties, dances, visits to Covent Garden and rides in Hyde Park. There seems to have been a mass of friends, male and female. There was his Hertford College friend, Buckingham, whose father was a parson-squire in Devonshire. Father used to visit there often and fell in love with Buckingham's sister Ellen.

Suddenly in the diary the whole pattern changes. A new and serious note comes into the entries. There are references to church services and prayer meetings and a change of heart. Father never talked about this change, but judging from the rest of his life it must have been a deep one. It sent him, to the surprise of family and friends, to train for ordination and he became one of the first four students to belong to the theological college in Oxford, Wycliffe Hall.

I have dim memories of two of father's sisters, my aunt Sophie and aunt Con. I see them as two round little ladies, one married and one single. They both suddenly became Roman Catholics to the alarm of the family. My father, although a staunch evangelical, always stood up for them and liked to have them to stay. Aunt Sophie Worlock had a grandson, my cousin, who has become a notable Roman Catholic Archbishop. I sometimes wonder whether, if Aunt Sophie had not made her dramatic switch to Rome, Derek might not now be Archbishop of Canterbury. He would have made a good one.

Father married the sweetheart of his university days, Ellen Buckingham, and they had five children including twin sons and one daughter. He became the headmaster of a school for boys and girls, with their own children as pupils of the school. Father and his wife led happy days at full stretch.

Then Ellen died after a long illness, leaving a busy impoverished parson with five teenage children. He did not feel he could carry on with the school, which was at Limpsfield, close to Tenchleys, so he moved as far away as possible and took a busy, working-class parish in Liverpool. But he did not move away altogether. He often remembered Tenchleys, a home where there were three charming and lively daughters, a place where there was always a warm welcome, where children were always at home, where laughter abounded and faith was practical and strong.

He took a trip back to Limpsfield, walked across the common from his old school to Tenchleys, and asked my mother to marry him. She was thirty-three at the time. He was nearly fifty. Mother was used to a life of some comfort with a certain amount of money and lots of servants. Father was a busy parish priest with a run-down vicarage, a small salary and five lively, and in some cases, rebellious teenage children. It was quite an assignment. Mother said 'yes', and there followed as fruitful and happy a marriage as one could find. It was not so easy to win the love and confidence of a pretty seventeen-year-old daughter who had been taking the role of mistress of the house. The twin boys were at Liverpool College now and were quite a rumbustious pair, with the added advantage of being able to fool their teachers and friends through being absolutely identical. Very soon I came along to join the family and later my sister Kitty. By that time we were seven, with the older boys needing to go to Oxford and later prepare for ordination. Another brother emigrated to Canada. It was before the days of university grants. None of us proved much good at winning scholarships. How my parents did it I do not know. I do remember back in the Liverpool days, when mother had to have a tooth out, she walked to the dentist to save money on the tram, and then had the extraction without anaesthetic, local or otherwise, so as to save on dental bills.

Everyone talks about the generation gap nowadays but from the earliest moments that I can remember to the last moments of their lives my parents were building bridges of affection and trust, and of listening, that stood firm and strengthened with every new development of our lives. The fact that four out of five of my father's sons followed him into the ministry must mean that either he was a formidable dictator or a shining example. I believe he was the latter. There are pathetic, phony kinds of parsons. There is also the real thing. When he died, the hundreds of letters that

38

poured in were not much about his sermons, which were good, or his public achievements, which were many. They were all about what he had done for people. We never knew, for instance (because he never talked about it) that he would occasionally lay his hands on sick people and they would recover. We knew little about the timely visits to people in trouble, or the outpouring of care for people in their greatest joys, temptations and sorrows.

When my sister and I were young children my mother developed cancer of the breast. She had one operation. Then the doctors called for another. We travelled with her and father as they went to London for this second operation. We were to stop off with the family at Tenchleys. All along the journey mother wrote us messages in backwards or 'looking-glass' writing which we could hold up to the mirror and read. The messages grew funnier and funnier and more fascinating. She wanted to leave us with a specially happy memory. It was an entrancing journey for us and a courageous one for her. Father, who was a man of strong and simple faith, read in the Bible that when one of your number is sick, you should pray over them and anoint them with oil and they will recover. We knew nothing of this until years later after father had died, but then mother told me how father had proposed that he should do this for her. She was not very keen on the idea, somewhat embarrassed in fact. But she agreed to it, finally, partly to satisfy father. Father did as the Bible said, and all I can report is that mother lived in robust health until the age of ninety-one.

4

Mrs Charles

Nearly seventy years later I can still live through every detail of those first journeys to Windlesham House. The unutterable, sickening nervousness and anticipation as my mother and I travelled to Brighton, cooped up in an old-fashioned third class carriage, with no escape to a loo that beckoned me urgently between almost every station. Then a blessed hour's respite in Brighton when we visited a local cinema, a real flea-pit, where I could lose myself in a flickering silent movie, and thrill to the adventures of a heroine tied and bound to the railway track, while the piano accompaniment throbbed with excitement as the express train loomed up on the horizon. But the clock beside the cinema screen moved relentlessly on, and the dreaded moment of separation drew nearer and nearer. For the heroine there was always a last-minute rescue. For me there was none. It was goodbye, not as now with free weekends, half-term holidays and frequent family visits; then it was a twelve week stretch, uninterrupted and unrelieved. And that, for a nine-year-old, was the equivalent of a life-sentence, with no remission in sight.

Equally clearly I remember my actual arrival at the school. I was greeted personally by a lady who gave me a warm and motherly hug and promptly popped a sweet into my mouth to save me the embarrassment of having to try and say something. Perhaps my career at Windlesham does not bear out any great theories of the merits or otherwise of boarding school education. But one thing is certain. It brought me into close contact with one of the most remarkable women I have ever met.

Windlesham House can claim to be the oldest preparatory school in the country. Lieutenant Charles Malden of the Royal Navy retired at an early age. He was not cut out for a life at sea, but his expert penmanship and his success as a cartographer suggested a scholastic career. He and his young wife settled in lodgings at Ryde in the Isle of Wight, and he started to take in pupils to coach for the Navy. In 1837 he bought a school at Newport, whose owner had suddenly packed up and left, and within a week or two opened up with nine boarders and three or four day-boys. The school at Brighton which had developed from this beginning was unique in that it was a preparatory school for boys of under fourteen years of age. Its aim, greatly encouraged by the great Dr Arnold of Rugby, was to spare them some of the rigours of the public schools of those days, and to concentrate on those early years so vital in a child's development and so neglected in the rough and tumble of *Tom Brown's Schooldays*.

Windlesham House has not only the distinction of its age, but also the remarkable record that from its first founding to the present day it has remained continuously in the charge of the Malden family. In 1958, a young, handsome, progressive Charles Malden, direct descendant, fifth generation, of old Lieutenant Charles, took over the school, and is today the headmaster of a much enlarged, go-ahead, and in many ways mellowed and broadened Windlesham, catering for some 240 boys and 120 girls.

Charles Scott Malden, grandson of the original Lieutenant Malden, founder of the school, succeeded his father to the headmastership in 1888. Five years before he had married his father's first cousin, Grace Gilbert Gibson. He was a large, jolly man with a burly athletic figure and a keen dark eye. He combined natural friendliness with strict discipline. He did much to bring the school up to modern requirements. He started to build the school chapel. Sadly, before it was completed, when he had only been headmaster for eight years, he suddenly died.

His widow, 'Mrs Charles', was left with a leaderless school on her hands. She had a young family of five of her own, including a baby of six months old. There was just £30 in the bank. What to do?

The idea of a woman head of a boys' school was far-fetched. Academically at any rate her qualifications left something to be desired. When she was ten years old she was threatened with meningitis, and by doctor's advice all book work was dropped. 'Instead,' she once wrote, 'I learnt many useful things—to ride a horse bareback, to follow the hounds on foot, to skate, play cricket and football; the blacksmith showed me how to weld horseshoes, the bell-ringer how to ring *Bob Major*—and in course of time, the best of husbands and schoolmasters taught me how to manage a school.'

Prudence suggested that she sell the school, but the path of prudence never appealed much to Mrs Charles. Encouraged by a few parents and friends, she decided to keep the Malden flag flying over Windlesham and carry on.

It was unfortunate that just at that very time the Revd J E C Welldon, headmaster of Harrow, speaking at the Conference of Headmasters of Public Schools, had made a slashing attack on prep schools run by ladies. He said that no lady understood how to deal with the moral difficulties of boys. How could they? And he ended up by suggesting to all other heads of public schools that if they wanted to avoid gross immorality in their establishments they should make a point of refusing all boys sent up from a preparatory school kept by a lady.

This meant ruin for Windlesham and for Mrs Charles. She instantly went into the attack. One of the old boys of Windlesham was at Harrow in Dr Welldon's house. Mrs Charles got him to beard the great man in his den—a considerable feat for a schoolboy—and fix an interview for her on the spot. Mrs Charles duly arrived. It was not long before lunch. Long enough, thought Welldon, to deal with an importunate widow. 'Look here Mrs Malden,' he said, 'if we are to thrash this thing out, I shall have to talk to you as one man to another, and I hardly want to do that with a lady.' However, this was exactly what Mrs Charles wanted to do with him. The lunch bell rang. The matter was still only half-thrashed. She stayed to lunch. They then adjourned to the study. At the end Welldon said, 'Mrs Malden, I believe you have been sent to me by God. I want you to go round to the heads of all the public schools, and to say that the headmaster of Harrow is going to help you, and that he hopes they will help you too.'

So Mrs Charles began a pilgrimage to most of the other leading schools. Eton was by no means cordial, but Dr James of Rugby, Burge of Winchester, and Furneaux of Repton all promised their support. Dr Pollock of Wellington sent a message to say that he was engaged. Mrs Charles asked the butler to say that she could quite easily stay at Wellington for the rest of the day in the hope that there might be an odd five minutes when he was not engaged. He found that five minutes and Mrs Charles told him that she was head of Windlesham House. 'Windlesham?' said Pollock, 'I don't seem to remember the name. I have thirty-three preparatory schools preparing boys for Wellington, and I cannot recall that name among them.'

'Well now, Dr Pollock, that's strange, as Windlesham is quite the best of the thirty-three. What's more,' she added, 'you have three of our boys right now, and I wouldn't be surprised if they weren't some of the best boys you have.'

Dr Pollock laughed and asked her to stay to lunch. So Wellington was added to the list of supporters. Haileybury under Dr Lyttleton followed, and as Lyttleton later went on to Eton, that was added to the list too. So Mrs Charles turned what was to have been a disaster into a crowning triumph, and the sex which had seemed a fatal bar became her great asset. On one occasion she even stormed her way into the Admiralty in Whitehall to tell them that their examination board had made a stupid and fatal error in turning down one of her boys for the navy as the result of an interview. Starting with the first clerk she could find, she gradually worked her way up through various departments until she reached Admiral Cochrane himself. It took her heaviest artillery to persuade him that this little thirteen-year-old boy was one of whose services the Royal Navy simply could not do without. In the end the Admiral promised to look into the matter. In due time a notification came from the Admiralty that, 'the examination for candidates for the Royal Navy will be held on such and such a date when the presence of . . . is again requested.'

The boy they wanted to reject had an outstanding record in the Navy. Among other things, in World War I he was picked to go on the heroic adventure of the attack on the Mole at Zeebrugge, where he was put in charge of the starboard side of *Vindictive*. Perhaps the single-handed attack of one woman on the Admiralty was an equally daring adventure.

'In a way,' writes her great friend and senior master G H Wilson,* (to whom I am indebted for much of this chapter) 'this story of the storming of the Admiralty is a little cameo of Mrs Charles herself. It shows her impulsiveness, her knowledge of man (by which I mean men and not mankind, for I don't think her knowledge of women was nearly as keen or as accurate), her self-reliance, her power of will, and her utter refusal to accept 'No' for an answer.

'As may be gathered . . . Mrs Charles is rather a terrifying personage, especially to those over whom she is in authority . . . To find out what she really is you have to be in a hole, and the deeper and more miry the hole the more you will find what a friend she can be . . . With all her sympathy for the unfortunate bemired one, and all her feelings of sorrow for his case, I think there is for Mrs Charles the same sense of excitement, I might almost say, joyous abandon, in attacking the troubles and difficulties of her friends, that she has in dealing with her own. I am irresistibly reminded of that noble passage on the war horse in the book of Job, "He saith among the trumpets, Ha! Ha! He smelleth the battle from afar." There is something, or more pleasurably, someone to go for. Such is Mrs Charles.'

As Mrs Charles greeted me on arrival so she would be apt to greet all boys, past and present, with the same hug. I have seen it with Bishops or Blues, with a future General Carver or a Michael Hordern, together, as likely as not, with some

* *History of Windlesham House School, 1837–1937*, by G Herbert Wilson.

shrewd comment on their latest activities. I never saw one who did not accept this treatment as completely natural and wholly right. They were all her boys.

On our first Sunday at school she summoned me, with the other new boys, to her study and talked to us. Much is debated nowadays about sex education in schools. Mrs Charles had a way of giving sex education that was all her own. It was extremely down to earth and where necessary explicit. At the same time there was with it all a sense of the wonder of life, of the beauty of genuine love and of God's provision for us all. 'One day you may want to tell your mother that you are grateful to her for what she went through in bringing you into the world.' There was often a touch of fire and brimstone in Mrs Charles' talks, but that is not what you took away with you as much as the positive adventure of a life of honour and purity.

I was at Windlesham during the First World War. Of course we had little idea of the difficulties and anxieties of feeding a hungry horde of growing boys when there was a much less efficient rationing system than there was in the Second World War. We laughed at or complained of rook pie, stinging nettle greens, black rolls with the odd bit of string in them that we christened 'elephants' eggs'. But there were treats on Sunday nights, when you were a monitor and sat at the staff table. There were scalding-hot fresh rock buns at the mid-morning break. All the same, there were times when we felt really hungry. I once managed to acquire a packet of gelatine, which when suitably diluted would provide a dish for ten persons. I ate the lot. Fielding on the boundary at cricket that afternoon was a hazardous enterprise. A sudden stretch or dash could have caused an explosion.

The teaching at Windlesham was good. Mr Wilson, the senior master, was that precious rarity, a born teacher. Mrs Charles' elder son, Gilbert, was a good classicist. As more and more of the masters were called to the Services we had to put up with some odd and interesting substitutes. Their efforts may have helped to deprive me of a scholarship to Marlborough, but they made up for it in other ways. One

American was a superb singer, with a repertoire from Bach and Schubert to Vaughan Williams and Roger Quilter. To lie on the floor of a crowded room and open heart and mind to a whole new world may have been worth a scholarship or two. From the start I loved music and had quite a good soprano voice. I hear myself taking the solo in school chapel. 'And God shall wipe away all tears, all tee-ears from their eye-eye-eyes.'

My time at school was a mixed experience. For the first year or more I lived in a state of semi-shock, as I struggled to discover what was happening to me in this new world into which I was so suddenly plunged. I lived mostly in a dream world of my own. When I told my friends that my father was an acrobat, I was not consciously telling a lie, though it must have sounded so when father came to preach in school chapel, and to the disappointment of the boys did not come in swinging on the chandeliers or doing flip-flops up the aisle. At one point Mrs Charles almost despaired of me and wrote to my father suggesting that I might do better elsewhere. However, I hung on, so did my father and so did Mrs Charles—and I ended up head of the school!

I suppose over the long arches of the years most of the important, worthwhile things I have forgotten. But the bits I do remember are so vivid: A stirring picture from some master of Charles Peace, the murderer, standing on the scaffold and saying, 'Now for the great adventure.' Then there were the soldiers whom Mrs Charles invited to camp on one of the rugger grounds. A cricket match was organized between them and some of the staff, whose numbers had to be made up by the music mistress, Daisy Estridge. She was brought up in a school house in Repton and learnt cricket at an early age. To start with the soldiers gallantly bowled her lobs and dollies. By the time she had sloshed several boundaries and made over seventy, they were hurling down their wildest. Miss Estridge was my cousin, and I basked for a little in reflected glory. She taught me to swim, walking up and down by the deep end of the pool, holding a kind of fishing rod with a belly band attached to my tummy. I learnt to high dive. No one *had* to climb the steps to the highest diving board. But if you did there was only one way down. I remember Armistice Day, 1918, and half the school in bed with flu. Some of the rest of us went down the school drive to the bus stop where 'Mademoiselle', a much teased and long-suffering stop-gap French teacher, stepped off the bus punctually at the same time each day. I hope amid painful memories she treasured the experience that day of being escorted up the drive by a guard of honour singing the *Marseillaise*.

Then there was the master who wrote on my best attempts at writing, 'Avoid hooks.' This was followed by 'Hooks again.' And later, 'Write out fifty lines, "Why more hooks?"' The real problem never occurred to either of us. I had not the slightest idea what 'hooks' were. Drawing was another blank spot in my education. It still is. 'Draw a map of Britain putting in various towns, rivers, etc.' My outline of our shores was unrecognizable. As for the various landmarks, I inserted a number of heavy inkspots but felt it advisable not to name them, but let the spots remain anonymous. My teacher described my efforts as a 'three-toed sloth with chicken-pox.'

I recall Sunday afternoons with a book and a rug on the grass. All Saints' Day when a bunch of friends could share a picnic in such unlikely places as the empty swimming pool, or the highest branch of a big walnut tree! End of term, and the pillow fight on the last night, led occasionally by the Bishop in Jerusalem, an ardent Old Boy!

At the centre of the school and its life was the chapel. It had originally been acquired in a very Mrs Charlesian way. She and her husband, already an invalid, were visiting Oxford in 1896. As they drove in a cab past Carfax, they saw that the church which had stood there for centuries was being demolished. The perennial Oxford traffic problem was even then beginning. There was a notice to the effect that the remains and appurtenances were for public sale. Leaving her husband in the cab, Mrs Charles went into the derelict church. She found a bunch of workmen gathered in front of what had been the high altar watching some kind of prize-fight. Soon she was asking the firm of demolishers what they would take for the lot. After a consultation with Mr Charles

47

she offered £150 for everything. There was window tracery for five windows and enough old oak for a roof and a gallery. The three-decker pulpit was an extra but was bought by friends. The pulpit was cut down to a single-decker, and the long winding steps that led up to the top deck became the stairs leading up to the organ loft of the chapel.

So the remains of an old Oxford church, where William Shakespeare once stood as godfather to Sir William Davenant, has become the chapel of a modern school.

The chapel was always the heart and core of Mrs Charles' life and faith. It was an unpious religion, but it pervaded everything. Every day at twelve o'clock the chapel bell rang for two minutes while all over the school silence was kept to think about the Old Boys who were serving in the war. Every Sunday night the names were read of a growing list of those who had given their lives. By the end there were 65, nearly one complete generation of the school.

Mrs Charles never spoke or took an active part in the chapel services. She got her sons, as they grew up, to do that. There was also a school chaplain for Sundays. Her talks to the school were practical, dealing with some point of discipline, or with the moral life or honour of the school. Sometimes they put the fear of God into you. There was a leather thong that hung behind her study door. It was not often used, but there were times when she commanded what she called 'a jolly good spatting'. To start with this was administered by Nobby Clark, ex-marine and school butler. Mrs Charles would stand behind him telling him how many strokes to give. Sometimes Clark would interrupt and say, 'I think you are wrong, Mum, begging your pardon. He ought to have more than that.' Later, in my day, the spattings were given by one of the Malden sons.

But this is not the note on which to end, and it is not my memory of our Head. I can see her now talking to us, the boys leaving the school. She was very realistic about us, but at the same time rather proud. She would talk to us about the public schools we were going to. Her advice would be a mixture of keeping your bowels open, morals, faith and commonsense. When she kissed you goodbye for the last time (that is until you saw her again) you knew you had a friend who would never let you down. Perhaps her ways would not work with a modern generation. But there is a host of ageing gentlemen all over the land who remember her as though it were yesterday, and who know that she has put some mark on their lives that is hard to eradicate.

5

Bunny and the Boss

It was 1949, and my old school friend Bunny Austin and I were entertaining some film people from Hollywood. Everyone was performing, and Bunny and I rashly agreed to sing our old school song. It would be fair to say that Bunny's proficiency in holding a tune is about equal to mine in holding a tennis racquet. The walls resounded with the familiar Latin words:

> *Carmen Repandunum,*
> *Te canemus unum,*
> *Vita dum manebit . . .*

The tune did not seem so familiar. At the end one of the American actresses said, 'Are you two boys sure you did go to the same school?'

I arrived at Repton in the summer of 1920. Bunny came one term later. My arrival passed unnoticed; his made something of a stir. Although only just fourteen he had already won the schoolboys' tennis championship at Wimbledon. It seemed at times as though his head barely topped the net, but he nipped about the court with marvellous speed and precision. I remember bumping into a tall, athletic member of the staff a few weeks after Bunny's arrival. He prided himself on his coaching of the smaller boys at tennis. With much surprise and some chagrin he said, 'A most extraordinary thing has happened. I've just been beaten by a little shrimp called Austin.'

By one of those fatuous public school traditions, long since

(I imagine) swept away, it was not considered 'done' for a boy in one school house to make friends or even talk with a boy in another. So Bunny and I saw little of one another until our last, more privileged year, when I was wearing a speckled straw hat as a member of the Upper Sixth and Bunny was playing cricket, football and fives, as well as tennis, for the school. He and his friend Brian Valentine used to go in first to bat for Repton and they put on several century opening partnerships together. Valentine went on to play for England at cricket and Bunny, with Fred Perry, won the Davis Cup for Britain four years running. He is still the last home player to appear in a Wimbledon Men's singles final. He was, without doubt, in the thirties, one of our best-known, best-loved national pin-ups. Back in Repton days he was an unusually modest, relaxed athlete, and he and Valentine—together with their housemaster, the Rev. Jack Carter—set the pace for a more human and liberal Repton during our time there.

To start with in my house, *The Mitre*, life for a small boy could be fairly grim. In our first term a close friend, Archie Dunbar, and I were the smallest boys in the house and we would be made to fight each other to the finish, while the rest looked on and placed bets on the result. There were no intervals and the loser would finally collapse from exhaustion. Masters, except for housemasters and of course the Boss, were not allowed to practise corporal punishment, but senior boys could. Often the announcement would be made by a prefect, 'Towels have not been hung up in the changing room' (or some equally heinous offence). 'Will the following come to my study immediately after prayers.' Prayers would take on a certain urgency that night.

The fagging system was in full operation. Boys in their first two years were expected to clean boots, polish army buttons, light fires, scramble eggs, make toast etc, for the senior boy in his study. This was a useful but hazardous training for anyone as unpractical as I was. When a roar rang out from a house prefect, 'Fag!' every single junior boy in earshot was expected to leave whatever it was he might be doing and rush to the point of call. The last one there got the job. I can remember a pair of white doeskin cricket boots being thrown at me by a god-like member of the school Eleven with the words, 'You, clean these, at the double!' How to clean white doeskin boots, when you're much too frightened to ask? I chose warm, soapy water. It was a grey sodden mass of pulp that I presented to my lord and master just before the match. 'You blank, blank . . . idiot! Come and see me after prayers.' I realize now that the wretched cricketer was probably just as miserable as I was, having to turn out for the first Eleven shod in a kind of mud poultice. This particular story had a happy ending. The sun shone hot. The cricketer bowled well. Looking down, after he had taken a particularly important wicket, he beheld his feet encased in sparkling white. He returned the hero of the match. 'All right. This once we'll forget it. This once, mind you!'

Gradually you learn to adjust, then to enjoy, finally to revel in life. Take those august and awe-inspiring prefects, some of whom actually needed to shave; one day you discover that you are one of them. The house, the whole school, after the stern discipline of the war years becomes, or to me seems to become, more mellow, more tolerant, more varied and creative. You do not have to be good at any game to become a 'person' in your house. There is scope for originality, for experiment, even for mild eccentricity. A boy in my study who, on the classical side of the school seems one of the dullest members of society, is taken in hand by some imaginative master and introduced to the science block and the labs. Later he is to become one of the Cambridge physicists who pioneered the splitting of the atom. An older boy in my study is Michael Ramsay, later to be Archbishop of Canterbury. Looking at that almost ageless figure lumbering along today, it is hard for me to believe or to persuade my friends that we were actually at school together.

Ramsay was not only an outstanding classical scholar, he was a personality. His main interest then was in politics more than the Church. He was a devoted Liberal and saw himself as a kind of reincarnation of Mr Gladstone. When there was a General Election in the country, we held a mock election in the school. Ramsay was the Liberal candidate, and made his election speech before the whole school, attired as Mr Gladstone and speaking with Gladstonian passion and in Gladstonian prose. Although the Liberals were dwindling in the country, Michael won the school election hands down. He was a brilliant speaker. He and I, largely for fun, defended Prohibition in a house debate. We won. Quite an achievement in an English public school in the twenties. We also used to sing Gilbert and Sullivan duets at the end of term in house concerts, normally extremely dreary affairs. I suppose we brought the house down with encore after encore because of a general relief at finding performers who could let themselves go and did not mind making asses of themselves. Ramsay's interest in religion began to show itself in odd and unexpected ways. He used to make up collects for various masters, referring in Elizabethan periods to their various characteristics or mannerisms. 'O God, who has endowed thy servant so-and-so with various singular or peculiar gifts . . .' (specified in detail). Beneath it all there was a warm heart (how many times he helped me with a Greek verse or Latin prose), a deepening faith, a growing seriousness, perhaps a sense of vocation.

Ramsay was the third Archbishop of Canterbury in a row to come out of Repton. First there was William Temple, the greatest of recent Archbishops, but not the greatest of Repton headmasters. He was too kind perhaps to be a good disciplinarian, too brilliant to get completely involved in the details of running a school. My headmaster, Geoffrey Fisher, was the second. He was a magnificent headmaster, who perhaps suffered at Canterbury from the fact that he never quite got over his headmastering ways. He has been described as 'the greatest schoolmaster, and the greatest schoolboy, who has ever sat on the throne of St Augustine.'

He became headmaster at the age of twenty-seven, a month after the outbreak of Word War I. One can imagine the difficulties of a man in an ancient school, where some of the assistant masters had spent as many years at Repton as Fisher's whole life. Then there were the constant heartaches and tragedies. Three hundred and fifty-five Old Boys were killed in the war, again nearly one entire generation of the school. He had to weather a particularly difficult storm when Victor Gollancz, later of publishing fame, joined the staff and with severe and passionate pacifist idealism (but with a heady, and at times ruthless intolerance) almost split the school in two and caused something of a scandal at the height of the war.

By the time I arrived in the school the war and all these dramas were things of the past. Fisher was firmly in the saddle, and in his prime. 'The Boss', draped in winter in an enormously long and thick overcoat covered with his Oxford gown, with a mortar-board perched at the back of his head, was a familiar, friendly, but still formidable figure. Whoever you were, however small, however short the conversation, you were given the sense in those few moments that you were important, that you had his whole attention and care, that he listened to you as well as talked, that he enjoyed you. His encouraging 'well done' must have given many a boy heart when he needed it, just as the thunder would roll and the lightning would flash when that was needed too.

Even in his discipline you could sometimes sense an element of astringent humour that healed as it hurt. At the centre of the village of Repton there is an old market cross with a spike on top of it. On the first day of a winter holiday, as the light came up on an empty school, there was seen to be an article of bedroom furniture reposing on the top of the ancient monument. Term was over, but Fisher's resourcefulness was not. The offending 'jerry' was removed. By its make it was traced to one particular house. There was a check-up in each dormitory until one such article was found to be missing. Other deductions were swiftly made. The result was that a boy who had actually left the school for good early that day arrived home to find a telegram saying 'Return Repton immediately'. And as Fisher described it with great relish at a subsequent Old Reptonian dinner, he had 'the extraordinary experience of caning a boy in plus-fours'.

There were moments in the Boss's classes when sparks of imagination were struck and fires were lit. I can hear him talking about Tennyson and Browning, and reading that remarkable poem, *Instans Tyrannus*, adding at the end, 'I think I'll die in the Browning ditch.' His lessons on St Paul were a revelation. You could see and feel Paul passionately dashing off a letter to those 'dear idiots of Galatia' as he hurriedly took to the road again, fighting for a great universal conception of faith against the small-minded proponents of an exclusive church. Years later I was to write the Boss a somewhat passionate letter myself, reminding him of this and asking him to open his mind in a new way to Moral Rearmament. I never got a reply.

A modern philosopher has attempted to interpret the meaning of life in terms of 'peak experiences', a more satisfying and luminous conception to my mind than to concentrate on the neurotic or the abnormal. When I think of peak experiences in my own life, some of them go back to Repton. L A Burd, a classics master of great scholarly antiquity, bends over the big Liddell and Scott Greek Dictionary to look up a word. His short-sighted eyes behind thick glasses almost touch the page as he follows the small print back and forth, up and down. Then he looks up and says, 'The dictionary is nearly right.' Suddenly an enormous chasm of doubt opens at my feet. The dictionary *nearly* right? I had thought dictionaries were always right. That is what they are for. There was an astonishing tingle about the whole thing. Life would never be so safe or so predictable again.

The neighbouring town of Burton-on-Trent does not suggest a city of enchantment, a palace of the arts. But it was there that for me one of life's great revelations was vouchsafed. Gilbert Stocks, music master at Repton, used to conduct the Burton Choral Society 'on the side'. He invited a few boys to come with him to the annual concert. The Birmingham Symphony was in attendance. The main choral work was Coleridge Taylor's *Hiawatha*. As an hors d'oeuvres, the orchestra gave a performance of *Die Meistersinger* Overture. Imagine the effect on an impressionable boy of sixteen hearing for the very first time a live orchestra blaze forth these monumental opening bars. The gramophone records of those days were a mere scraping echo of the real thing. I was shot out of my seat, and as the great themes twined and combined in a glorious towering crescendo my blood raced, tears came into my eyes, and I was caught up in a peak experience that had never been conceived by me before. 'For a long time now,' writes J B Priestley, 'I have believed that the symphony orchestra is one of the greatest achievements of Western man. Perhaps it is his noblest achievement.' It certainly seemed to be true in Burton-on-Trent that day.

'Where has my childhood gone?' sings the hero in the film *Goodbye, Mr Chips*. (Not the far-better version with Robert Donat and Greer Garson, a film which was shot with Repton as its setting. Some eighty boys volunteered to stay on for part of the summer holidays for the background shots. None of them received a penny. Equity, O Equity! I believe that MGM did give the school a new cricket pavilion.) Most of my Repton days are far beyond recall. Of all the lines of Euripides or Homer that we learnt by heart (twelve lines at a time every single evening, plus of course all our other prep) I cannot now repeat a single one. But I'm thankful for many lessons that do remain, and realize that they are only the tip of the iceberg, while nine-tenths of what I owe to my school probably lies hidden beneath the surface.

I thank Repton for some unforgettable golden moments; crumpets by a roaring study fire after a long, cold run; the little cubicles in the music school where I went to practise the piano, shut myself in and knew, God willing, that no prefect, no master, no rule or regulation would disturb me for a whole blissful hour; lying on my stomach with a bag of cherries, while the evening shadows grew longer and a school match came to an exciting finish; the school library, a glorious place of oak beams and long mullioned windows, where I encountered for the first time in my life G K Chesterton, Bernard Shaw, and a host of others; play-readings on a Sunday night; Crommelin Brown, an English master, at the last lesson of term suddenly bidding us put away our indigestible set book, Browning's *Ring and the Book*, and relax over our desks while he read Keats and Shelley aloud superbly, and we caught a taste of an almost intoxicating flavour; Dr Stocks' piano recital after Sunday morning chapel, where one listened or read a book, or even ate chocolate quietly and was introduced to a whole repertoire of classical music. You could do anything within reason except talk. 'I never play when people talk. It's rude to play when people talk.' A good old Sunday night roar in chapel, where Dr Stocks again (one of my heroes) had written a whole series of hymn tunes in an original popular style, now much imitated but not in my opinion surpassed by modern hymn writers. I still think Stocks' setting of Milton's great poem, *On the morning of Christ's Nativity*, among the finest hymn tunes ever:

> Ring out, ye crystal spheres,
> Once bless our human ears
> If ye have power to touch our senses so;
> And let your silver chime
> Move in melodious time;
> And let the bass of heaven's deep organ blow;
> And with your ninefold harmony
> Make up full concert to the angelic symphony.

My ears still ring with the sound and my blood still tingles.

6

Encounter with Frank Buchman

I have spent some years of my life in theological colleges for the training of clergy. I have been both student and tutor. They are strange places. I have known there brilliant scholars, selfless Christians, affable pipe-smoking men of the world, gloriously outrageous rebels, and I think at least one genuine saint. One of my pupils became the editor of several brightly-coloured and very successful magazines for children and did both well and good with them. Another was a retired naval commander of twice my age who always called me 'Sir' in our tutorials. One or two have become bishops. Most are hard-working, conscientious clergy. One was a murderer. You can never be sure what will come out of a theological college. For a time Stalin studied in one.

In my years as a student we seemed to have a particularly varied and colourful crowd at Wycliffe Hall. In the small, cell-like sitting-rooms along our corridor I recall an English country squire, a vividly dressed American who played the banjo and drove an enormous sports car, an Arab who became the Vicar of Nazareth, a shy young Chinese who became a bishop. There was Francis Goulding, brilliant linguist, just back from a teaching job in Persia, and Hallen Viney, a high-powered executive who had left a position as manager of a factory in New York in order to enter the Ministry.

There was also my friend Bernard. Bernard Chutter had been one of the rebels and a delightful one at that. He was rotund and bespectacled, a poet, a delightful companion and a lover of the good things in life. I had often laughed at his good-natured cynicisms about the world around us and the college in particular.

We had not seen each other for some time and it was, I think, on the golf course where I first noticed that something had happened to him. It must have been somewhere around the eighth green (our golf was of the sketchiest and seldom went beyond nine holes) that he dropped the surprising remark that the only thing that gave life any point was to give everything.

'And you propose to give everything?' I said, as I approached the delicate matter of a very short putt. For once he answered me without a smile. 'Yes', he said, 'I think I do'.

I missed the putt. 'May I ask for what?' I said. He did not reply and sank his.

On the way home I kept glancing at the well-upholstered figure of my friend Bernard. Without a doubt there was something new about the set of his shoulders. For the first time he looked like a man who knew where he was going. I asked him to tell me more. He mentioned that he had recently met some people. They had made him think. They were interesting. They were perhaps the most interesting people he had ever known.

'If they are so remarkably interesting,' I said rather tartly, 'perhaps I might meet them too.'

Bernard did not smile. 'I don't know,' he said. 'I shall have to find out.' Of course he could not have found a way of intriguing me more.

In fact I had to raise the matter with him again before he admitted that he had mentioned me to his friends and if I cared to come along with him to so-and-so's rooms after lunch some day, it would probably be all right.

The greatest vistas are often reached through the humblest approaches. I arrived at the turning point of my life clattering up a dingy staircase of somebody's digs through a typical aroma of boiled cabbage and half-hearted drains.

The dozen or so men assembled in the room upstairs were warm in their welcome, but sufficiently reserved in the Oxford manner to avoid embarrassment. One or two were in rowing togs, with heavy sweaters knotted by the arms round their necks; an obvious freshman, straight from a lecture and a hurried lunch, was still in his new and shiny gown. There was a South African Rhodes scholar with a black moustache and alert, sensitive eyes; one or two Americans, and a German student with a high forehead, balding head and thick glasses.

I can scarcely remember a word that was said. But I do remember that after a short discussion, silence fell on the room, silence without awkwardness. Some of those present pulled out a scrap of paper and made a thoughtful note or two. After a while someone rather surprisingly remarked 'Amen', and conversation broke out again.

After that more or less everyone spoke in turn. It frankly puzzled me. It was like hearing snatches of a play when you did not understand the plot. Thoughts about the state of the world, the life of the University, fragments of a conversation, and once in a while a sincere conviction that obviously cost the speaker quite a lot and was somehow moving, or perhaps disturbing. It was a vivid string of colourful beads but where was the thread? I had never heard people talk with the same naturalness, and reality and humour about themselves and about God.

My friend Bernard, when his turn came, remarked that his great need was discipline. I could have told him that but it surprised me to hear him admit it.

A friendly goodbye, a warm invitation to drop in again, the clatter down the stairs and that was that.

'Well, I must say,' I began as Bernard and I bicycled along St Giles.

'What must you say?'

'I mean, what do you think they are up to?'

'I rather think they are out to change the world.'

This seemed too far fetched for comment.

'But all this paper and pencil business? What was that?'

'If God can put a thought into your mind, don't you think it might be worth writing down?'

'But half the things I could have thought of anyway. Yours

about discipline, for instance. Anyone could have told you that.'

'Oh, they have,' chuckled Bernard. 'Ever since I can remember, they've told it to me for years and years. But this is the first time it's registered.'

We cycled on in silence.

My whole instinct was to run a mile. It was preposterous and presumptuous. It was also extremely inconvenient. I was a busy young man of twenty-two with examinations to pass, concerts to attend and half a dozen other delectable fish to fry. But for some reason I came back again to that same room at the same time the next day.

There was a larger group gathered that day and I was introduced to several new people. One of them was an American, an alert, round-faced, bespectacled man of about fifty. When he heard my name he looked at me in a friendly, half-laughing way and said, 'Oh, Alan Thornhill, I know all about you.' My immediate reaction was, 'Does he? How ghastly! Had Chutter been indiscreet?' For at that point in my life I was careful that no one ever knew too much—let alone all—about me. But as I looked at the man again I had another thought. 'Does he? How wonderful!' It was not more than a flash. But for an instant it felt as if it might be a relief to have someone who did in fact know all about you and yet seem as unjudging and ungrudging in his friendship as this complete stranger seemed to be. His name was Frank Buchman.

In the conversation that followed, people recounted experiences they had had during the previous days in their life in college. Normally this could be boring. 'A bore,' according to one definition, 'is a man who talks about *him*self when you want to talk about *your*self.' In this case I found it interesting. There was a thread running through the conversation that I had not noticed the day before. It was the word 'change'. That people could and should be changed, in their human nature, seemed to be assumed. People apparently were being changed in this way in the colleges of Oxford. Stories were told to this effect, sometimes by the very person concerned, right there in the room.

I was again both intrigued and disturbed. Intrigued because the stories were human and sincere and interesting. Disturbed, because there was very deeply ingrained in me a philosophy of live and let live as far as activities in Oxford were concerned. I hated the thought of a zealous meddling in other people's affairs. But this was different. It was living a life that was infectious. If you were convinced and convincing in the way you lived, others might want what you had.

Besides, I had to admit that the philosophy of live and let live could sometimes have the effect of live and let die. I remembered the look on the face of a friend of mine who dropped into my rooms once and told me, with much embarrassment, that his 'people' (i.e., his father and mother) had just decided to get a divorce. I could tell that it was a terrible shock. The bottom had dropped out of his life. He seemed to be groping for something to hold on to. At one point he broke a long silence by kicking the fireplace and saying, 'You know, Alan, I'm incredibly irreligious.' It was all very public school and self-conscious, but I actually know it was a stifled cry for help: 'For God's sake show me a faith.' But in my mumbled, diffident reply there was no faith, and I could see my friend go away empty.

I know my Bible well enough to know that it stood for the exact opposite of all that. People who came to Jesus or his disciples did not go away empty. They were healed. They were transformed. In spite of my excellent upbringing I had never known anything like that happen to anyone. It certainly had not happened to me. I looked at the roomful of men, at my friend Bernard. They looked reassuringly ordinary, not fanatical, not pious, and yet . . .

Once or twice during the conversation people turned to the American for a lead or an answer to some question, but my impression was that he did not say much. He listened rather than talked, gently teased or interjected rather than lectured or advised. Then suddenly he asked me what I had to say. I had nothing to say to match what I had heard but groping for something—anything—I recounted an experience I had had the night before.

I had a youthful passion for the theatre and more of my time and money than I like to admit had been spent hugging my knees in the top-most balcony; drinking in plays, good bad and appalling, with almost impartial fascination. The mere smell of the theatre, the darkening lights, the swish of the curtain, the liberty to stare at other people and listen to them talk, was enough for me. I was always trying to get some compliant soul to go along with me and share my enthusiasm, and the previous night I had inveigled my Chinese friend, a quiet courtly man, to be my companion.

The show turned out to be the crudest kind of burlesque, greeted by ribald cheers from the undergraduate audience. My friend, who became a bishop on the Chinese mainland (and God knows in what terrible dramas he found himself engulfed in later) became more and more withdrawn and embarrassed. At one point when a line of chorus girls pranced on stage behind the leading man, he turned to me with much mystification and whispered, 'Are they his concubines?'

I suppose I'm a showman at heart and thrive on an audience. Anyhow the story lost nothing in the telling and went down rather well. It seemed at the end to require some point of conclusion, so I turned to the American, who had said nothing up to then but who was laughing wholeheartedly, and asked him what he would do in this situation. Would he leave the theatre, explain things away to the oriental mind, protest to the management, or what? It was a silly question. I was trying the man out. By this time I could almost see myself as some kind of archangel with a flaming sword charging onto the stage, scattering a covey of startled chorus girls into the wings.

To my annoyance, Buchman only went on laughing and then said, 'What did *you* do?' To my somewhat feeble reply, 'Nothing', he laughed the more and everyone joined in. Then suddenly serious he looked at me and said, 'Of course the theatre is a tremendous force. It could help to transform society.'

The incident is worth recalling because it illustrates one side of Buchman well. I was brought up in an academic tradition that tried to give logical answers to logical questions.

Buchman often seemed to skip the question entirely, especially if it were an irrelevant one. He concentrated on the questioner, and with uncanny precision put his finger on a vital spot. That remark about the theatre meant little to me at the time, but twelve years later it was to prove another turning point in my life.

By 1928, when I first met him, Frank Buchman was becoming a well-known figure in Oxford life. He came from Pennsylvania. His ancestors were of Swiss origin—what is known in those areas as Pennsylvania Dutch (Dutch = Deutsch). He was a Lutheran and an ordained minister. He had taught and worked in American universities. He had evidently travelled a lot, especially in the East.

He held no official position in Oxford. He gave no lectures, had founded no society, was not at that time identified with any movement. He was just a man who appeared from time to time and got to know people. He had friends among the intellectuals and the athletes, the drunks and the dons, the pious and the popular. He also got to know people in a deeper sense. He would stay as a guest in a college, or rent some lodgings, and very soon there would be a chain of visitors knocking at his door. Some came bristling for an argument, some came weighed down by a private worry or a hidden fear. Some were just curious or bored with a life that was too small.

However you came and whoever you were, you usually left with the knowledge that there was one person at least who understood, saw through you, and at the same time believed in you. He was a man, strangely enough, who had little advice to give, few answers to offer. He had no power or standing of his own. He was not bursting with charisma; to many, not immediately attractive. But when you thought about your time with him you might know you were face to face with the challenge or the chance of a lifetime. You could take it or leave it; it was up to you.

In those first meetings with Frank Buchman and his friends I felt like a man standing in the wings of a theatre during the performance of a play. There, quite close to me, almost within my reach, were people enacting a drama. They were men and women like myself, but there was a great gulf between us. They were caught up in events greater than themselves. All they said and did was part of a whole. Whether that part was small or big, whether they seemed to do little or much, they were somehow in character, in a continuous relationship with one another, and with the play. In the true sense of the word they were 'acting', that is to say they were filling a role not of their own making. The play was the thing and they were on stage. Everything they did or said mattered, every gesture counted.

I, on the other hand, only a few yards away, was alone. I was in the dark. What I might say or do was my own affair. It had nothing to do with the play. And yet (and this is what began to dawn on me that winter in Oxford) supposing I were to hear my cue, some word or act that would be a summons to me to take a step forward, only a step maybe, that might be a step out of darkness into light, out of a monologue into a drama, out of the wings and on to the stage? When I talked to Frank Buchman, I got the feeling that I was about to hear my cue.

It took me several months to begin to see the pattern of Buchman's life or to unravel the two-fold thread which wove it. Like the Athenians of old we in Oxford had intense curiosity for any novelty ... and like the Athenians we had a strong disinclination to do more than talk. Buchman listened more than he talked. When, in my early meetings with him, he did have things to say they as often as not struck me as unconnected, even contradictory.

One side of him, to my hypercritical academic ear, sounded crude and trivial. Sometimes when one of his followers had gone off individualistically and done some particularly silly thing, he would say, 'The banana that leaves the bunch gets skinned'. 'But Frank,' I would protest with all the student seriousness of youth, 'that's what a banana is for—to get skinned and eaten.' As likely as not he would just repeat, 'The banana that leaves the bunch gets skinned.' Infuriating! Then suddenly there was a delicacy and sensitiveness that made you feel like a clumsy ox. Late one night a young man in considerable trouble decided to go and knock on

Buchman's door. He found him up and waiting, with a kettle on the hob and two cups on the table. 'I thought you would come.'

Mahatma Gandhi used to recall that when he was living in the East End of London he called on Buchman at Brown's Hotel. As he was leaving Buchman hailed a taxi and paid the driver Gandhi's fare home. No words were said but Gandhi needed that taxi and the money to pay for it. Few at that time thought to act that way.

Undergraduates, for all their assumed sophistication, are very easily shocked. Buchman knew how to administer the shock. What we were learning at that time to call repression, or a complex, or fixation, he old-fashionedly called sin. 'Sin is anything that comes between me and God, or me and another person.' It was also a fact of life as crippling and deadly as cancer. 'Oxford is not intellectual,' he once said impatiently, 'it's immoral.'

'Learn to deal with sin. It's not a fly-swatter you need but a rotary street broom.' He knew that sin could be cured. 'Sin is the disease, Christ is the cure, the result is a miracle.' And this he not only said but demonstrated.

What gripped me in those early days was not so much his meetings as the miracles. The meetings often annoyed me. Young men and women who had discovered a new meaning and direction in life sometimes seemed horribly exuberant and cocksure about it. 'One thing I know, once I was blind, now I see.' All the reactionary in me rose up in protest. Surely they could not have been as blind as all that. Surely they did not now see as well as they thought they did. But when all was said and done, there were the young men and women genuinely different. They had come alive. There was a freedom, a selflessness about them that could not be denied. And that, I would argue to myself, must be a good thing, if not for me, at least for some of my friends.

There was one particular friend of mine, an American called Sidney, whom I used to take along to Buchman's meetings in the hope, Pharisee that I was, that they would do him some good. Sidney was a charming companion, who nevertheless seemed to me to be wasting his time and his scholarship, lounging around Oxford, smoking far too many cigarettes a day.

It was on a Sunday in the following spring that everything began to make sense. Buchman had invited a number of us to spend the day with him at a hotel by the river at Wallingford. So far, whenever I saw him, he had been very much in the background. On this day he did a lot of the talking. I cannot remember exactly how it happened but suddenly it dawned on me with a chill and a thrill, 'this man is a revolutionary'. Here for the very first time in my life I was at grips with the genuine article; or rather, he was at grips with me. Radicals I had known, free-thinkers abounded, sincere Christians were my upbringing. But here was something different. This man not only talked about an entirely new society, he expected it to happen. He meant it to happen and I knew he would go to any lengths in the way of personal sacrifice to see that it did. And what he had decided for himself he meant to reproduce in people like me. We were to be ready to go anywhere, forego anything, give everything to make Christianity relevant and revolutionary in an age that was becoming more and more Godless.

'What we are going to do now,' said Buchman, as the day drew to an end, 'is to rivet, rivet, rivet.' I did not fully grasp what he meant, but I knew it had to do with steel-like decisions of the will, whereby life would never be the same again; decisions that might lead to miracles.

It was all clinched for me as we stood in the lobby of the hotel waiting to drive home. I ran into Sidney. He seemed a couple of inches taller as he looked me in the eye and said, 'You know I always said I didn't believe in miracles. Well, I believe in them now. One has happened to me.'

Two days later we walked round and round the Parks, having it out. It turned out that during the Easter vacation Sidney had accepted an invitation from Buchman and his friends to spend a weekend together somewhere in the New Forest. He had gone, intrigued by the people there, but still extremely sceptical and critical. This was all the more so when some there had experienced an undeniable change of heart. They had come alive. This kind of experience is far more recognized and recognizable nowadays than it was in the Western world in the 1920s. Sidney remained unconvinced. 'A thousand shall fall at my side,' he had muttered grimly, misquoting the psalms, 'and ten thousand at my right hand, but it shall not come nigh me.' Then walking with a friend the real Sidney had broken through. Under the veneer of sophistication and triviality was a very lonely man, unsure of himself or his vocation or his true identity. It was all told to me that day in the Parks with honesty, with humour and with a complete lack of preachiness.

Of course I was glad for him. He was so obviously a more satisfied and convincing person. It was exactly what I felt he needed. And yet he left me more and more disturbed. 'You little beast,' I thought to myself. 'You've let me down.' The truth became more and more clear. We were alike. The man whom I had often patronized was myself, except that now Sidney was more honest and humble than I was. As we talked I felt like a man on the roof of a rotten-timbered, collapsing building, with a chance being offered to jump clear. And yet almost fanatically I resisted. 'It's no good,' I said at last, 'You're talking about something I know nothing about. Call it rebirth, call it revolution, I don't like it. I don't understand it, and I'm not sure I want to. In which case,' I added as my final barb, 'the most honest thing is for you to go your way and for me to go mine.' Sidney did not bat an eyelid. I expected some kind of protest or personal appeal but he just said, 'If you feel that way you're probably right.' And he turned and left me.

It was that evening in St Mary's Church, heart of the medieval University where Cranmer, Latimer and Ridley spent their last night before they were taken to Broad Street to be burnt at the stake, where the young Wesley wrestled with his calling and Newman thundered from the pulpit, that I (a theological student who was tempted to give up the idea of the ministry; a parson's son with three elder parson brothers, sheltered in a loving home, in protected schools and academic groves) answered the call that men and women have heard all down the ages. A sentence from the Psalms that Buchman had repeated several times out at Wallingford

68

came quietly back into my mind: 'Great peace have they who love Thy law, and nothing shall offend them.' Suddenly out of my turmoil came a great silence and a great peace. It no longer mattered what others thought or said or did. It was not so much that I felt a miserable sinner. That came later. I was being offered a free, undeserved gift. I would be an unutterable fool to turn it down. I would be worse than a fool, a coward.

Yes, Buchman was right. I was called to be part of a revolution. I knew little of what it might involve. It might mean to stay right on in Oxford studying for the same exams; it might mean going to the ends of the earth. It was a case of 'Rivet, rivet, rivet.' A cold decision of the will. But far more, it was 'Accept, accept, accept.' I seemed to fly up St Giles on my way back to college. For the first time I knew God's power to free me from myself. It was all wonder and worship. In one sense it had nothing to do with Buchman. I joined nothing, I signed nothing, but I had picked up my cue. From then on I was part of his oft-repeated challenge: 'New men, new nations, a new world.'

Here were the two great strands of his life, the individual and the world. Not for a moment did he lose hold of either. They were the axis on which everything revolved.

'Alan,' he would say to me in the years that followed, 'you should read fewer books and more men.' By this time I was a don and chaplain in one of the Oxford colleges, preparing my first course of university lectures on 'The Kingdom of God in the New Testament'. My rooms were lined with books and it is true I found them a great deal easier to handle than the young men all around me. You can shut up a difficult book. It is not so easy to shut up a difficult man. You can skip with a book. You cannot skip with people.

'Have an intense preoccupation with the individual man.' But how? Everything in me revolted against the proselytizing, 'Brother are you saved?' kind of invasion of someone else's personality. And yet the fact remained that a place like Oxford was bursting with intelligent, gifted people who were self-absorbed, caught in a routine, vague, directionless, if not actually defeated by life and utterly miserable.

69

Everybody talked about the new society. People still banked on the League of Nations. But at home we had followed the General Strike with a major depression. There were disquieting rumbles in Italy and Germany. The disruptive forces under Hitler, Mussolini and Stalin were acquiring a strategy. The constructive forces had none. Buchman had. It was people. I heard story after story of people from India or China, from the universities of the United States or South Africa, whose lives were transformed. I even had a part in this miraculous God-given process myself.

There was nothing remotely pious or sentimental in Buchman's dealing with people. His vision for those he was out to win seemed limitless: 'The interesting sinner can become the compelling saint.' 'All Buchman's geese are swans,' said someone. If so, Buchman had few illusions about either geese or swans. It was a fascinating experience to see him at work with people.

The only home that could be called Frank Buchman's own when I first got to know him in those early days was a roomy first-floor sitting-room and bedroom in Brown's Hotel in London. It seemed to me surprising in an unorthodox, not to say revolutionary man, that the place he constantly returned to and seemed to like best was a discreet, conservative setting like Brown's. You did not raise your voice in Brown's. You were greeted at the desk with dignity and restraint, whether you were a firebrand from the East End or the Emperor Haile Selassie, whether you were Stanley Baldwin or an untidy young Oxonian like me. But Buchman had greatly helped the son of the Swiss owner of the hotel, so there was always a room for him there.

'I've got a holy man from India coming to see me,' said Frank to a bunch of us on one of my first visits to Brown's. 'You'd better come and join us, and see what you make of him.'

Soon a party of a dozen or so were gathered in front of a cosy fire, with an impressively austere, fakir-like figure, and of course, Frank. Our visitor, it appeared, was making the rounds of the bishops, archbishops and other dignitaries. He was soon well away in a hypnotic sing-song of which I can only remember a fragment. 'The microcosm is greater than the macrocosm, the microphone is greater than the megaphone,' and so on into the more obscure depths of Oriental philosophy. How to comment if I were called on for a contribution? I need not have worried. Frank seemed content to listen at length until at long last the visitor paused for breath.

'Tell me,' said Frank, 'what kind of a curry do they give you in London?' The face of the holy man suddenly took on a gleam of humanity. 'Not good! Not good!' he said with feeling. 'I remember a curry I had in Bangalore,' said Frank. 'It was so good. Never to be forgotten.' 'Yes,' was the reply. 'My home was in Bangalore.' For a few moments the conversation came down to earth. That is, until the holy man remembered his mission. Once more we were plunged into the inscrutable. This time Frank did not allow him quite so long an innings. 'You must throw your voice out more,' he interrupted. 'I don't get all you are saying. Throw it out. Throw it out.' Again the conversation took on a more human tone. There was even a laugh or a smile or two. At length our visitor rose to go. 'Thank you, Mr Buchman. It is always a pleasure to meet with holy men.' 'Oh, these are not holy men,' said Frank briskly. 'They are a bunch of scoundrels, every one of them.' And he handed his departing guest a copy of the best-seller about his work. It was entitled *For Sinners Only*.

He was one perhaps of a dozen visitors to meet Frank at Brown's that day. I was interested to read in the Press later that the gentleman in question had left the country rather hurriedly, having been suspected of fraud in collecting money from well-wishers for his own somewhat unspiritual purposes. 'You must learn to read people,' Frank would say, 'like a page of print.'

During these years of the thirties I was to see Buchman's work and to share in it in many situations and countries—from the riot-ridden streets of East London to the stately, tension-filled halls and palaces of the League of Nations in Geneva. In one six-week Easter vacation before I was to deliver my first university lectures in Greek New Testament, he invited me to go with him to America and

71

Canada with a number of others. I pleaded the excuse of work and yet there was a strong urge to accept. After all, a few weeks with Buchman in his own country would be an adventure; it might conceivably throw light on the Kingdom of God and the New Testament.

Looking back, I marvel at the grace and patience of the man. We were an awkward and uncomprehending crowd. He not only organized our journeys, bought our tickets, allocated us our sleepers, found our hotel accommodations and arranged interviews and meetings, speaking engagements and assemblies; he had to put up with our poor manners and many stupidities.

Then there was the Press, with which Buchman had considerable though not always considerate experience. In one Canadian city he warned us especially to be careful what we told the Press about future plans and such. Feeling that these warnings obviously could not apply to an Oxford don in his twenties, I found myself in long and wordy conversation with a personable stranger, in the course of which he asked when the Oxford Group was going to Russia. I didn't know but gave as my opinion that we were bound to go sometime and that a friend of mine was learning Russian for the occasion. That night there were headlines on the front page: 'Oxford Group to visit Russia. Students learn language. Don' (with picture) 'discusses coming project'. Running into Buchman that night I was covered with confusion and tried to explain that of course I had not told them all the things they had printed. 'Ah,' he said, with a twinkle, 'but you told them something.'

He never referred to the matter again. He was like that. When you most deserved a thunderous carpeting, he forgave you with a smile. Sometimes when you felt you had done really rather well, he was trenchant in pointing out what you could have done better. His principle was to give people not what they deserved, but what they needed, the thing that would help them grow the most.

That tour with Buchman was a breathless round of meetings, overflow meetings, overflow overflow meetings, preachings, speakings, assemblies and above all, talks with people.

You found yourself booked up half-hour by half-hour, like any busy doctor, with personal interviews with young and old, who spoke about their lives with the utmost freedom, who desperately wanted to be effective and who, with God's help, would often go away different. It was in fact a fragment of the Kingdom of God. 'If I with the finger of God cast out devils, no doubt the Kingdom of God is come upon you'.

Prominent in all of this was the distinguished Oxford psychology and philosophy professor, Professor L W Grensted. Grensted, as speaker, lecturer and private consultant, was in demand from morning to night and it is fair to say he had the time of his life. On the last day we met with Frank in the hotel to say goodbye and go our various ways. 'Well,' said Buchman, 'it's been a marvellous time. The best teamwork yet. But after all,' he added, 'it's just normal living.' At which point Grensted exploded. 'Frank,' he said heatedly, thinking of the past six weeks and of years in Oxford stretching ahead, 'it is *not* normal living.' Frank only laughed and repeated several times, 'I think it's normal living.'

Another visit to that room in Brown's took place in 1937. I had been offered a new job in Oxford, as chaplain of my old theological college, Wycliffe Hall. I was also head over heels in love with a young lady who was not so enthusiastically devoted as I was. I was feeling somewhat bruised and confused. I decided to go and see Buchman in Brown's Hotel. Just to keep a well-rounded perspective on the affair, and having time to kill, I visited the famous Windmill Theatre for such spiritual sustenance as I might find there. By the time I arrived for tea with Frank, I had decided to leave out any reference to that part of my programme.

We were sitting down to talk. John Vinall, one of the porters at Brown's, had brought in crumpets and tea when Frank suddenly said, 'Alan, will you straighten that picture on the wall.' I did my best. 'No, no,' said Frank impatiently. 'More, more. No, now the other way.' I grew more and more confused. It was only after quite a struggle that Frank was satisfied. 'That's better,' he said at last. And as I resumed my comfortable armchair, he added, 'I hate being in a room with something that isn't straight.' I laughed. The ice was broken. I talked. A great deal came out. The sublime and the ridiculous. Wycliffe Hall and the Windmill Theatre.

As so often with Frank, the talking gradually stopped and we were quiet. Frank picked up a couple of pieces of scrap paper, handed me one and we both paused and thought and wrote down our thoughts. I had expected advice on whether to take the new job or not. I never got it. I don't remember what my thoughts were. Two things Frank wrote down I have never forgotten: 'Alan needs persecution', and, 'Nothing less than the spirit of St Francis'. A far cry from crumpets and tea. A far cry from the rest of my life. And yet . . . how often those two short sentences have stirred up the embers of my conviction and purpose.

Cruttwell

The Oxford train slowed down, paused for a moment opposite the cemetery, then crawled past the famous view of the gas works towards the spires and towers of the city. As I reached for my bag I felt the old familiar tingle of anticipation and excitement, with that slight touch of fear. I have arrived in Oxford hundreds of times from North, South, East and West by car, bus, train or motorbike but seldom without a tightening of the nerves.

This time a little fear was more than usually justified. I was returning to my old college to preach a sermon. I pictured the scattered array of bored undergraduates in their short black gowns, the scholars even more bored, white surplices comically festooned over 'plus fours' or 'Oxford bags' and at the end of the chapel, facing me in the seats of judgment, the dons. I knew fairly well who would be there; the aesthetic popular dean, the enigmatic philosopher, the meticulous ancient historian, the abrupt, lovable classicist. The lawyer and the mathematician on principle would stay away. And then there would be Cruttwell, my old tutor, now Principal of the college—a strange and remarkable man.

'Crutters' had been made Principal since I left. I had run into him once on a visit to Oxford. 'How are you,' he had said, eyeing my dog collar with a kind of sheepish leer. 'Growing in grace?' Then he hurried on. Yet I was touched with the invitation to preach and felt I did not merit it. I could imagine Crutter's rough explanation to his colleagues for having chosen me. 'May as well have the little so-and-so; he's harmless enough.'

It was such a short time ago that I had faced the same men, sitting in much the same way at the end of every term, in an ordeal that was known as 'Collections'. It was never quite clear to me what was being collected, except the scattered wits and tattered reputations of the students who would file in one by one to occupy the solitary chair on the other side of the long table, in order to receive a report on their term's work. T S R Boase, another of my tutors, would glance up from his papers and in graceful, if slightly weary tones (after all there were 130 odd undergraduates to get through) would address himself to the matter in hand. 'Mr Thornhill,' he might say, glancing down the table at his colleagues, 'has really been trying quite hard this term and if the results so far achieved are not altogether in proportion to his efforts, that is perhaps not wholly his fault.' Cruttwell's verdict would be briefer. 'When Thornhill gets something to write about, his essays may not be too bad.' A word of just and appropriate comment from the then Principal, and so out again into the friendly Quad and the wild dash for the London train.

As I stepped out into the cold, damp Oxford air that winter Sunday I could not help feeling as though once again I were heading straight for 'Collections'.

A few minutes later I was in college chapel. I thought with homesick longing of the hot, crowded Sunday night service in the South London church where I had been working for the last year; the friendly faces, the familiar smell of oil heating, wet coats and steaming umbrellas, the loud singing of well-known hymns. I pictured old Luck, the enormous ex-guardsman verger at St Mary's, his crushing handshake and his hearty 'You'll do' after my first sermon. Those were my friends, that was where I belonged, not in this austere chapel with its delicate Italian marble and carved woodwork, where your voice seemed to echo as in a vault, and the polite, inscrutable faces of your congregation seemed to leave your words freezing in the empty air.

And then it was all over and I was sitting with the dons at High Table while Henry the butler kept the glasses filled, and over Dover sole and roast pheasant the conversation was witty and elusive and about everything under the sun except anything that had to do with the world I had been living in for the last year.

After port and coffee in the senior common room, Cruttwell invited me to his study. We chatted about some of the news and latest gossip of college life. He told me of the impending departure of the present chaplain, a shy and scholarly man. Then the thunderbolt fell. The Fellows, he said, had talked over the matter of a successor at a college meeting and had decided that they might offer the job to me. I was staggered. My academic record was moderate in the extreme. I had no pretensions to being a real scholar. I was sure I was in no way cut out for a don. As I hesitated and expostulated Cruttwell became more and more genial. Under the awkwardness and abruptness of his manner I felt the warmth of the man. He has since been the object of a savage attack by Evelyn Waugh, another Hertford man, in his autobiography. (Waugh expressed his dislike by naming one or two minor and somewhat unpleasant characters in his novels, Cruttwell.) I can only say that I owe him a lot. He had taken me on when I first came to the college as a raw schoolboy, starting from scratch in a new subject, and had made the study of modern history a challenge and a delight. He had one of those phenomenal memories that could recall every detail of a book that he had read, even the number of the particular page where the information was to be found. Yet he never was bogged down in detail. His thinking seemed to bestride the centuries like a Roman aqueduct, planting massive piers of insight into the marshlands of conjecture, and conveying the clear water of truth from the earliest times down to the present day.

Memories came flooding back as I faced him that night in his study. I had heard him when, as Dean, he was responsible for college discipline, quell a drunken undergraduate party, without bothering to get up from his bed. 'Will you be quiet, you something, something so-and-so's,' he would roar through his open window. 'I know who you are. I'll see you in the morning.' And it would have the desired effect.

I recalled games of tennis which he played with ferocious

intensity, a small exhibition which he recommended for me in the college as my work improved, an invitation to his home in the New Forest, an offer to take me on for an extra year in the hope that I might scrape a 'first'. He had the reputation of being the rudest man in Oxford but his actions were always so much more generous than his words.

'There are the usual services in chapel,' he was saying, 'but otherwise the job is what you care to make it—getting to know the men and so on. You ought to manage it all right. As I remember you were rather less poisonous than some.'

This from my old tutor was a distinct compliment and I thanked him warmly. Then I thought I had better try to tell him a bit more about myself.

It was only four years since I had 'gone down' from Hertford, but so much had happened in the meantime. I had travelled twice to the Near East and had spent several months in Jerusalem. I had been to a theological college. I had reversed not only my collar but also my way of thinking on a great many subjects. I had spent the happiest year of my life amid the drab homes and lovable people of South London. I had met Frank Buchman and the Oxford Group.

I paused, wondering how to explain this last. Evidently I did not make a very good job of it, for his only comment was a grunt, and then, 'That's all right. I don't mind what you do in your spare time.'

'Well, it's a bit more than a matter of spare time,' I said. 'You see, some of us feel that this Oxford Group may turn out to be one of the important developments so far in this century. It may lead to a great spiritual awakening.'

But nothing would shake his mood of tolerant complacency. 'That's all right,' he repeated. 'Might be a very good thing. As a matter of fact something of the sort is overdue. They come about every two hundred years.'

'Anyway,' I concluded, still eager to drive home my point, 'whatever it is, I think it's going to affect everything I do, not just my spare time.'

But Cruttwell was getting restless. Likely as not he was thinking of the detective story or the P G Wodehouse novel which he would swallow in one sitting before going to bed.

With a final injunction to think it over, and the hint that after a year's probation the college might even consider making me a fully-fledged Fellow and tutor, with freedom to lecture on the Theological Faculty, he bade me a curt goodnight.

The late-night stragglers were long in bed before I could sleep in the college guest room. I didn't want to leave London. I did not want to return to Oxford. I was alarmed at the thought of becoming a don, and yet I could not get away from the thought that I would probably have to say 'Yes'. As the days went by, the conviction grew in me to accept.

Through it all was the half-humorous, half-disturbing thought: I had been up for 'Collections' after all.

The Oxford to which I returned in October 1931 was as gloriously beautiful as ever. The trees in the park were a golden brown, the brilliant red creeper on the ancient stone walls shone in the autumn sun. All the same, the University itself was fast becoming a very different place from that of my undergraduate days. The famous 'Oxford bags' were giving way to the shabbiest of grey flannels and the dingiest of red ties. Politics were replacing art as the major pre-occupation of the intellectuals; the 'hearty' of course in every college continued to play games, enjoy their friends, imbibe beer and occasionally smash windows. But even the hearty was apt to develop a social conscience. The economic crisis had hit Britain. Ramsay Macdonald had saved the country or betrayed the workers, according to one's point of view, by heading a national government. When undergraduates crowded the streets it was less likely to be for some 'blind' or 'rag' than to welcome the hunger marchers as they tramped through the city, singing lilting Welsh hymns and songs or delivering fiery, desperate speeches at the Martyrs' Memorial.

The Communist 'October Club' was becoming the liveliest and probably the largest political club in the University. The college secretary of the October Club in our college was one of the most charming, popular men in the whole place. He got on equally well with the aristocrat and the worker. He mingled with the Boat Club, he was a favourite at 'bump' suppers and college celebrations. But he seldom lost a chance to recruit men for his cause or to insert a shrewd piece of Marxist ideology into an otherwise lighthearted conversation. 'Join the October Club,' he would say to a cheery rowing man. 'Of course you must. They have the best-looking girls in the whole University and, between you and me, most of them are "available", if you know what I mean. It's all part of our philosophy.'

I had everything to learn about understanding the men, 130 of them or so. Historians, classicists, medicos, athletes, bookworms and diletantes; born aristocrats from the great public schools, men from workers' homes, fighting their way through on hard-earned grants and scholarships; American Rhodes Scholars, a few from the Orient, devout churchmen and militant atheists. It was for me a tougher proposition than any slum in London.

I began by calling on the freshmen. At least we had our greenness in common. One of the first rooms I visited was occupied by an enormous Punjabi, reputed to be a champion hammer-thrower. He told me he was a vegetarian, and in case I might doubt the effectiveness of his diet he threw out his chest halfway across the room and hissed, 'Look at me!' I was quite ready to take his word for it. The only decorations he had added to his room were a wooden statue of Mahatma Gandhi, a framed portrait of Stalin and a great wooden crucifix. 'My Trinity,' he announced proudly. I was duly impressed and we had several discussions of a political and religious character. Unfortunately, a few months later my friend suddenly departed from Oxford, leaving his bills unpaid and taking with him a girl from one of the women's colleges. Presumably his Trinity was enlarged to a quartet. I realized sadly that I still had a good deal to learn about human nature, and I remembered Frank Buchman's early remark to me, 'Read fewer books and more men'.

Other visits, I am glad to say, were more fruitful. One or two men in the college were profoundly affected and now can look back on lives of outstanding faith and public service.

I failed to influence the majority in Hertford College, but God honoured in unexpected ways the work in the lives of a few.

One of the disturbing elements in my life at this time was the behaviour of my friend Cruttwell, the Principal, especially in chapel. He was a most regular and faithful attender at the services and hardly ever missed a day. I found, however, that he was a man of violent likes and dislikes with regard to hymns. There were certain favourites in which he would join with a sardonic fervour. I can see him now, mouthing out Cowper's wonderful poem, 'God moves in a mysterious way His wonders to perform'. I'm afraid I was guilty at times of choosing this or one or two others of his favourite hymns, just to put him in a good humour. But if God moves in a mysterious way, so also did Cruttwell. If the hymn chosen was not one to his liking, he would shut the book with a slam, bang on the pew in front of him, snort with disgust and throughout the singing stare at the rafters in moody silence.

At first these performances alarmed me, as I felt they were precipitating some serious crisis in the life of the chapel, still more of the chaplain, but I would find the Principal that night genial and mellow, and after a time I came to take these outbursts as a matter of course. In fact I would often feel inspired to choose some well-known favourite, such as 'How sweet the name of Jesus sounds' or 'Jesus shall reign where'er the sun doth his successive journeys run', knowing all too well what the violent reaction at the other end of the chapel would be.

But then Cruttwell's opposition began to take on a much more serious and threatening nature. Among the handful of men in the college who had been finding a new faith in God and, as a result, a new aim in life and a new kind of lifestyle, there happened to be some of Cruttwell's favourite pupils.

One such man who had taken to dropping in to my room from time to time, especially interested me. Hugh Elliott was essentially a nice fellow, a fair scholar, idealistic and charming. I summed him up in those days as delightfully well-meaning but a trifle weak. Like everyone else, he loved

81

to discuss and argue, and long and late were the nights we spent, elbow-deep in the problems of the world and the ultimate issues of our life on this planet.

He talked a good deal, and I came to realize that much of the weakness came from an unhappy home. He had a deep longing to be a man, to stand on his own feet and to be free. He wanted to know what he was living for, but then again he would relapse into doubts and fears.

As I had discovered for myself, the crucial point in a person's relations with God is often a deliberate effort of the will. You cannot ooze into the Kingdom of God; beliefs, longings, good intentions will probably not get you there. Sooner or later you have to decide. Either you accept God's will for your life, or you do not. And in the end, if you do not accept it wholly, then you are still the final judge whether you will or whether you will not trust and obey. It is all or nothing and the choice is yours. It is true also that having decided, it is still all up to God. Only he can forgive you or transform you, but by the very nature of his love he will not do these things unless you ask him; and to ask him sincerely is to decide that from now on in everything God is the ruling partner and not you. He has the last word and the first as well.

Again and again we went over all this ground with my friend Hugh. It began to have clear and practical implications for him. He would have to stand firmly for what was right in his family, and to take a clear moral stand with his friends. Popularity might have to go, wherever it depended on compromise. Those were the days when you could be a fully-fledged member of the October Club, attend college chapel regularly, enjoy semi-drunk college celebrations, fiercely denounce the callous indifference of the rich and privileged, and end up a wild evening by a corporate jump in the men's bathing pool known as Parson's Pleasure, complete in white tie and tails. I told him my own battles over compromise and asked his help. He was studying for the Colonial Service and hoped one day to go to Africa. We talked of what it could mean there to have a white man, an official, living selflessly and thinking more of others than of himself. His whole being would light up in response, but then just at the crucial moment, back would come the fears, the old story of compromise and defeat and with it the intellectual doubts about God and moral standards and everything else.

One of the hardest things for most of us in trying to help another man is to risk hurting him. That is certainly true for me. I hate to hurt another person partly because I hate to be hurt myself. I hate to be severe because I love to be liked, and yet Christ at times was very severe. He risked losing his dearest friends by the stern things he said to them. To avoid all pain is to avoid the Cross.

So one night I was direct and severe with my friend Hugh. I talked about the tragic cost of compromise, for ourselves but even more for other people and for the world. Once again I put the issues just as fairly and squarely as I knew how, and then I said to him, 'Look, Hugh, I don't think I am going to talk about these things ever again. We have both said all we need to say. You will always be welcome in this room. I hope we will be friends, but in future we'll talk about something else. Good night.' I shan't forget the look of reproach on his face as he left the room, or the sinking of my own heart at the thought that by my clumsiness and impatience I might perhaps have let a good man slip for ever. I prayed for him during a large part of the night.

Meanwhile some of Hugh's friends in college, men whom he knew intimately, had begun to change. They had taken the plunge before him and they challenged him strongly to do the same. 'Hugh, why can't you put the same guts into your faith that you put into your politics, your hurdling and your hockey?' The combination of my words and their example acted on Hugh like an electric shock. He took an honest look at his life and decided he must take action to put things right. One morning he knocked on my door. He seemed a new man, a man of inner strength and conviction. He knew what he was going to do with his life, and that life, poured out for Africa and beyond, is one of the finest I have known. It started a process which set him on a new course with far-reaching effects, including, after some years, a transformation in his family. His father and mother were reunited after a break of twenty-eight years.

But the result that was of immediate interest was the effect on Cruttwell. To do him justice, I suspect that he had a genuine fear that an undergraduate's work would be affected by too much involvement in religion. (In fact, he told Hugh three years later, when Hugh was on leave from Africa, that he had been one of those who had done not worse but better than he had expected.) He probably resented any outside interference with men whom he regarded as his special concern. But the chill towards me was obvious. The differences were slight to start with, but gradually he who had been my friend became my enemy. There would be a marked and brooding silence when we sat together at High Table, a sarcastic cut or a pointed comment in the senior common room, an angry snort in college chapel when the attendance was thin or my sermons not to his liking. Several times I knocked on his door. But I could not get through to the man or feel free with him. There were times when even in his silences he could exercise an almost hypnotic control over the people around him.

For a whole year or two Cruttwell scarcely spoke a word to me. A sense of sheer hatred seemed to possess the man. It was no surprise to me that after my five years of appointment as chaplain and Fellow of the college my contract was not renewed, and I departed to another job in another place.

But that is not the end of the story. There is a sequel and very few people know it. I think that neary fifty years after his death it can be told now.

Not long after I left Hertford, Cruttwell became seriously ill. He had been a victim of shell-shock in the First World War. He was a man afflicted by deep wounds of body and spirit. He was divided between a bitter hatred of many people and of much of life, and yet at the same time he had a longing for something new. They say he kept a copy of St Augustine's *Confessions* beside his bed and would read from it every night. One or two of his sermons in college chapel were moving and unforgettable.

Nobody could diagnose his medical trouble, and he eventually was sent to a nursing home in Bath for some special treatment.

One morning in my time of quiet a compelling thought arrested me: 'You must go and see Cruttwell today and put things right with him.' I discovered his whereabouts from the college and set out on a long and round-about train journey to Bath. I was not eager for the encounter and I still did not know what to say to him. Some of the old fear remained. I could only seem to think of the slogan, 'Say it with flowers', and I bought a bouquet on my way from the station.

At the nursing home I was informed that I could only see him for a few minutes; 'Mr Cruttwell is not at all well and very disturbed in spirit'. I walked into a large half-darkened room, the flowers clutched in my hand. I could see him looking up, gaunt and grey, in the bed. I put the flowers in his hand. At last he saw who I was. We sat there quite a long time in silence, his hand resting on my arm, the flowers between us. Very few words were said. I know that I apologized for having been too cowardly to be the friend to him that I might have been. I can't remember much else, but I can see now how his eyes filled with tears and I can hear his voice muttering again and again words that sounded like 'It's very good of you. Very good of you.'

A few days afterwards a clergyman in Bath, entirely independent of me, made some visits to this nursing home, which was in his parish. He knew nothing of Cruttwell. He was not an intellectual man—in fact something of a simple, timid soul. But he was a good man and just recently, only a few weeks before in fact, he had attended some meetings of the Oxford Group and had experienced a renewing of his faith. Somehow, this man, a complete stranger, found his way to this particular room.

When Cruttwell saw him, he asked the nurse to leave him, and then to this visiting priest he said, 'My whole life has been a sham and a fraud. What I need is a simple experience of Jesus Christ. Will you help me?' I learnt this much later.

An intellectual discussion would have been completely

beside the point. A sermon would have been hopeless. This man had the simplicity and faith to do what was required. 'We will pray,' he said. 'I think you are only ready so far to pray the Lord's Prayer. Let us say it together.'

I can only guess what followed, but I do know this: not long after another Hertford man visited Cruttwell. He said he had seldom seen anyone so transformed. He seemed, as it were, washed clean. He was as simple and open as a child. He was at peace. Not long after that he died.

> God moves in a mysterious way
> His wonders to perform . . .
> The bud may have a bitter taste,
> But sweet will be the flower.

8

Sumi

The phone rang in my rooms in college and it was Professor B H Streeter on the other end. Would I consider taking another pupil? He was a Japanese who had just come up to Magdalen. He was a younger son of a wealthy industrial family and his name was Takasumi Mitsui. What did he want to study? He didn't so much want to study, B H explained, as to talk.

'Talk about what?'

'Oh, English and England; anything you like—even God.'

Streeter, I knew, had lectured in Japan. He was well-known there in academic circles. He was President of the Oxford University Japan Society. He gave a helping hand to Japanese students who appeared at Oxford. I said 'Yes'.

A few days later a stocky, smiling Japanese appeared at my door. I welcomed him and asked him to sit down, a feat which could not be accomplished without several bows and much ceremonial politeness. My pupil bowed. I, not wishing to be outdone, bowed a little lower. Mr Mitsui promptly bowed lower still. I followed suit. Before long, tutor and student were almost encircling one another on their hands and knees.

My pupil's English was limited and for the first tutorials there were more bows than any articulate conversation. Any learning or enlightenment was certainly more on my side than his. My ignorance about Japan was deplorable. About the famous Mitsui family I knew nothing.

'How many workers does your family business employ?' I enquired studiously.

'About a million.'

I gathered that the Mitsui enterprise included a bank.

'When was your bank founded?'

'In 1684, ten years before Bank of England.'

Even these startling pieces of information gave me no real conception of what the Mitsui family had meant, and still did, in the history of Japan. In fact it is only since studying a large and detailed history of the family by John G Roberts that I have begun to grasp the fantastic background of wealth and influence from which came the polite and modest pupil, in his short undergraduate gown, to my rooms in Hertford.

It was in the year 1616 that Sokubei Mitsui, the ruling head of the family, came to a momentous decision. Born of the aristocratic warrior class and now a gentleman of leisure, he foresaw a long period of peace and prosperity in Japan. Warriors might be on the way out and traders on the way in. In spite of the fact that commerce was looked down on and merchants ranked in esteem only just above the outcasts, who were not classified as human beings, Sokubei gathered together his family, who were falling on financially evil days. Bowing to the family shrine and clapping his hands smartly, he declared solemnly:

'A great peace is at hand. No more shall we live by the sword. I have seen that great profit can be made honourably. I shall brew sáke and soy sauce, and we shall prosper.'

From this humble beginning the business extended from selling sáke to money-lending, and then to the selling of cloth. The house of Mitsui sold large rolls of fabric. But they were not too proud to sell also small lengths to the ladies for their kimonos, and in their establishments there appeared for the first time the signboard, which remained for generations the hallmark of the Mitsuis: 'Cash only. Fixed prices.'

By 1700 there was set up in Tokyo what was probably the world's first department store, with a staff of forty, where customers would remove their shoes or sandals, recline on silk cushions, drink ceremonial tea and engage in polite conversation while bolts of material were brought from the warehouse for their inspection.

By wise business methods, by carefully planned marriages,

by constant attention to even the smallest details of personal behaviour, the house of Mitsui had grown, by the time I knew Takasumi, into a massive complex of businesses, which was a great national institution with an influence in many ways equal to that of the government, and a dignity only surpassed by that of the Royal Family.

Sumi's father, Baron Machiroemon Takamine Mitsui, lived in a great mansion and estate in the heart of Tokyo. Here, amid groves and gardens, shrines and pagodas, with rockeries set with exquisite planning amid brooks and water-falls, there stood a house so vast that it is said that one servant had to be employed full-time to open and close the sliding doors that covered every window. By the time many hundreds of windows were opened up, it was time to start closing them again. Here entertaining of the choicest and greatest kind took place. Beside the opulence there was a genuine care for each individual guest. 'On one occasion Baron Mitsui asked each foreign guest what bit of landscape in Japan he liked best. The choices were recorded and two years later each guest received a picture painted by one of the outstanding Japanese artists, and beautifully framed.'*

When Edward, Prince of Wales, made a State visit to Japan in 1922, Takamine was given the honour of entertaining him at a banquet. Although he was only given a month's notice, he drew up plans and built an English-style banqueting wing, capable of seating more than a hundred guests at dinner. It was completed just in time. Sumi, like the other Mitsui children, was not allowed to sit at table but they met the guests, were introduced to the Prince of Wales after dinner, and sneaked into the kitchen to sample the good food, every detail of which was supervised and directed by his father.

So this was the sumptuous setting from which my pupil came. How little of it he revealed! How little I grasped or understood! But there was another side to the family background. Sumi's father, alone with his family, was a quiet, gentle and sensitive man who listened more than he talked; who treated his wife, and all women, with deference and

* *Mitsui* by John G Roberts.

89

respect; who was more of an artist than a business man. He was engrossed in painting, in silk collage and calligraphy, and especially in the Noe drama, for which he had built a special stage in his house, and in which he and his family often performed.

Gradually I got to know and admire this gracious, sensitive side of my pupil's character. I was invited to supper to meet his elegant and petite wife Hideko, herself a Mitsui and connected also with the Sumitomo family. There were two adorable children, Naoko aged seven and Yori some years younger. There was another child on the way. We ate raw fish and sukiaki, specially brought from the Mitsui head-quarters in London. We began to talk more freely. Mrs Mitsui was in urgent need of help with the children. Could I suggest anyone?

Some months previously I had been speaking in a church in Bournemouth. After the service two teenage girls had come up to talk. They invited me to their home for supper and I had spent a refreshing and delightful evening with their family. One of the girls was a good pianist and we shared at that time a passion for Elgar. They introduced me to his cello concerto, and I had fallen in love with the music and with the whole family. They likewise peppered me with questions about faith and change and the Oxford Group. We had kept in close touch, and at this point, when the Mitsuis talked about help in the family, I thought of Margaret, one of the daughters, who had been disappointed in an engagement which had failed to mature and was looking for a worthwhile job.

Soon Margaret Aldridge was in the Mitsui home, and soon after that some remarkable changes began to take place in the Mitsui children. Margaret vividly remembers being intro-duced by their father to the two children. 'These are my children, Yori and Naoko. I want you teach them listen to God.'

Any religion that there was in the family seemed to be related to the Shinto faith. My efforts with my pupil to discover what this meant in practice had not got me very far.

'Do you actually look on the Emperor as God? Do you worship him?'

There was a long pause and then the answer came: 'I was at school with him.' I had begun to discover that Sumi, with his limited language, had a knack of conveying much in a few words.

Now, however, the Mitsui children were learning about God. They discovered that their English nurse was praying on her knees. What was she doing? Whatever it was, it seemed to make a difference. Could they learn it too?

They could indeed. What's more, prayer could be a two-way experience. They could talk to God but God could also talk to them. Whatever the truth of this remarkable assertion, the results were undeniable, and for a busy bewildered Japanese mother in a foreign country, extremely gratifying.

Hideko Mitsui still kept much of the old tradition. When Sumi walked through the streets at Oxford on his way to a lecture, she might walk behind him carrying his books. When the lecture was over, she could be there to follow him home. Respect and authority were the keynotes of the home. That did not prevent two lively youngsters, tasting the freedom of Western life, from making an occasional nuisance of themselves. There had been threats, tears and tantrums. The generation gap was widening. Hideko could not refrain from asking questions when the children under their new nurse became happy and obedient.

When staying in the Hyde Park Hotel, their London home, Yori, aged six, strode towards the lift door, leaving Margaret and Naoko to follow. 'Ladies first,' said Margaret automatically.

'No', said the six-year-old defiantly. 'In Japan, men first.'

'Yes, but you are in England now'.

The stocky little boy stepped aside and the ladies got into the lift.

The children were soon talking better English than their parents, so that it was with their help as interpreters that Margaret began to answer her mistress's questions. Soon mother and children were starting the day together, reading stories from the Bible and listening to the thoughts that God

91

can give to the youngest as well as to the older of his children. Hideko was learning what it means to be a Christian.

It was when she was in London awaiting the birth of her third child that Hideko came to the decision that this child should be born of a Christian mother. She was prepared for baptism. I was invited to the ceremony and had the unexpected thought to take with me my church robes. By some mishap the local vicar failed to turn up on time, so I had the unexpected privilege of performing the baptism. A few days later the baby was born.

Not long after that, Sumi came to my rooms for his weekly tutorial. I had sensed that he was a disturbed man. His wife's decision had affected him deeply. Not only had she taken a momentous step in her life—that was bad enough. Much, much worse was the fact that she had done it first without waiting for him. Was he, a Japanese husband, head of a distinguished branch of a great family, supposed to follow his wife?

That morning I had been thinking much of the Mitsuis and had written down a few thoughts on the subject of pride and forgiveness. I began our lesson by reading them to him. Then I read the story of the Prodigal Son. Having done so, I had the sharpest warning not to add one more syllable but to wait until my pupil spoke. There was what seemed an interminable silence. Then at last: 'So it does not matter how much we sin. God is always ready to forgive us.'

Still silence. Five minutes. Ten minutes. It seemed eternity. Then, right out of the blue:—'I am proud and selfish man, and I come from proud and selfish nation.'

'Mr Mitsui,' I said, 'I am a proud and selfish man and I come from a proud and selfish nation.' We knelt and prayed, he in Japanese and I in English. I understood nothing and yet understood everything.

From then on it was as if a door that had been tightly shut stood wide open. We discussed everything from our personal lives to world issues. So often Sumi was the teacher and I the learner. We were talking one day about God having a plan for the world. Sumi, again out of the blue, said, 'Japan

in China, God's plan?' The Sino-Japanese war was at its
height.

'That is a question for you to answer,' said I, careful not
to fall into a trap. Another pause.

'I think, *not* God's plan.'

'Well,' said I, pleased at this admission, 'I believe you are
right. It's not God's plan.' Another pause.

'Britain in India, God's plan?'

So our mutual education advanced.

There came a day when Sumi, with his three children,
Naoko, Yori and the baby Aiko, were baptized in Iffley
Church, Oxford, while Hideko stood as their witness. I was
a godfather to Yori, who by now was a smart little schoolboy
in the famous Dragon School at Oxford.

We all became fast friends. They got to know Frank
Buchman and took an increasingly active part in the life of
the Oxford Group. Sumi's gift of saying much in a few words
became a legend. One day during a tutorial he remarked,
after one of those long silences, 'At home, rather a dictator.'
An enormous social revolution was implicit in those five
words, but with Hideko and the children's help they worked
it out.

He could be as incisive with others as he was with himself.
Travelling in a taxi one day with some big industrialist who
poured out his many criticisms of all and sundry without
drawing breath, Sumi at long last got in two words of his
own: 'Purity, perhaps?' Enigmatic, but possibly relevant?

He travelled the country in his big Armstrong-Siddeley,
nicknamed *The Battleship*, speaking briefly but effectively at
meetings and attending the 'house-parties' which were the
setting for much of the work of the Oxford Group in the
thirties. It was at one of these at Eastbourne in the spring of
1938 that he, with his family, decided to return to Japan and
fight there for a new policy of peace. 'Sumi must become a
peace-maker,' was Frank Buchman's thought for him.

Back home in Japan, it was no easy time for such a
message. Anti-British feeling was at its height. There was a
national move to suppress Christianity, 'a device of Jewish
ideas which threatens to encroach upon the spirit of the

Japanese race.' Christian teaching was forbidden even in missionary schools.

Undaunted by this Sumi boldly proclaimed publicly and privately the faith that he had found. He gave a series of lectures on the Oxford Group before business men's clubs and to an imposing audience of two hundred Mitsui executives.

Then came the war and the long silence, with no news of the Mitsui family.

It was more than five years later that I discovered that Sumi, although his family firm had been deeply involved in war production, had at considerable risk even of his life, refused to have any part in it. Instead he founded a school close to the Mitsui mansion in Tokyo. It was a school specially for the children of diplomats and business executives who had been recalled from the West. There was a special emphasis on the teaching of English. He was preparing for the day when the wounds of war would have to be healed. He also became President of the vast Mitsui charitable foundations. He was one of the first of his people who got to the West after the war was over. He looked a good deal thinner, though with his dark hair and round face he was still remarkably young for his age. It was a long time before I had discovered that my most respectful pupil was in fact some years older than I was.

He spoke little of the hardships they had all undergone in Japan. The famous Mitsui firm had been virtually disbanded and split up into small independent groups.

'How does your brother, Baron Mitsui, now head of the family, live?' I said to Sumi.

Sumi smiled. 'Like the onion,' he replied. 'Every time gets hungry, sells another family treasure. And every time he peels a skin he cries.'

Little Aiko, the herald of the family's faith, had died. There had not been enough to eat. 'And Yori, my godson?' I asked.

Sumi smiled again, this time sadly. 'Yori, rather a playboy.'

Sumi's loyalty to the work of Moral Re-Armament had

remained unshaken, and now his determination was to bring the leadership of his country into touch with the ideas on which he felt the new Japan must be built. By this time a great conference centre had been established at Caux in Switzerland, and each year Sumi and his family would travel to Caux or to the United States bringing with them delegations of businessmen, labour leaders, and politicians, which grew larger and larger. The deep wounds of war needed to be healed. Pearl Harbour on the one side and Hiroshima on the other stood like an impenetrable wall between us. Forgiveness could never come easily. Too many had suffered too much.

> Let the healing streams abound,
> Make and keep me pure within.

These words of Charles Wesley became more than a familiar hymn. They were a living experience between nations as well as between individuals.

In the summer of 1949, thirty-seven Japanese leaders came to Caux, including the first Socialist Prime Minister. Next year seventy-six came, the largest delegation at that time to leave Japan for Europe. There were Members of Parliament from all the main parties. They also included seven Governors of Prefectures and the Mayors of Hiroshima and Nagasaki. On their way home they were received in Washington in both Houses of Congress and their spokesman addressed both Houses and apologized to the American people for the wrongs that had been done. They were received with a standing ovation, and the *New York Times* next day had a leading article saluting this new step in statesmanship.

This world mission only five years after Hiroshima had its humorous moments also. The problem of language was naturally a great one. The delegation brought with them one or two official interpreters. I remember a day in Caux when we decided to show our guests a performance of my play, *The Forgotten Factor*. I recall vividly the serried rows of unsmiling Japanese each with his headphones clasped to his ears in order to follow a simultaneous translation of the play in

Japanese. The first act of the play, which is usually regarded as humorous with quite a few laughs, was received in complete silence. Not one smile. Not a gleam of response. Somewhat worried I went up to the translation booth after the first act.

'Do you think they are getting it?' I asked.

'Very sorry,' was the reply. 'Have not been translating play. Gave instead latest news from war in Korea.'

Before returning to Japan, the delegation issued this statement (22 July 1950): 'We realize that Japan has caused great suffering through her pursuit of false ideas and false roads. We hope in future as a nation to show by our deeds that we have found a change of heart and that we can make our contribution to the remaking of the world ... We appeal to the governments and people of the West to ... make themselves expert in the philosophy and practice of Moral Re-Armament, which is the ideology of the future. Then all Asia will listen.'

At the heart of all this tumultuous activity were the Mitsui family. Sumi's contributions to meetings and conferences were as apt and colourful as ever, and now Hideko would join him on the platform. Speaking of their life together as a married couple, he would say, 'I was like coconut. You know coconut? Hard on outside, very soft on inside. My wife like peach. You know peach? Soft on outside, hard on inside.'

And then one notable day in Caux they were joined by their playboy son, Yori, who added, 'I was like banana. Soft on outside and inside, and very slippery.'

But Yori, my godson, was the greatest miracle of all. Too young to fight in the war, he had attended the famous 'Peers' School', where his father, like the Emperor, had been a pupil. Yori had become increasingly cynical and disillusioned. With Japan's defeat, life for a proud aristocrat seemed hopeless and pointless. The coming of the American Forces to Japan brought a whole new world of bars, night-clubs, prostitution and the black market. Yori plunged deep into it all. He even hired a bodyguard to protect him in his various nefarious activities. But he had come to Caux with his parents and sister, and he found hope and healing and a passionate faith and conviction from which he never turned back.

This was in the summer of 1948. Yori had only three more years to live. The war had taken a terrible toll. He developed a cancer of the bones for which there was no cure. Bit by bit his life was eaten away. But what an amazing three years he made of it.

I have never known a young man who poured out his flagging strength so freely to serve others and serve his country. As these delegations travelled the West in Switzerland, Germany, Italy, Britain and America it was Yori, day after day, who arranged their transport, collected their baggage, secured tickets and visas, shepherded, befriended, inspired, or occasionally scolded the travellers. He burned with an intense though dying flame that they become the leaders that Japan and the world needed so desperately after the war. Men like Prime Minister Kishi, who later were to visit other countries apologizing publicly for the wrongs Japan had done, pioneering a new kind of diplomacy of the humble heart, owed much to the care and self-giving of a young son of privilege who became a troubadour for God.

Here are some extracts from the notebook which Yori used regularly, writing down the thoughts that came to him day by day. They were written early in the morning in days of constant travel, long hours of unseen work in the background, sometimes from a sick bed, usually in pain, often battling with temptation, opposition and discouragement.

'Remind yourself more often that you are in a revolution and that you have no time whatever to waste. Always be free in heart that the Lord can guide you through His plan.'

'Faith is an idea that changes people. An ideology is an idea that changes nations. You won't keep going without a faith. You will not change a nation without an ideology.'

(In bed.) 'Lazy, undisciplined creature, you have not one minute to waste. Broaden your knowledge. Know the facts. Pray more. Fight more. Never lose against your illness.'

'Do not ever try to look like a big shot, because you aren't one.'

'Have at least one hour to an hour and a half of listening

97

to God each morning. That means you've got to win those sleepy battles in the morning. Never pity yourself. You won't get anywhere. Don't dream about the future or about anything. Live in the present and be absolutely guided now. Have no fear whatsoever about your health. Be absolutely honest about it.'

'Don't think you are doing a mere job, because you're not. You're serving *me*.'

'You are hard with other people, and damned soft with yourself.'

'The Cross represents Jesus Christ giving everything, and it becomes real when you give everything.'

'The Cross means to identify yourself with God's battle for the whole world.'

'You must fight for a new Japan, a Japan re-born into the family of nations, a Japan that is willing to give and not get.'

'You've got to go through the bitter salt before the flower blooms.'

I saw my godson in the Mayo Clinic a few weeks before he died. His body was wasted away but his spirit burned like a pure white flame.

These were the last thoughts that he wrote down:

'You need Me now. Ask for forgiveness and come back to Me. Surrender everything to Me, for I shall take full command of you. Grateful to Mum. Pray for Naoko and Sei' (her husband). 'Make them great. Have no fear.'

A few hours later Yori died. He is buried in a cemetery not far from Los Angeles. His parents and family visited that grave faithfully almost every year.

The story of Sumi has, for us, an unexpected postscript. We frequently saw Sumi and Hideko as they visited Britain or came to the great conferences in Caux. The years went by and we all became older. Sumi more and more took on the stature of an informal but influential and respected senior statesman and ambassador of his country. Many times when we met in London, Sumi would say with a smile to us as we parted, 'You must come Japan.' We would smile and bow, knowing full well that we would find it very hard to find the money to make such a trip. And so the years went by, and it seemed less and less likely that we would ever 'come Japan'.

And then one year in his usual way as we parted in London, Sumi smiled and bowed, saying as before, 'You must come Japan.' Only this time he added, 'I send you tickets.'

By this time the Mitsui firm had gradually become re-established as a considerable power in Japan and in the world. It was never again to be the mighty force it had been in the past before the war, but it was a thriving international business. Sumi was as good as his word. Through the Mitsui office in London we received round-the-world tickets for Barbara and myself, not only to visit Japan but to return through America, and to make various stops along the way.

And so at long last, after such a close connection with Japan, we arrived at the busy airport and boarded the bus into Tokyo. The bus journey took several hours and we discovered right away that traffic jams in Japan can even surpass the traffic coming in and out of London. But there were Sumi and Hideko to meet us. They drove us to a charming International Club in Tokyo where we stayed the first few days as their guests. Later we moved to the Mitsui home in the town of Odawara, about an hour's journey from Tokyo. It was a great rambling mansion full of treasures, with a lovely collection of Japanese dolls and costumes. It was a fascinating mixture of East and West, where you could either take a Japanese bath in traditional style, or enjoy Western plumbing and convenience.

Sumi and Hideko were wonderful hosts. Day after day, always in taxis hired by the Mitsuis, we would travel the country, one day getting beautiful views of Mount Fuji emerging from mist into glorious, sun-capped peaks of snow, on another occasion travelling by the famous high-speed 'bullet' train to the historic city of Kyoto, where we were entertained in the exquisite house and garden of the Sumi-tomo family (another great industrial family) members of whom were close friends of the Mitsuis and also devoted adherents of Moral Rearmament. We would return from busy days in the Mitsui School or from visiting friends in

99

Tokyo to join Sumi as he rushed to his television to watch baseball or the famous Sumo wrestling, or perhaps golf, all of them great delights of his older age.

Many were the leisurely conversations we could enjoy together such as we had never had since those days forty years ago in Oxford. Above all, my wife and I learned to know a little about and to love Japan, in a way that tourists seldom can.

We sometimes explored on our own and were amazed how the kindness and graciousness of strangers and passers-by would surmount the barriers of language and help us on our way.

One day we went to a bank in Odawara to change travellers' cheques. The young girl cashier, looking to us not much older than a schoolgirl, explained in very limited English that this bank unfortunately did not deal in pounds, only dollars. We were a little crestfallen. In a moment, she came across from behind her desk (and in Japanese banks there were none of those bullet-proof glass barriers to protect the cashiers but just a simple, open table) and with many bows beckoned us to follow her. She led us out of the bank into the street. She walked with us, smiling and with a very few English words, introducing herself to us. She came to a crossroads and turned down another street. It was after quite a long walk that she led us into another bank, took us upstairs and explained to a similar young lady clerk our need for pounds. She finally presented to us a little gift of Kleenex and matches, bowed and smiled and went back to her work in her own bank.

This kind of thing seemed typical of a graciousness, offered specially to strangers, that is a less-known element of what we regard as the thrusting, competitive, technical life of Japan. Western thrust and technology, ruthless competition for foreign markets, all the harsh commercialism that we associate with modern Japan, have not destroyed an extreme delicacy of life and graciousness that is deeper than mere formal politeness. It has a love of beauty and a sense of giving and receiving from which we in the West can learn so much.

100

I came across a Japanese saying the other day which seems to me to sum much of this up. 'When you pass a bowl to a friend, you pass the whole universe.' We noticed especially in Japan how carefully, almost lovingly, a waiter in a restaurant or hotel will place your cup or your plate or your bowl on the table before you. It never seemed to be shoved down in front of your face as so often happens in the West. It was almost a ceremonial act just to serve a dish or plate for a customer or a friend. You learned a little of the graciousness of giving, and so of the receiving that was the other side of giving.

When in a shop someone hands you your change, it is done with a bow and a certain sense that you are receiving a gift. We discovered that it is not polite in Japan when you are given change to count it carefully, as we do in the West to be sure there is no mistake. The Japanese are lightning calculators and they often use the old abacus. They seldom seem to make a mistake. You accept the change with a bow. Maybe outside in the street you count it to be sure a mistake has not been made, but it is not polite to question or calculate the change you are given in the simple transaction. Giving is gracious. Receiving must be gracious too. I learned something from all this about our relationship with God; to give without counting the cost, to receive without counting or calculating the gift.

On one of our last days in Japan, Sumi turned to me and with his usual laconic, economical turn of phrase, said, 'When I die, what kind of funeral? Christian? Family graves and ritual?' I realized this was a serious question. The tradition of the Mitsui graves was very strong and a great historic family bond. I considered my reply. 'I think,' I said finally to Sumi, 'when you die you ought to have a glorious, triumphant Christian funeral, proclaiming to all your faith in Jesus Christ, the Resurrection and the Life. After that,' I said more hesitantly, 'perhaps God does not mind so very much where you are buried. Perhaps you should join the Mitsui family graves that go back so many generations and mean so much.'

As we spoke, I little knew that within a few weeks of our memorable visit to the Mitsuis in Tokyo my beloved friend

Sumi would in fact die. His energy and vigour had amazed me. He was in his late seventies, moving ceaselessly and rapidly, playing a vigorous game of golf, constantly caring for many concerns and people.

He made one last trip to Europe and we had the pleasure of entertaining him and Naoko in our home. It was in all a golden time together.

Suddenly his heart failed and in a few days he was gone. He did have that triumphant funeral in the Anglican Cathedral in Tokyo. A devoted friend spoke glowingly of Sumi and his faith at that service. He was then buried in the Mitsui graveyard and rests with that historic family amid his ancestors.

My friendship with the Mitsuis stretched over many years, surviving the horrors of the Second World War, the upheavals of a great city like Tokyo, twice razed to the ground by earthquakes and by Allied bombing, the enormous changes and chances that now make Japan one of the most powerful forces in the world. Our relationship remains a personal treasure and also a link with the country I have come to love.

I still keep on my mantlepiece a wooden cross made out of camphor wood from a tree that survived the blast of the first atomic bomb. It was given to me at Caux by the Mayor of Hiroshima, one of several that he gave as a symbol of forgiveness between us and our nations. I look at that cross. I think of my friend and pupil, Sumi; of Hideko, who looks as fragile as porcelain but who has a lion heart; of Naoko who has inherited some of the business genius of the Mitsuis; and of Yori, my godson, 'rather a playboy', who laid down his life for his friends and his people.

9

B H Streeter

The cold grey waters of the Atlantic rose and fell and rose again. Somewhere they met a cold grey sky. The *Aquitania* patiently pushed her way eastward in the month of April, 1934. At the rail of Deck A two figures stood alone; a younger man and an older.

The older and taller of the two was wrapped from head to foot in an enormous black overcoat. Between its turned-up collar and the peak of his cap pulled down over his forehead, little could be seen of the wearer's face—little but a thick beard, grey and wavy as the Atlantic itself. Somewhere in the background loomed a nose, and somewhere remoter still, behind burly eyebrows and thick spectacles, a pair of eyes, exceptionally blue and alert. The final noticeable thing about this figure was its feet. They were telescopic feet. At the place where the normal foot stops they seem to have decided to start all over again. Encased in shiny, black, crinkly boots, they seemed all of a piece with the long overcoat and the thick grey beard. You smiled with them rather than at them. They had something to do with those unusually blue and alert eyes. Boots and eyes seemed to be enjoying a private joke together.

Turning to me, for I was his companion, with an expressive wave of his hand toward the waste of water below, the figure said, 'You know, this kind of thing creates in me complete disbelief in God and the universe and anything else.'

'Over in America,' he added, 'I was asked to contribute to *The Atlantic Monthly*. I shall reply that I have been contributing to the Atlantic daily.' Then with an odd little laugh (or

103

was it only a sniff?) he turned and strode away. I stayed for a moment or two looking out over the sea and then I too walked, rather uncertainly, below. In my cabin, as my dressing-gown swung mournfully back and forth on its hook, I flung myself on the bed and tried to think.

So far things were not turning out very well. I had banked a good deal on this voyage. On the last day in New York I had paid out my last hundred dollars to transfer my return ticket to England from tourist to first class. I had done it suddenly against all my natural habits and instincts. I had done it entirely on account of the tall black figure with the beard and the twinkling eyes.

To me at that time, B H Streeter, Doctor of Divinity, Provost of Queen's College, Oxford, author of *Reality*, *The Four Gospels*, and a number of other works, was not in any way a personal friend. It is true that we were both teachers in the same university—colleagues if you like—but I was a beginner, a junior Fellow in one of the smaller colleges, just about to deliver my first course of lectures; whereas he was perhaps the leading man in his field of New Testament study, and one of the few really original and creative thinkers of his day. He was never a one-subject man; philosophy, history, comparative religion, psychology, ethics, mysticism, he had written on them all. There was a book on old chained libraries written for relaxation, which is the last word on its subject. 'The only book of mine that'll last,' he used to say.

But better than all the books was the man. I had had a glimpse of the man earlier, when as an undergraduate I had attended a conference of the Student Christian Movement at Swanwick in Derbyshire. I was at that time rather a half-hearted spectator of the proceedings. Streeter impressed me. The talks he gave were scholarly, human and humorous. His answers to questions were dry and to the point.

He was what everyone, especially students, enjoyed; a profound scholar and a rich character in one.

I remember one meal-time in the conference food marquee. The heat was stifling; the commissariat had broken down; the sweltering multitude was getting impatient. As often happened a cry went up, 'We want a limerick from Canon Streeter.' The reply as usual was instantaneous:

> This conference leaves me dead beat.
> I can't even get something to eat.
> If for verses you call,
> I tell you to go all
> To the one place that beats this for heat.

But all this had been several years earlier. Now on the *Aquitania* the voyage was more than half over. Four precious days had gone by. The ship had groaned and plunged; sea-sickness had not encouraged friendliness, and beyond that little encounter on deck, I had seen nothing of Streeter. Yet I had had a strong inner compulsion that I must get to know this man; that I had much to gain from him, and (strange thought this) something to give as well.

The next day the sun came out, and with it the deck chairs and the deck games, the scandals, the romances, the gossip and the photographs.

All day long in the sun we sat side by side. Streeter had volunteered to look through the notes of the lectures I hoped to deliver the following term. It was a gruelling experience, as Streeter's critical faculties were sharp and probing. It was like having a dentist tap and explore his way round your occasionally crumbling teeth. For him it was a pure labour of love, a gracious gesture undertaken at the cost of precious hours of rest between a strenuous lecture tour in America and a heavy summer's work in Oxford. But he did not spare himself, and it was not until evening that the work was done.

Next day was the last at sea. We had dined together and talked a good deal. Something of a friendship was springing up between us. We were in a corner of the smoking-room when suddenly Streeter began to talk again, this time about himself. He felt, he said, that his main job in the world was now done. He had given his life to try to make the great truths of religion understandable to the thought of today. He had written about all he had to write. There were jobs to be done in Oxford, of course; there was plenty to keep him from being bored, and yet, five, even twenty years might seem long and a trifle sad for one who had to go on living and growing old when he felt that his work was done and that he was only marking time.

I swallowed hard. This was the moment I had been waiting for. This explained the hunch—or that more than hunch—back in New York. This, in some way I could not fully see, was part of a plan, a plan that embraced Streeter and myself and everyone else in the whole world, a plan for which of late I had learned to listen every day,

I swallowed again, for I was shy. Then I said, 'You know, I believe that, far from being finished, your greatest job in life hasn't yet begun.'

'What's that?' Streeter, the critic, the terrier of truth, was fully awake now.

'Well,' hesitantly, 'you've given your life to make eternal truths plain to men's minds. Now you will make them effective in their lives.'

There was silence. A few more miles of ocean slipped back into the night. At last Streeter spoke again. 'Let's go to my cabin and pray about this matter.'

We began a friendship that was to ripen under the sunny skies of an Oxford summer term. I gradually got to know his passion for truth, his rapier mind, his shy but confiding smile, his sidelong glance to see if you were shocked or only amused. 'You know,' he would say, 'there are things you can get away with if you have a beard like mine.' Underneath it all you recognized his simplicity and humbleness of heart.

With a select group of more senior scholars I was invited to attend a seminar in Streeter's study on the synoptic gospels. He was what was known at that time as a 'Modernist'. Some of the faithful would ostentatiously get up and leave Hereford Cathedral when, as a Resident Canon, he got up to preach. Actually, some of his independent and original research has turned out to be a bulwark of the faith. At his seminar every word of every verse of the first three Gospels was put under a microscope of discussion and analysis. I happened to be present one day when we reached the last word of the last verse. It had taken fourteen years' work since the beginning. Some had been present throughout. Streeter looked up over his spectacles and with the barest smile had said dryly, 'I imagine we may as well start at the beginning again.' The pages were turned back and the work went on.

Occasionally we would run into one another amid the crowds and bicycles of Oxford traffic. He had a way of stopping abruptly and, without preamble, coming out with the thing that was on his mind at that moment.

'You know, Thornhill, the Christian and the Buddhist are alike in one thing. He has each discovered a fraud. For the Buddhist it is the universe. For the Christian, it's himself. Good afternoon.' He was on his way.

It was at some of the informal meetings of the Oxford Group that I had got to know him best. The larger public meetings he seldom attended. But we would find him occasionally at a smaller informal group where some of us met together on Monday nights. There, in an atmosphere of outspoken honesty among friends who trusted and understood each other, he would watch the lines of a spiritual strategy being laid down, not only for the University but for the whole country, or listen to the latest report from South Africa or Switzerland or Canada; or meet visitors passing through from Scotland or the industrial north, talk with some of the unemployed hunger-marchers, or revolutionaries from the East End of London. He could see the emergence of a philosophy, not in academic debate, but in relation to a hundred and one practical problems of life.

He was a good listener, instantly and obviously bored at the slightest trace of unreality or cleverness for cleverness' sake, but alert for any grain of truth or spiritual experience, no matter who gave it or however crudely it was expressed. He seldom spoke himself, but near the end of a meeting he might casually throw in a remark to clarify a point or sum up a discussion. These remarks had a habit of sticking. I certainly have never forgotten an occasion when I, taking myself too seriously, announced the discovery that I must be ready to make a fool of myself for the sake of the cause. '*Make* a fool?' said Streeter with a chuckle and that mysterious little sniff. Everyone laughed, including me and Streeter, who when he laughed would throw back his head, his beard pointing skywards like a spreading plant, and his mouth open wide in proportion to the size of the joke.

He loved the sense of a family, perhaps because he had not had much family life himself. He liked the sense of battle. He had always been a fighter in his own way. He understood the mixture of daring faith and shrewd commonsense that he found on those Monday nights. Gradually he began to dream, to hope, to believe, that here might be an answer for the world after all.

Then I was invited to the Provost's House at Queen's where he had taken up residence. Irene, his wife, had recently returned to him and I met her for the first time. Their life of late had been lived mostly apart. It had worked out better like that. He, with his bachelor ways, in his book-lined study littered with papers; she, the Puritan, the independent, disapproving of his books, disapproving of his habits, living mostly abroad and going her own gait. He seemed too clever, too original for her; she too practical, too rigid for him. So he took refuge in his books and hobbies and research; she in her strict principles, her good causes and her points of view.

But lately there had been a remarkable change. Irene had joined him in the Provost's home. It was there he needed her most as hostess and companion. No one had been more surprised than he at the job she was making of it. He marvelled at the graciousness of her hospitality, the care in her housekeeping, the new understanding of him, the sense of a home such as they had never experienced before. She didn't lecture him any more, or disapprove, or set herself on a pedestal. Instead of that she was alongside him, willing to help and understand, saying less and laughing more, eager that they pioneer and build something new together.

At first acquaintance she was a rather forbidding figure, with her straight black hair and her heavy masculine features. Everything about her was large and stern and strong. But there were times when her whole face would light up with a smile as if the sun had broken through dark clouds. And every now and then there was a gleam of battle in her eye.

And then one day she talked to him from her heart. Fearing another lecture he had tried, as he often did, to parry her with a sly joke or a piece of sarcasm. But she was not to be parried, and this was no lecture.

Rather she told him of her own failure, begging his forgiveness for the way she had deprived him of warmth and affection and had laid down the law. The shyness and reserve and disappointment of years began to melt as he listened. Eagerly he asked her questions. She told him how she was learning to listen. She, who had preached and prayed and organized good works and given God his orders along with everyone else, had been finding that God had things to say to her. In the Oxford Group she was learning to start at the bottom again as an ordinary sinner like the rest, to learn how to be humble and flexible and take her orders from God.

Now he was deeply moved. Here was the spirit which he believed might change the world, coming into his own house. He had written a book called *Reality*. Was this reality for him? There was another book, *Adventure*. Was this adventure beckoning at his own door?

He talked with many friends. He asked innumerable questions. Like the scholar he was he tested the evidence at every point. His friend Bishop Roots of Hankow, China, was staying with him in Oxford. Often they talked and prayed together late into the night. At last he made his decision.

'Would you be good enough, my dear,' one day he said to Irene, 'to tell your friends in the Group that I would like to say a few words, if I may, at one of their public meetings?'

His tone was deliberately matter-of-fact, almost casual. Her reply equally so.

But on her knees she thanked God for His miracle-working power and prayed for strength for them both to carry through for the rest of their lives.

It all came to a head on July 11th, 1934, three months after the encounter on the Atlantic voyage. The Town Hall of Oxford was crowded to the doors. People were there from forty-five countries. Turbans and tartans, open-neck shirts and stiff white shirts, tall intellectual foreheads, rough work-hardened hands, children, parents and grandparents, leaders of today, leaders of tomorrow. The common aim, 'a new world civilization'.

I was present at that meeting and shall always remember the moment when a new speaker was introduced. There was the tall black figure and the twinkling eyes, those monumental boots and the quiet, half-diffident voice.

'My attitude towards this movement,' it was saying, 'has been what diplomats call (sniff) a benevolent neutrality.'

A peculiar mannerism, that sniff. You couldn't tell whether he had a cold or was making a joke at his own expense.

'In speaking to some of my friends I have compared this attitude to that taken up towards the early Church by Gamaliel, that most amiable of the Pharisees.'

The crowd laughed, though they did not all understand what he meant. 'Suits us in Oxford all right,' I thought. 'Hello, what's this?'

'. . . say publicly,' went on the voice, with almost the dry monotone of the lecture, 'that I ought now to cease from an attitude of benevolent neutrality towards what I have come to believe is the most important religious movement of the day.'

Silence. The audience was held, gripped by a sense of something happening, important beyond their understanding. In the front row, listening intently through a large ear-trumpet, sat Irene. With straight back, head erect, grave motionless features, she looked like a guardsman at his post.

'The world situation . . .' I had missed the last bit. 'Hope somebody's taking this down,' I thought.

'. . . more and more full of depression, full of despair.' The voice was stronger now, with more ring in it. 'There is a great deal of goodwill, but there is not enough of it to solve our tremendous problems—war, class war, economic breakdown. And the men of goodwill are losing heart. They carry on but with lessening hope. And, speaking broadly, the churches have been losing heart.'

A bishop stirred in his chair. He had heard that before; probably said it himself last Sunday. Why had he seldom felt the truth of it so keenly?

'This movement,' the voice went on, 'seems to be able not

merely to change bad people into good, but also gives new heart and a new courage and a new sense of direction to those who are already men of goodwill. That is why I have come to the conclusion that in an age of growing world despair it is my duty to associate myself with it.'

Some of the older men looked puzzled and uncomfortable. They were friends and colleagues who had come that night partly out of courtesy, partly out of curiosity, knowing that Streeter was to speak. They felt perhaps as he did. But should they be doing as he was doing? There was much to weigh carefully in the privacy of their rooms.

'May I add,' came the voice, again more diffident, 'that I come to the Group, not as a person with perhaps some little reputation in his own sphere of study, or as the head of an Oxford College. I come as one who has already learned something from the Group, and hopes to learn more, and who hopes that by doing so he may be of a little more use than might otherwise have been the case.'

He sat down. There was silence. My mind was far back in the ship's cabin. I seemed to smell the air from the engine room and hear the creak of a thousand beams as they took the strain of the Atlantic. So this was it.

'By 1934 I had seen enough of the Group to realize that it was making bad men good and good men better faster than any other movement; and I decided it was my clear duty to step into the boat and handle an oar, instead of continuing to shout from the tow-path a judicious mixture of criticism and encouragement.'

So wrote Streeter three years later, just before he died.

From shore to boat is a little step, but it may be a step to another world. The Town Hall speech at Oxford was Streeter's step into the boat.

Outwardly life went on much as before. Another University year began. The usual college boat races came round and Streeter, as he had done for twenty years, stood at the starting point and during the last seconds before the gun recited a limerick to encourage his crew. He did things in his own way—you expected it of him. Besides, anything was a help that took your mind away during those last ticklish seconds. One year, when Queens rowed behind Corpus, he contented himself with announcing, 'Habeas Corpus'. And they did.

Outward things were much the same, but there were changes too, most noticeably in the home. It was a large austere building where you instinctively lowered your voice and put on your best behaviour.

But now Irene's hand was at work, letting light and air and colour into every nook and cranny. There was a constant stream of visitors. The usual student tea-parties, instead of being a typical Sunday afternoon bore, became fascinating occasions where everyone was included and you instinctively gave of your best.

But it was some of the private visits that counted the most. Men had always gone to Streeter for advice, but now he was giving them more than advice. Cautiously, to begin with, he was practising the art of life-changing. One morning the phone rang in my room. Streeter's voice was at the other end. 'I think you had better come over,' it said, with more than the usual number of sniffs. 'There's a young man come in to talk and I rather think I have got him at least half-changed.' I declined to go over and urged him to finish the good work himself. Next day a new recruit was to be seen at the after-lunch meeting. The change had taken place.

Sometimes, late at night, a shaft of light would pierce a private back door out of Queen's, and a hurrying figure slip out into the darkness. For Oxford had, here and there among its great ones, a Nicodemus who came face to face with reality secretly at night.

For Streeter it was all part of a new and fascinating family life. He was no longer Professor Streeter, the patron, the spectator, the distinguished visitor. He was BH, the loved and lovable father of a big family—the whole Group in Oxford. He came more often to the meetings now and usually sat in the front row next to Irene with her big ear-trumpet. He was giving leadership and direction to the whole work, and yet he was also its newest and rawest recruit. No one paid him undue deference. No one put him on a pedestal. No one took him for granted. And that was what he liked.

Occasionally he made time to visit other cities and talk about the Group. He would take a few of us with him in the car and we would speak together as a team. BH was adept at answering questions, and he was never happier than when there was opposition in the meeting. 'I rather think the Lord has delivered him into our hands,' he whispered to me while an opponent was delivering a virulent attack. When his turn came he would deal with the point with a minimum of words and a maximum of effect. At a large meeting of clergy someone delivered a tirade about some act of foolishness on the part of one of the Group. BH was asked to reply. 'After all,' he said slowly, gazing round the hall, 'you know each of you has at least one mad person in your congregation.' Discussion moved on to the next point.

At times the fire would burn in him and he would give his audience all he had. I remember when one speaker, who had acknowledged that in the Group the Spirit was at work, had urged that we must guide the Spirit into safe, familiar chan-nels, he spoke with burning passion. 'Who are you to guide the Spirit of God? When are you going to let the Spirit of God guide *you*?'

Then there was the drive back through quiet, green countryside and a chance to relax, to fight the battles of the day over again, to check up on mistakes, to say what was most on our hearts in the frank but costly give-and-take that builds an unbreakable fellowship.

Spring came late in 1935. Mussolini, Laval and Macdonald were getting together at Stresa. They were going to do something at last, it was said, about this fellow Hitler. That April Anthony Eden had been on a grand tour to visit Hitler and Stalin. Stalin had asked him if he thought the prospect of war within a year was greater or less than it had been in April 1914. Eden thought it was less. Stalin said he thought the opposite.

All asked questions. Few had an answer. One or two were shaking their heads over a place called Abyssinia which, somebody said, was a member of the League of Nations.

On April 1st that same spring, BH and Irene took the *Lapland*, newest airliner on the London-Copenhagen route,

113

to join the Oxford Group's campaign in Denmark. The tall bearded intellectual alighting from his plane and hurrying within the hour to address the crowds—crowds which were flocking day after day to the Odd Fellow Palace—caught the imagination of the Press. Next day the newspapers dubbed him in a headline, 'The Flying Professor', and the name stuck.

'I want,' he said, 'to join the Group once more in its daily work.' And the work was stirring indeed. For it was a spiritual advance in whole nations; small nations, true, but nations which might one day play a vital part in the remaking of Europe.

I was part of a team of more than 300, including BH and Irene, as we moved rapidly each day through a series of meetings, parties, receptions, Press interviews, private conferences. It was exacting work. Much had to be done through interpreters. The spiritual hunger was extreme. The clamour was always for more speeches, more interviews. BH would leave a solemn conclave of Lutheran ministers still arguing over a point of theology and rush in a fast car to talk at a late cocktail party for the smart set. Early next morning he would be off with Frank Buchman to meet a statesman or industrialist in another city.

Sometimes he and Irene would speak together. I remember one such occasion before a large audience in Copenhagen. Streeter had spoken at some length with his usual charm and penetration and had been greeted with enthusiasm. When Irene had responded to an invitation to add a few words, her robust incisiveness, her unpretentious forthright tone had brought the audience to their feet. BH was surprised and, to be honest, a little shaken. But his true reaction was one of delight.

'You know, Thornhill,' sniff, sniff, as we walked away from the meeting, 'strange as it may seem, there are times when my wife shows distinct signs of genius.' It was his own Oxonian way of signalling, 'She's quite a woman, and I'm proud of her.'

From the pulpit of the little English church in Copenhagen, before a congregation including the American and

British diplomatic Ministers, BH gave voice to his convictions. It was Palm Sunday, and he read from the Bible the story of Christ weeping over the city of Jerusalem. Then he turned to the fate of modern cities.

'There was some limit to the "devastated areas" in the last war; in the next war London, Paris, Berlin, and hundreds of other cities will be "devastated areas". Revolution after revolution has resulted from the last war; it is perfectly obvious that the next one, whoever wins, will be followed by revolutions on a far larger scale. In some countries Communism may get to the top; in others some kind of military dictatorship. But whichever prevails will do so after a civil conflict of a kind which will leave behind it many times as great a legacy of bitterness and hatred.

'If Christ rode today into London, Paris, Moscow or Berlin, might he not again weep over cities who knew not the time of their visitation?'

Here in the quiet cultured accents of an Oxford professor was the voice of a modern Amos. And his message was the same. 'Repent. Change.'

'Respite is not cure,' he said, 'if, when the thing comes, it will be worse than if it had not been postponed. But there is one chance. Can we somehow or other make use of such respite—and it may be quite a short one—to do something which is going to bring about in Europe a fundamental change?'

Then still quietly, but with burning conviction, Streeter spoke of his faith. A new spirit was abroad in the world, as in the days of the early Franciscans or the Wesleys. Here was the possibility of saving civilisation. The heart of this new spirit was change, the change that God works in a man when he is honest and admits his faults and puts himself at the disposal of God completely.

A few days later the Streeters left again for Oxford. They were given a royal send-off by their Danish and other friends. There were songs and poems and speeches and a guard of honour from the hotel to the car. In a few short weeks 'The Flying Professor' had become a nationally known figure.

His words of farewell were in the form of a limerick:

115

I'm not very sure that I'm changed,
But my inside's a bit rearranged.
  So no longer I'll trifle
  But shoulder my rifle
On a world front the battle is ranged.

Like all his limericks it was composed in a few seconds. But it was a confession of faith, and he held it to the end.

Later that year, again with BH, I joined a large international group in Geneva. The League of Nations was sitting. The flags of the nations fluttered over the various hotels along the lake-front. People craned their necks to get a glimpse of Anthony Eden, the League's best-looking, best-dressed representative. In the Assembly, Sir Samuel Hoare in studied tones upheld the sanctity of the League. The Genevese, cultured and close, went their way. BH and I were among four hundred guests at lunch in the Hotel des Bergues, invited by shrewd, intellectual Edouard Benes, President of Czechoslovakia and that year's President of the League, to hear Carl Hambro of Norway and others speak of the relevance of the Oxford Group to international affairs. My most vivid memory of the occasion was the sudden appearance of sly, sleepy-eyed Laval standing in the doorway taking in the proceedings. He watched and listened for a while and then suddenly turned away.

Night and day, all around there was nothing but talk, talk, talk.

Streeter found it all unreal, oppressive. At any rate he saw it clearly; a noble monument to human wisdom, a vision that had failed. And he knew why. It had not come to grips with the root of the problem—human greed and selfishness. 'A race that has grown up intellectually,' he said, 'must grow up morally or perish.' And not all the machinery of the Covenant or solemn deliberations of the Assembly could alter the fact by one iota.

He was unusually silent during those days in Geneva. The turmoil around him threw him more and more on the simplicity of his experience of God. He had fought for this experience, for he had never found faith easy. He had seldom known the warmth and glow of a clearly felt Presence. His recent decisions had been more cold decisions of the will than any Damascus Road revelations. Yet those decisions had been honoured. He had a genuine, a growing experience of God. 'For one who has had this experience,' he wrote, 'there is no longer any question of believing or not believing. It is the clearest reality, as exact as any scientific idiom.'

So there was kindled the need, the desire, to incorporate his new convictions in another book. The basic material was there in a course of lectures which he had been giving to the learned lawyers of Lincoln's Inn. Now he felt that the lectures, like the lecturer, needed, if not to be changed, at any rate to be 'a bit rearranged.' He was learning to know the fact of God's guidance as a daily experience. The book, which he called *The God Who Speaks*, must challenge the reader to listen for himself and to obey to the limit the truth so far as he grasps it. Above all, the book must be related to the desperate needs of a dying civilization. 'Is there available for man,' he wrote in his preface, '. . . guidance on his dark and dangerous course from some Wisdom higher than his own?' Then with typical Streeter understatement he added, 'A study which may point the way to an answer to that question is one of more than academic interest.'

Soon after this he became desperately ill. Those large feet of his were in reality no joke. Ever since he was a young man they had been a source of weakness. More than once they had literally let him down. This time an infection in his feet spread rapidly through his whole body. Within a few days he was suffering from acute blood poisoning and lay at death's door. Irene hurried to Hereford where he had been fulfilling his usual term as Canon in Residence when he was taken ill. Friends in Oxford and all over the world waited in anxiety as the reports grew worse. For a week or more it was touch and go. But at last the poison was fought back and BH was saved—though almost too weak to speak or move, or to consider work for many months ahead.

It was a long winter that he spent at various south coast resorts, away from Oxford and his friends and from the active life for which he longed.

It was not easy those days to lie helpless, too weak to write or even to talk for more than a few minutes. Irene visited him frequently and brought him news of his friends in Oxford. Now he was more than ever grateful for her robust, practical faith; her brusque dismissal of doubt or fear; her quick disposal of difficulties about which he tended to worry. 'All these people need is to be thoroughly and soundly changed,' she would say. It was to her he turned when things went black. Besides, he recognized more and more her warm, dauntless warrior spirit. It was Irene who led him along the slow, difficult road to convalescence. She stood at his side to encourage and protect him when in the spring of 1937 he at last returned to Queen's where, lying on a couch, and looking like a gaunt, grey effigy in stone, he slowly began to pick up a few threads of college business.

By the summer he at last began to feel he was coming to life. He managed to make his usual appearance at the start of the College Bumping Races and composed his usual last-minute limerick.

But as the term ended, the doctors ordered a further long period of rest in Switzerland. The usual Oxford Group summer house party was beginning in Oxford. Frank Buchman and a group of old friends had just arrived from America. BH paid them one or two visits at Lady Margaret Hall, one of the house party centres. The last and one of the best pictures of him that exists was taken outside the college as, with Irene beside him, with twinkling beard and battered old hat complete, he waved his friends goodbye.

None of those who shared that holiday at Lauenen will ever forget it. As always in such a fellowship of honest, costly sharing and waiting on God, answers were found to personal problems, recent or long-standing, as well as insight into the needs of others.

Through all there was a colourful pattern of expeditions and talk and argument and laughter; of mornings spent walking on the high pastures; of afternoons sometimes too stormy for expeditions, when the whole party would gather on the wooden balcony facing the Wildhorn, and read poetry or try to write it, while the thunder crackled among the mountains; of evenings when Madame, the ever-friendly proprietress, would bring in a neighbour or two and try to teach her guests how to yodel.

There were the meal times when everyone gathered with appetite whetted, not only for the good Swiss fare— mysterious soup with dumplings swimming in it, tasty stews, never-failing salads in wooden bowls, delectable coffee and cakes—but for the conversation which outdid the feast.

It was the family life for which BH had always longed. His care and thoughtfulness for each one knew no bounds. As he grew stronger he would stroll up the valley with each one in turn, focusing all his wit and wisdom to suit that individual's special interests or needs. A conversation with BH usually left you with one pungent comment or pointed remark that summed the matter up. It might be a piece of profound wisdom or a little scrap of elementary common sense, but it stuck in your mind and was hard to forget. On one such walk he was passing on to Christine Morrison, tutor and lecturer at St Anne's College (then the Society of Home Students) all that his experience had taught him of how to lecture. On her remarking that she needn't fear over-work as she was as strong as an ox, he said with a twinkle, 'Ah, but you mustn't make the ox an ass.'

He was constantly thinking about a new book in which he might give to the world his maturest convictions. He often talked about it. One morning he fastened on a sentence from a book review which said, 'The only lesson of history seems to be that men never learn the lessons of history.'

'I want to show,' he said, 'that there is one lesson of history which men may yet learn—the lesson of God-control.' But that meant that the great democracies must get back to the real source of their greatness. The struggles for freedom in Britain and America had been struggles for the freedom of the individual, not to do as he liked, but to do what he felt God wanted him to do. Streeter contrasted the materialistic conception of freedom which had spread in Europe since the French Revolution. How to present the fact of God's guid- ance as a practical working alternative to chaos for individuals and nations? That was the supreme question of the hour.

As summer drew on, he began to talk of his plans for Oxford. All his love of adventure was knitted with his vision for the youth of his country, and especially of Oxford. He had a sense of pride in his college and in the fact that its men were going out and taking up leadership of world significance. He had a great longing that new leadership, and spiritual leadership, should be given to the world through the men of Oxford. Yet none knew better than he did that the going would be hard. Oxford was his 'Jerusalem', where he would meet opposition and persecution. His was not the courage of a man who did not care. He knew what fear was, but he knew it could be overcome.

So the last day dawned. After breakfast, lunch was packed up in rucksacks and everyone walked to the Lauensee, its waters deep under a clear sky. They ate lunch by the lake and walked back in the late afternoon. At one point they stopped and sat down together on a bench facing the Wildhorn where a waterfall poured down its precipitous cliffs. All at once BH began to pray, thanking God for the beautiful weather and the joys of the holiday which was just coming to an end. It was the longest walk he had undertaken since his illness. Striding along side by side with Irene, he finished strongly, flourishing the shooting stick which he always carried. He turned proudly and said, 'Well, I think I may officially describe myself as cured.'

That evening he prayed a prayer which had something prophetic in it, thanking God for the interesting life he had given him, the people he had met, the places he had visited, the work which he had been able to do. Next day they would take the train to Berne and then home to England by plane.

The brilliant sunshine had suddenly turned to fog and rain. It was almost as dark as night, this Friday afternoon, as the twin-engined plane on the Berne-Basle service flew blind through a five thousand feet bank of mist.

At the controls sits one of the best pilots in Switzerland. He has had fourteen years' experience of aircraft. In front of him the airspeed indicator shows nearly a hundred miles an hour. He knows every hill on the route. But the conditions are unusually bad. It is hard to gauge the force of the wind. He must be over the top of the range by now. He leans over to the operator by his side. 'Tell them at Basle we are going to drop a thousand feet through this fog to see where we are.'

Behind in the eight-seater plane the couple sit alone. They are the only passengers.

Suddenly the tail of the aeroplane catches some saplings near the mountain top. In an instant the plane spins violently to the ground. The heavy engines with their ring of cylinders smash through and splinter large trees like twin thunderbolts.

At once the end comes to the two sitting in the cabin and to the pilot. The radio operator survives. By a merciful anaesthetic of oblivion even he is unconscious for four hours until the rescue party finds them.

The plane fell without burning. It made a clearing in the trees on the meadow crest. From the spot one looks over three countries – France, Germany and Switzerland. You can stand there and see, as it were, a continent in the breaking and the making. Yet the place itself is peaceful. It happens that it is a favourite haunt to which tired city dwellers of the region come for refreshment of body and mind after the week's work. In winter, skiers meet at this very point before swinging down over the slopes to the valley. It is a spot fitted for a wayside place of prayer and encounter with the Christ who there took two of his friends to live with him.

They were laid to rest in the quiet village cemetery close by. After the service Frank Buchman and others of their friends met to thank God for all they had done. I felt moved to read to them the story of how Mr Valiant-for-Truth crossed the river.

'Then,' said he, 'I am going to my Father's, and though with great difficulty I am got hither, yet now I do not repent me of all the trouble I have been at to arrive where I am. My sword I give to him who shall succeed me in my pilgrimage, and my courage and skill to him that can get it. My marks and scars I carry with me, to be a witness for me, that I have fought His battles who will now be my rewarder.'

10

Another Stage

The place, a small barn theatre on Mackinac Island in the great lakes of Upper Michigan. The play, *The Forgotten Factor*. It was one of the first performances of the first play that I had written. It was Labour Day 1942. Visitors had come up from the great war plants of Detroit and beyond. Close to the stage in the row in front of me sat Victor Reuther and his wife. He and his brother Walter were two of the outstanding labour leaders of America. Much of the war effort on both sides of the Atlantic depended on men such as these.

The play dealt with some of the human and ideological clashes during a tense strike. As the scene over the labour leader's breakfast table between man and wife developed into bitter argument—with fears and resentments spewed out across the couple's little son trying to eat his cereal—I noticed Reuther's young wife in front of me, totally absorbed with her head going backwards and forwards, as though she were watching a tennis match. Suddenly there is an unexpected knock at the door. 'Come in!' cried Mrs Reuther in the audience, and then, realizing what she had done, clapped her hand to her mouth in great embarrassment. That unexpected interruption meant more to me than critic's approval or the audience applause. This simple unpretentious play was real to some of the people for whom it was written. It was meant to be more than a play. It was meant to be a force to help change the thinking and living of people of responsibility at a time of crisis.

It seems to me that these words 'Come in' express what

theatre is all about: involvement in the drama, some fresh insight or illumination, comic or tragic, trivial or profound, that makes a theatre-goer say 'Come in'. And before that can happen a writer needs to say 'Come in' to some influence or inspiration that may come to him or her from who knows where.

And so it was with me. It originally came like a kind of explosion, and it has brought a host of friends. Friendships in the theatre can be drenched in 'darlings' and droolings and be as brittle as they are brief. They wax and wane with the passing show. They also can go deep in loyalty and love.

First in a list of theatrical friends must be Frank Buchman. Not that he ever wrote or produced a play or stood on a stage. Part of his genius was always to fire and inspire others to do things that he could never have done himself. He did launch and sustain a considerable theatrical enterprise, and incidentally helped to nudge me into a new and unexpected career.

The 1930s had been a period of rapid growth and expansion of what had become known as the Oxford Group. Oxford University had remained a recruiting ground and training centre for the leadership of a world work. The conferences or 'house parties' held each summer in Oxford attracted hundreds of visitors from all over the world. As the war clouds gathered, as the nations began piling up armaments, the urgent need for moral and spiritual rearmament gripped minds and hearts as the only sanity in an insane world.

With his call for Moral Re-Armament Frank Buchman began an expansion of his work. It was launched in the East End of London in the summer of 1938. Then in the spring of 1939 he took the programme of Moral Re-Armament to America. Inaugural meetings were held in Madison Square Gardens in New York, in Constitution Hall in Washington, and then, on the West Coast, 30,000 poured into the Hollywood Bowl. Thousands more failed to get in. There was focused all the strength of a world movement. Later, over the first weekend of December, there followed through a network of continental broadcasts, a massive appeal for 'Listening'. War had broken out in Europe. This was a moment above all for people everywhere to listen to the voice that speaks in the heart of the individual; call it conscience or sanity or the voice of the living God. Millions of people listening. This was the challenge taken up and followed through in countless churches, meetings, homes and personal experiences. Europe seemed locked in phoney war, America was still a sleeping giant, unprepared for the test of total war. With Stalin in league with Hitler, the Communists and all the followers of the party line joined forces with the isolationists to cry 'keep out!' How to unite industries, shaken by strikes and lock-outs, often torn by violence and bitter confrontation? How to help prepare a nation for the testing times that lay ahead?

It was that crucial stage when movements of the spirit can go astray, where a genuine springtime of the spirit can be promoted, organized, filed, and in the process, filleted.

It was then I came to realize in a new way something of Frank Buchman's unique quality and greatness. He steadfastly refused to think in terms of membership, of organization, of money, of a human movement. The question that preoccupied him was not how to promote Moral Rearmament but how to prepare people and nations for a war of arms, yes, but still more for the peace that must in the end follow. It was quality that mattered, not quantity. It was not to spread a vast organization but to deepen the lives of those who were ready, so that in turn God might use them to influence many. How to match men and women with the hour? How to live through the terrible days of testing that were to come to one and all?

And so there came a time in the summer of 1940 when Frank gathered in from all over America the leaders of his work, called a halt to the whole range of pleas for promotion and expansion, and for several months, in a secluded spot in the mountains, spent unhurried time to pray, to dig deep into human motives, to search out the hearts of all who were at work with him, to begin to turn a group of loyal workers into a blood-bought, undying fellowship of sinners, cleansed and redeemed by Christ. For those of us who spent that summer together, it was a daily experience of rugged honesty, of quiet, sober thought about the whole world and the great ideologies at war, and the fresh challenges that an all-out war would bring to America, and looking far beyond that to the creation of a new kind of world that must be built out of the ruins and devastation of the present.

This is what I hungered for in my own spirit. This, though I had not realized it at the time, was why I had left my job in Oxford and answered Frank's call to come to America.

The times that I remembered and treasured most were when a comparative few of us would gather together with Frank, with laughter resounding round the room at some piece of unexpected honesty, of the tears that accompanied true repentance, of the pageant of world thinking and planning, all combined with detailed care and thought for the tiniest detail of every day. It was life all in one piece. Times with Frank were, as someone once said, a glorious mixture of a Christmas party and the Day of Judgment. Nothing was too small to be excluded, nothing was too great to be accepted. Time and again, sitting with Frank and his friends, I would think 'Yes, this is sanity. This is what life is really about. This is not talk, this is the Holy Spirit actually changing people, not with some momentary emotional response, but deep down in the very roots of human nature, down in the very depths of sin and shame, up to the glorious heights of Christ's full grace and forgiveness, joy abounding and unspeakable, no limits, no reservations, the whole world.'

It was here by the shores of Lake Tahoe in Nevada that a new element came into our work, certainly an unexpected turn in my own life and in my relationship with Frank Buchman. Hospitality, always a keynote of life with Buchman, was a constant feature of those summer months, stretching on and on into the crisp, cold air of the autumn mountainside. At supper we would gather in the rustic setting of a large chalet built out over the lake, and our friends and neighbours as well as visitors from farther afield would join us round tables with red and white check gingham cloths for a simple, tasty meal. We got into the habit there of putting on entertainment for our guests. There happened to be considerable dramatic and musical talent in the party. There was Marion Clayton Anderson, a rising young Hollywood starlet, with her husband Bob; George Fraser, an irrepressible fount of humour and melody alike; Cecil Broadhurst, lanky cowboy singer and broadcaster blossoming into a considerable theatrical talent, and many others.

Out of this came the birth of a revue that subsequently played hundreds of times throughout the United States. It was called *You Can Defend America*. Frank, well in the background, but concerned with every detail, showed the gifts of an impresario; a constant spur, critic and promoter of a new theatrical enterprise which has since covered half the world. It was a new stage in his life and ours.

My intense love of the theatre stirred within me. I had never been backstage in my life, or on one. I had never dreamed of writing for the theatre. 'What are you writing Alan?' said Frank to me out of the blue one morning at this time. 'Nothing,' I replied innocently. My writing up to then had been confined to reviews of theological books, Sunday services or lectures on New Testament Greek. Frank looked up. 'You're a fool,' he said almost casually, and turned to another subject. Something that he had said to me about the theatre twelve years before rang out of a deep echo-chamber in my sub-conscious. We were living in a world of drama, immensely serious, yet with a spark of hope and faith in a setting of ideological struggle and confrontation. Why not a real full-length play? Why not find a real playwright? No one responded.

'You're a fool.' I felt more than ever a fool when waking up early one morning by those lake shores, I reached for a block of rough paper and scribbled those alluring words 'Act One Scene One'. I had mulled over a possible theme, based on things I had actually seen and experienced in American family life. But how to encompass a play? 'Begin', whispered an inner voice. 'Begin and I will show you how.' So for a whole day I wrote. My pen flew faster and faster. I missed breakfast, I missed lunch, I even missed tea. No one missed me. I wrote in the white heat of a furious volcanic outpouring. I never even took time to number my pages, and by the evening my room was littered like a snowstorm with sheets of paper scribbled over and cast aside.

'What have you been up to?' said my room-mate Bunny Austin, as he hopped into bed that night. 'Actually,' I said, trying to sound as casual as I could, 'I've written two acts of a play.' And then with a budding author's irresistible enthusiasm, I added, 'Shall I read them to you?'

Bunny is a Christian gentleman. It was late. He climbed somewhat wearily into his bed, propped his head up on to several pillows. 'Of course. Go ahead.' His eyes were some-what glazed and full of doubt. He knew the professional theatre from the inside. He also knew me from schooldays. Theological dons seldom burst into drama. Two whole acts in one day? It was absurd. Undeterred I launched in. When an hour later I came to the second act curtain, we were both very wide-awake. 'Tell me,' said Bunny, shaken but still sceptical, 'can you write the third act?' 'I don't know,' I said. 'I think so.' 'Well, you'd better do it at once; as long as this, whatever it is that's got hold of you, lasts.' It did. I did. So was born a play in which, for the moment, nobody except Bunny was interested and which I carried around in a brief-case for nearly two years. Then suddenly in a typically theatrical turn of fortune, everything came together. The birth of *You Can Defend America*, life on the road touring the country in a fleet of station wagons and cars travelling at 30 mph as a national petrol savings scheme, had produced some pretty hardened, experienced, resourceful actors and crew. We were on Mackinac Island for a conference. There was a barn ready to be converted into a charming theatre. There was even a laundry room beside it for dressing rooms and props and scenery. There was a demand from the highest quarters for fresh theatrical weapons to arouse sleeping America, to help break the bottlenecks in industry on which the life of the free world depended. Here was the challenge. Where was the play? Faithful Bunny remembered. 'Alan has a play.' 'Let's hear it.' 'Why haven't we heard of this before?' 'When can it go on?' 'Saturday week?'

So we took to the road once more, this time with *The Forgotten Factor*. Artists, craftsmen, technicians, seasoned

127

professionals of the theatre, beginners and amateurs alike, each found his or her part in a common enterprise. We were lucky enough to have two or three stars. Phyllis Konstam, Bunny Austin's wife, was a top-level West End actress. She was to go on to play the part of the labour leader's wife nearly a thousand times—never stale, always buoyant, never giving anything but a moving performance. Her opposite number Howard Reynolds, the Canadian actor, as the labour leader, was a fiery yet utterly human character. He would often go on from a performance in some industrial centre to stay with an actual union leader, where they would battle out the philosophy of the play in real life into the early hours of the morning. Marion Anderson gave up her whole career so that she and her husband Bob could devote themselves to this new kind of theatre. In addition to acting, she had a genius for a special kind of directing, dealing alike with professionals, teenagers just out of school, inspiring novices to be real and draw on their own experiences to portray a character, good or bad. The play ends with an enraged mob bursting into the home of the manager. There were plenty of volunteers for the mob. Together they managed to erupt in a scene of such convincing fury that on one occasion the mayor of a small town where the show was being given hurriedly sent out a call for the local police, thinking that they were breaking up the play.

Before every performance cast and crew would meet backstage to prepare for the play and pray together. 'O God,' prayed one youngster, as he got ready for his role in the mob, 'please put the devil into me for the next couple of hours.'

It was all a daring adventure of faith. No one drew a cent of salary, no credits were given to individual actors or to the author. No charge was made for admission. The play was given as a free contribution to the war effort. We did it first for the Ford factory people, with Henry Ford and his wife in the audience. Then we went further afield. Harry Truman, then a Senator, Roosevelt's right-hand man for breaking industrial bottle-necks, saw the play in Philadelphia, together with a Republican Congressman on the other side of the

House. Together they agreed to sponsor a national première in Washington. 'This is the most important play', said Truman, 'to come out of the war. There is not a single bottleneck in industry that could not be broken if these ideas are given the green light to go ahead.'

Someone has said that if a bomb had fallen that evening on the National Theatre, much of the war effort might have been suspended. So many in high responsibility at that time were in the theatre. After the play was over the explorer, Admiral Richard Byrd, sitting in a box close to the stage, rose spontaneously and called for silence. 'The forgotten factor', he said, 'is the decisive factor,' and he sat down as an extraordinary silence fell on the theatrical occasion. So we went out, sent with the official blessing of Washington and the powers that be, and with *The Forgotten Factor* and our big national revue *You Can Defend America*, we covered the country playing in great cities and small towns, meeting youth in uniform, workers just out of the factory, wives, families, the great and the small, even the delegates gathered in San Francisco to found the United Nations. Not only through the plays but by what we could do in the days that followed in smaller sessions and seminars, discussions and debates, we were able to play our part in the war effort. But it was much more than that. As well as the war of arms, there was a war of ideas. The war of arms ended: the war of ideas went on.

The play became part of our lives, our almost daily programme. Frank would come to see it again and again, sometimes with a half-hidden seat in the box where he could turn his chair around and take in the audience as well as the play. He was fierce in his backing of the play. To someone rash enough to suggest that the production was not fully professional he would shout, 'Not professional? It's super-professional.' To the young man playing the lead, if Frank saw him busy with other work on the day of a performance: 'Why aren't you resting? You have important work to do tonight. The most important thing you can do.'

Frank was a master of the humorous, affectionate take-down of every form of self-importance. I was complaining once at the very short time we had to put on an extra, sudden performance for some special guest. 'We need time for rehearsal,' I said with urgency. 'Rehearsal! Rehearsal!' Frank said with a twinkle. 'I think that's an Oxonian conception!' Woe betide us on the other hand if the performance was not perfectly polished.

He was an artist at heart. His early paintings show that. Still more important was his eye for detail. The arrangement of a dining table, his sense of décor in a room. How often he would go round every room in a house or at a conference where he was receiving guests, making sure that every detail was exactly right for the particular individual who would occupy that room! Above all, of course, there was an almost uncanny sensitiveness to people. With Frank you would experience being prominent and being utterly in the background, being featured and being ignored, being special and being ordinary. 'Friend, go up higher,' was so often his greeting to some shy individual hovering in the background. Equally, you might hear him say in no uncertain terms, 'Give this other man room.' Again and again in a crowded room Frank would pick out the one person who specially needed encouragement, or possibly a swift kick in the pants. No one could architect or plan a special occasion, be it a quiet dinner in his room, or a great meeting involving thousands, with a surer touch, a greater sense of atmosphere, above all a greater care for individuals.

When it came to theatre he very seldom interfered, or even made suggestions. His trust in and support for a person like me was unwavering. Sometimes I would go to him in his room and tell him of a new idea for a play, or even to read a scene that I had just written. On one such occasion, while I was reading, he was leaning forward in his chair with his back to me, looking intently out of the window as the long ore boats steamed slowly through the straits of Mackinac. After I had finished there was a long pause, and then he turned round and said, 'I think that holds attention pretty well.' I laughed and said, 'I'm afraid it didn't hold yours.' No reply. But later in the day he stopped me in a corridor and mentioned one tiny point that needed improvement. He had taken in every word. Just occasionally he would sum up everything in a single dismissive sentence. After a rather pretentious, artily, craftily lit scene full of 'symbolism' and hidden meaning, his comment was 'Couldn't see; couldn't hear.' The scene was dropped. But on the other hand, if some well-meaning 'expert' tried to mess about with one line of dialogue, one piece of business in one of our plays, 'Leave it alone' he would thunder.

In the autumn of 1942 Frank suffered a serious stroke. For many weeks he hovered on the edge of death, and it seemed little short of a miracle that, buoyed-up by the love and prayers of thousands he gradually fought his way back, not to full health (he remained partially crippled for the rest of his life) but to an activity even more profound and effective than before. By Christmas the following year Frank was able once more to entertain a host of friends. He had been lent a small, charming hotel in Florida on the Gulf of Mexico. I was one of some thirty fortunate enough to be with him there. It had been a tumultous period. The plays were in demand all across the country. The work of 'MRA', as it became known, was a hive of activity. Leadership seemed stretched to the limit. The great majority of the full-time workers were now enlisted in the armed forces. Once again Frank felt the need to deepen the commitment of a few, to feed faith and to heighten vision.

Sarasota, Florida in the winter season, was a microcosm of the American Establishment. It comprised jaded politicians, over-worked editors, high-powered business executives and union leaders seeking to recharge their batteries, members of the armed services on a brief leave, not to mention the Ringling Circus in its winter quarters and budding baseball teams limbering up in the sun. It was small-town America playing host for a few days or weeks to the powerful and the privileged, to the political caucuses or the Pentagon, to Wall Street or even the White House.

What a golden opportunity for us to be busy, to make propaganda, to announce a programme, to put on plays, arrange meetings, give interviews, write articles, cover the waterfront. Frank was not interested in any of these things. He invited a few neighbours to lunch or supper. One day he met the director of the Little Theatre. 'I think we'll give him sweet and sour pork and wilted lettuce', said Frank (favourites of the Pennsylvania Dutch folk, from whom Frank came). Over lunch the director's eyes lit up. He came, it was discovered, from Pennsylvania. This was his favourite dish.

Later on came the opening night of the Little Theatre's winter programme. It was a gala occasion for the whole community. Black ties, long dresses, the works. Frank bought thirty tickets and invited us all. Somehow, somewhere, we begged or borrowed the necessary outfit. 'We'll go early', said Frank, 'and watch the people arrive.' We were standing in the lobby when our friend the director appeared, harassed and ashen-faced. One of his leading actors had suffered a heart attack. There was no understudy. The show couldn't go on. 'That's all right,' said Frank. 'Cecil Broadhurst here will take the part.' Scarcely knowing what was happening, Cecil found himself ushered backstage, a script thrust into his hand and a hurried introduction made to the leading lady. He had assumed, hoped, that his part would confine him to carrying a spear in the background. Instead, he was pressed into the role of 'Jerry'. Jerry was, it seemed, the wolf threatening a happy marriage in the light comedy *Claudia*. To Cece's horror page after page seemed to be festooned with dialogue marked Jerry, Jerry, Jerry.

Meanwhile, the rest of us were taking our seats in the stalls, leaning back leisurely, so grateful for once to be at a show for which we carried no responsibility whatever. Shock and amazement followed when our own Cecil Broadhurst strolled into the scene of happy domestic life, smooth and sophisticated, the script in his hand somehow part of his nonchalanace, a look of delightful anticipation on his face as he quietly turned the pages discovering to his own and everybody else's delight what he was up to next. Cece had the temperament and enough experience to carry it all off perfectly. It was a dramatic tight-rope act that suited the part and the occasion. The applause at the end was tumultuous, the questions a crescendo of disbelief. Who was this debonair actor with a script? He had undoubtedly saved the show, rescued the evening. The director was almost in tears with gratitude and amazement There was only one fly in the ointment. The show ran several nights. Cece Broadhurst was due to appear before his far-away draft-board tomorrow. The stricken original Jerry was still stricken. Crisis, despair once again. 'That's all right,' said Frank. 'Bob Anderson will do the part.' It was again good casting. This time Bob was able to learn the role of Jerry, have a hurried rehearsal and perform in *Claudia* without script for the rest of the run.

Never had a welcoming door to a rather exclusive and wary small-town community been so widely opened. We were on the front page, invited to broadcast and to speak, to be special guests at every social occasion, questioned about our faith, our philosophy and our programme. 'Moral Rearmament' became a household phrase in Sarasota.

A few days later we entertained the whole cast of *Claudia* to a celebration party. It happened to be the birthday of one of our group. Barbara (not yet thought of as my wife) volunteered to make a birthday cake. 'I think,' said Frank unexpectedly, 'you had better make two birthday cakes.' Time was short, the small oven would only take one cake at a time. Barbara was a shade indignant. When the party was assembled and the first birthday cake was ceremoniously presented, someone whispered, pointing to the quietest, least prominent member of the cast, 'I believe it's her birthday too.' No one had known it. But when a second birthday cake appeared and a diffident birthday guest was honoured, she burst into tears. Haltingly she explained that she had come from a very deprived home. She had never had a birthday cake of her own before. Tears turned to laughter. She became like a child, blowing out the candles in wonder.

This may matter more than the fact that in subsequent weeks in Sarasota, the owner of a big Washington Daily, a Presidential candidate, the conductor Artur Rodzinski, an American Air Force Colonel home for a few days from the European battle-front, a Canadian Senator, the Press and the public all somehow swam into Frank's orbit. All were surrounded by friendship, most were directly strengthened with faith.

As always with Buchman there was an intense preoccupation with the individual person. Be he an interesting sinner, or an aspiring saint, a statesman or the liftman who took you to his office, he counted, he mattered, he or she was a child of God, a potential part of his Kingdom.

This was the essential theme of my friendship with Frank Buchman, from our first meeting in Oxford in 1928 down to the last months of his life—when he was over eighty, crippled and often bed-ridden, but still instantly alert to people, their needs and possibilities.

December 1960 in Milan seemed to have very little to do with sunny smiling Italy. The weather was dank and dark; condensation poured down cold stone walls. There was a sense for some of us of an oppressive gloom about the place. We were giving a play in a suburb outside the city, close to Sesto San Giovanni. It was a workers' quarter, notorious as red and revolutionary. We had many friends there and the play was a success. For me, however, I felt far from triumphant. Barbara and our daughter Susan were thousands of miles away on Mackinac Island. Frank was with us in Milan, but he had come to the end of a tumultuous and exacting year, sailing in the spring from America and then pouring out his strength and his heart during a long session at Caux, travelling himself through Switzerland. And now in his hotel in Milan he lay in bed. All his strength had ebbed away. He seemed at the very end of his tether, without the energy even to get up or dress. His doctor, Paul Campbell, was eager to get him away to sunnier climes where he might pick up in health, but he scarcely seemed to have the will or the desire to move. He just lay there. The thought of him added to my gloom.

And then one day for some reason or another I found myself with him in his hotel bedroom, and we were alone. He started to talk. 'I do not say,' he said, 'that I do not sin. But one thing I can say, that I live for one thing and for one thing only; that Jesus Christ be regnant in the life of every single person I meet, and that includes the waiter who will be bringing me my supper.'

I felt at liberty to talk freely about myself. 'I long to do that too,' I said, and then I added the thought that had been much in my mind during the previous weeks of discontent. 'I sometimes wish I could work as a chaplain in a hospital. I feel there one could be stripped of so many of the non-essentials of life, and meet people in obvious need in a crisis in their lives, and have a golden opportunity to do just what you have said. I wonder sometimes,' I added, warming to my subject, 'if possibly I might be cut out for that work. My father had a real gift of healing, although none of us knew it until we heard stories of him after he had died. I sometimes think I may have inherited just a little of that gift. I'd love to have a chance to try and see. Perhaps I would be nearer to God's purpose than I seem to be, helping to put on plays in Italy in December.'

There was a pause. Then with great vigour Frank suddenly said, 'Begin on me, begin on me.'

I was stunned by the challenge, but I rejoiced to rise to it. I went straight to his bed, I knelt down beside it; I laid my hands on his forehead and without premeditation or any formality I began to pour out my heart in prayer. All my love for the man over so many years, all my gratitude, all my faith in the way God used him and led him, all my longing that his life might go on and on in ever greater power, poured out in a flood—begging God to raise up this servant of his and give him the strength he needed to meet all that still lay ahead. The prayer was quite a long one. When I had finished Frank said a loud "Amen", and then in quite a cheery casual voice, 'Goodnight, see you again.'

Next day we were putting on the play as usual. I had arrived at the theatre early and was standing in the lobby near the box office, greeting friends and early arrivals. Suddenly I became aware of quite a stir and a considerable chatter going on by the door. I turned, and to my surprise, there was Frank in his wheelchair. He was sparkling with energy and enthusiasm, greeting people right and left, hailing old friends, making contact with new ones. Eventually they wheeled him into the theatre. He attended the play. When it was over he greeted several of us with great enthusiasm and invited us back to his hotel. It was late at night by this time. Dr Paul, rather amazed at this fresh outburst of energy said, 'Well Frank, you've had quite an evening. Shall we take you upstairs to bed?' 'Bed? Bed?' said Frank indignantly, 'Let's have supper!' So several of us joined him for a late supper party. It was a merry one, full of stories, reminiscences, fresh discoveries. On his 80th birthday, looking into the future and the years ahead, Frank's thought had been, 'Not many but merry.' Well, that evening in the hotel was one of the merry experiences. A few days later Frank was well enough to move out of Milan to sunnier climes where he could begin to rebuild his strength. That Christmas in the Assembly at Caux, he was exceptionally active and vigorous, conducting plenary sessions in the great hall, greeting new arrivals, attending many of the meals, and entertaining guests in his private sitting room. He had clearly taken on a fresh lease of life.

With Frank life was drama. The world was a stage, God the supreme dramatist. We are all participants, good or bad, in the greatest drama of all time, whereby the Cross of Christ will remake the world.

11

Artur

New York, November 7th, 1941. The New York Philharmonic Orchestra was giving its usual Sunday afternoon
concert, broadcast over the Columbia Network. The guest
conductor was Artur Rodzinski, conductor of the Cleveland
Symphony. I was high up in Carnegie Hall in the cheap
seats. We had Shostakovich's First Symphony, of all his
works the one I enjoy the most. Then came my favourite
piano concerto of all, Brahms' Number Two, a work of vast
symphonic proportions, with a monumental solo part, with
all sorts of extra delights thrown in. The ghostly horn
summons as the curtain rises on the whole drama; the heavenly 'cello theme at the beginning of the slow movement,
when the cello takes over as principal soloist. Artur
Rubinstein was the pianist. It was the first time I had heard
him in person. The vast audience was lost in another world.
At the end a tremendous burst of applause as the two Arturs,
Rodzinski and Rubinstein, were called back on the stage
again and again.

At the climax a man walked on stage, a paper in his hand.
He handed the paper to Rodzinski who looked at it, grew
pale and then handed the paper back shaking his head. And
so the stranger raised his hand for silence and read to the
audience: 'The President of the United States has just
announced that Japanese forces have bombed Pearl Harbour.
Our country is at war.' Gasps, tears, no one moved as the
orchestra, already standing, struck up the National Anthem,
Rodzinski conducting facing the audience, who rose to their
feet, some singing, some crying. Rubinstein joined in at the

piano. For me there was being born for the first time the clear certainty that Britain's solitary struggle was over.

There were so many different emotions at that terrible, heart-stirring moment. Many years later I re-captured one of them. After a Rubinstein piano recital in the Royal Festival Hall some time in the sixties, I went backstage to greet and thank him. I referred to this extraordinary experience in the Carnegie Hall on Pearl Harbour Day, and told the old man I had been there. 'Yes,' he said, with deep feeling, 'it was terrible!' 'Yes,' I said, thinking of the horrors of war, 'it was terrible.' 'I could not find the correct tonality to join properly on the piano in the National Anthem,' said Artur Rubinstein.

The other Artur, Artur Rodzinski, I came to know very well. He was doing a stint for a few weeks as a guest conductor of the New York Philharmonic. He and his wife Halina were staying in Essex House in a fine apartment looking far up Central Park, already powdered with snow.

How well I was to know his volcanic energy, his great bear-hugs of affection, his remorseless attention to detail in rehearsal, probing each soft spot or irregular reaction He may not have been the world's greatest conductor, though he was among the best, but for me he had the power to generate sheer excitement, deeply emotional and intellectual excitement, more than any musician I have ever seen or heard. All this spilled over into his personal and private life and he was prone to experiencing extremes of attraction and repulsion. Such a temperament always generated excitement and drama, but also took its toll in terms of leading to sheer emotional and physical exhaustion.

But little of this was apparent at an after-concert party at Essex House, when Bunny Austin and I were guests of the Rodzinskis. The one thing that stood out that day, and captivated me ever after, was his smile. It was a smile suddenly breaking through dark clouds, with a look of wonder, of guilelessness (or was it guileless?), like that of a young lover or a small boy. We were there because we were friends of a friend of his, a Dr Loring Swaim of Boston. Artur had been troubled constantly by a bad back and arthritic shoulder. Conducting, always a physical strain, had been agonizing. Someone had persuaded him to try Loring Swaim. 'The man is an angel,' Artur told us that day, 'the most wonderful human being. No one ever spoke to me the way he did that day.'

'What did he say? What did he give you for your back?'

'Oh, nothing for my back. But for me, everything. He asked me if I believed in God. "Well, I do of course," I told him, "but I let it trouble me as little as possible." '

'There's the point,' he said. 'Eighty per cent of these rheumatic pains are nerves. If you have no faith in a power greater than yourself, then you make yourself the centre of the universe, and of course you suffer agonies of frustration because the universe will not submit to your will. When you submit your will to a power infinitely superior to yours, a power that can change your heart and mind, and also the people you have to deal with, then your aches and pains will go away along with your frustrations and unhappiness.'

'And your back?' I asked.

'I tell you it is a miracle,' he said. 'But my dear, it is not just a healed back. It is a healed heart. Dr Swaim is proving that half the cause of arthritis and rheumatism is linked to bitterness.'

So for me, that winter evening in Essex House began a saga that has been one of the most dramatic, most humorous, most richly rewarding, as well as in the end, one of the saddest of my life.

I was to see more and more of Artur. He was Polish, the son of a general, an army physician. He himself had trained as a lawyer. In Vienna, where his father had been stationed and in his home city of Lvov in Poland, he had half-stumbled into the world of professional music. He owed less to formal training than to an innate genius, coupled with a passion for perfection and a ruthless attention to the smallest detail. He was merciless as a trainer of himself, and then when he began to conduct, merciless in training others.

First he had been accompanist and vocal coach for the Lvov Opera. Then he got a sudden, unexpected chance to conduct Verdi's *Ernani* himself. He knew the work by heart, but how to conduct he literally did not know. He was scared to death. From the concert master of the orchestra he learnt a few tricks. And then, hour after hour, day and night after day and night, with his first wife Ilse, herself a rehearsal pianist and coach, she at the piano, he conducting from the full score—cursing each other, shouting at each other—he learnt to conduct and made, with his first appearance, a great success.

Warsaw followed and the young Rodzinski, rehearsing to the point of exhaustion, driving everyone to distraction, produced performances that were alive with genius and electric with distinction. There in Warsaw he was 'discovered' by Stokowski, became his assistant in Philadelphia and later conductor of the Los Angeles Symphony.

By this time his first marriage had broken. Soon he was to bring to America his new wife-to-be, Halina Lilpop, herself part of a famous Polish musical family and certainly one of the most devoted and beautiful women I have ever known.

Soon after his meeting with Loring Swaim, musical New York and Cleveland were full of talk about the new Rodzinski. No more bully boy tactics with the players, common enough with many well-known conductors; a new openness and charm with the management. Even Arthur Judson, the tycoon manager not only of the New York Philharmonic but of many other musical institutions and a host of individual concert performers all over the world, had to admit that the temperamental Rodzinski was indeed a different man. This helped to bring about his appointment as permanent conductor of the New York Philharmonic Orchestra, the heir and successor to Toscanini, in one of the plum positions of the musical world.

As I got to know Artur and Halina better I was enchanted and moved by this loveable, unexpected and constantly faith-filled pair. I would drive with them to the big orchestral concert in Carnegie Hall on Thursday night, Halina in charge of a whole battery of equipment; the musical scores, extra batons in case one should break, an extra tail suit (should the first half of the concert drench him in sweat), extra shirts, towels, rubbing ointment, Coca-cola, pills and medicines for any possible eventuality, plus a series of mascots and good luck charms—a photo of his father, a model elephant and an old pistol belonging to his father, which was always crammed into a back trouser pocket before he went on stage.

Artur, thanks to his wife, would arrive at Carnegie Hall in what in military circles is known as 'a high state of preparedness'. But now there was something still more—a preparation of the spirit, a calmness and concentration that came from a direct sense of God's power and love.

One Thursday night I walked with Artur through the drab, unpretentious musicians' entrance upstairs through the soloist's dressing room to the inner sanctum of the maestro himself. The concert that night was an almost routine Tchaikovsky evening and the soloist was the French violinist, Zeno Francescatti. Zeno that night was for some reason in a terrible state of nerves. 'Maestro, maestro,' he groaned, 'it is terrible. I cannot play. It is terrible.' He looked terrible.

'That's all right, Zeno,' said Artur calmly, 'come with me. I can help you.' We went together into the inner room. 'Now we'll pray together,' said Artur blithely. The look on the violinist's face grew even more tortured. 'Pray! I cannot. I do not.' 'That's all right. Just stand here with us.' The three of us stood together. Artur prayed a most natural, original prayer. 'You know, Lord, how nervous Zeno is feeling. I feel it too. Calm us both. Help us to go out there and pour out our hearts with the joy and love of music.' An extraordinary peace seemed to pervade that drab, unpretentious room. The angry hoots of the traffic outside seemed to be stilled. Whittier's Quaker verse was a reality:

> Drop Thy still dews of quietness,
> Till all our strivings cease;
> Take from our souls the strain and stress
> And let our ordered lives confess
> The beauty of Thy peace.

It was a superb concert. Familiar, almost hackneyed, music came to fresh life. The orchestra seemed somehow to respond to something new, the audience was enthralled. Olin Downes, the respected, often feared music critic of the New York Times, was complimentary. The following day, the whole concert was repeated for the well-dressed, well-upholstered lady music-lovers of New York. Once again I accompanied Artur to his dressing room. Once again, as we passed the soloist's room, there was Zeno looking, if anything, more nervous than ever. 'Maestro, maestro', he begged, 'do for me today what you did for me yesterday!' He did.

It was my great privilege during the years that followed to stay often with the Rodzinskis, to visit them at their Stockbridge farm, to attend concerts packed into Halina's private box, Number 61—which, out of her generous, over-flowing spirit, she usually crowded with guests, always asking for more chairs than the eight allotted—even going occasionally to rehearsals, meeting the soloists, and discovering more and more of the fascinating, often cut-throat backstage world of top-class professional music.

So many memories and impressions crowd my mind. Fritz Kreisler playing one of his last concerts, now tragically old, the charm and dignity still there but a few unprecedented false notes and intonations creeping in too, and his wife standing anxiously in the wings, medicine in her hand for the very minute he came off. Artur loved this great man and musician. A little before, in Cleveland, they had given a concert together. At the rehearsal Kreisler had stood in his shirt sleeves and braces ready to start. Suddenly he turned to Artur. 'You know this concerto. I know it too. Let's go home.' And the concerto went perfectly well.

I can picture, in the Carnegie Hall soloist's room, Yehudi Menuhin, still young, but looking a bit travel-worn, performance-worn, smiling as they waited to go on and saying wearily, 'Well, here we go again.' And then you could see them both summoning up that extra inspiration and energy that made a fine performance.

I can see the two Arturs, Rodzinski and Rubinstein, each with his beautiful Polish wife, each wife having helped bring about the marriage of the other.

There were tours with the orchestra up and down the East Coast, familiar programmes repeated several times, and occasions on the road for a certain amount of fun and practical jokes. The programme usually began with a well-known overture, starting on a full chord, tutti, played 'ff' by everyone. One day Artur forgot or did not know that the programme had been changed. Instead of the usual opening, it was Weber's *Oberon* Overture. Artur gave his usual full-force opening beat, only to be greeted by a tiny, tenuous reedy solo. He almost fell off the rostrum.

There was a new, young assistant conductor always in attendance at the Carnegie Hall. He was handsome and charming but still a little uncouth and ill at ease, relying a bit on Halina's advice about dress and appearance—respectful, but ever alert and ready to edge himself in where compliments were flying or celebrities were collected. One Sunday Bruno Walter was scheduled for the big, broadcast afternoon concert. Artur was on holiday out at the farm. Suddenly a worried telephone message came through to say that Walter was ill and could not conduct. Artur must come at once. 'No,' said Artur, 'Lenny, the assistant must do it. That is what an assistant is for. It is his chance.' The concert was an enormous success. Olin Downes' revue notice was printed on the front page of the *New York Times*; a new musical star had been discovered. His name was Leonard Bernstein. I remember going with Artur to an early private performance of Bernstein's first stage musical, *On The Town*.

To be at the top of the musical or theatrical tree is often to be full of fears: Are you secure? Who are the young ones coming up who might replace you? Are you keeping your grip? I remember Artur telling me, with great honesty and humour at his own expense, how during his summer at the farm, the Philharmonic, his orchestra, was due to be conducted in a broadcast open-air concert at the Lewisohn Stadium by a rising young conductor, Fabian Sevitzky. The programme included one of Artur's favourite works, Shostakovitch's Fifth Symphony. Artur tuned in to check up on how the concert was going, and found it all terribly good. Genuine admiration soon turned to frenzied jealousy. This young man was conducting magnificently. All the tempi were exactly right. The performance was inspired.

'I have under-estimated this man,' he growled, as he paced the room in growing excitement and alarm. He had to telephone Koussevitzky, who lived nearby, so he might get excited too. By the time the symphony came to its climax, Artur was in a frenzy of admiration and competition. The music ended in a burst of triumph. Silence! 'My God,' thought Artur, 'the audience are so moved they can't even applaud.' More silence and then a voice, 'Owing to rain the open-air concert at the Lewisohn Stadium has had to be cancelled. You have been listening on records to Shostakovitch's Fifth Symphony conducted by Artur Rodzinsky.'

Rodzinski's first years with the New York Philharmonic were golden years for the orchestra and for him personally. It began with a drastic cutting of dead or ageing wood among the players—painful, but necessary. He was meticulous, unrelenting, super-professional in rehearsal; no flowery descriptions, no general exhortations, but a minute attention to detail. Then there were times in actual performance when a kind of volcanic energy, an outburst of lyrical passion and excitement, would pour out from the conductor to the players and pervade that now old-fashioned, but elegant and acoustically perfect Carnegie Hall.

The other day in New York, a friendly doorman let me in, turned on the lights and I stood on that empty stage and relived some of the past musical experiences of those years. I think of an all-British programme, a salute to Britain's gallantry in the darkest days of the war, a Vaughan Williams symphony and William Walton's dramatic and exciting oratorio, *Belshazzar's Feast*. There was also a piece by a young RAF Wing-Commander. He had attended a concert while on a special mission to New York. He introduced himself to Artur, both as a pilot and a composer. Artur struck a bargain with him. If Wing-Commander John Wooldridge shot down five German planes, Artur would perform one of his works. The Spitfire pilot more than fulfilled his part of the bargain, and Artur was true to his. I don't know if a *Solemn Hymn for*

Victory was great music. Certainly for one Englishman it added to a moving occasion.

Another stirring war programme was in honour of Czechoslovakia, thinking especially of the little town of Lidice, completely destroyed by the Nazis as a reprisal for Czech resistance. Martinus' *Memorial to Lidice* had its première at this concert.

As I stood on that Carnegie Hall stage I could see Jerome Kern standing on the identical spot, after the performance of his *Scenario for Orchestra on the Themes from Show Boat*, a piece which Artur felt just as worthy of a serious concert performance as works by Offenbach or Johannes Strauss.

An empty concert hall; silent, brooding and full of ghosts.

For one memorable concert, on January 2nd 1944, I was not present in Carnegie Hall but listened spellbound on the radio. It was while we were in Sarasota with Frank Buchman during his illness. Among the Christmas guests had been Artur and Halina Rodzinski. Their presence gave the celebrations a Polish flavour, with boiled fish on Christmas Eve, the dining table covered with straw. A Christmas play was written and performed, with an American-Indian Nativity scene, with Artur as Big Chief Down Beat and Halina as an adorable Indian Madonna. I have the picture still.

The following week was Artur's fiftieth birthday. I have a feeling that it might have actually been his fifty-second, but with celebrities and performers you have to give or take a year or two. The birthday was on a Sunday, the day of the usual nationwide Philharmonic broadcast. While down in Florida, Artur had the thought to ask CBS and his sponsor if he might speak for two minutes on the air during the interval. He and Halina worked and re-worked on that speech, drawing extra help and inspiration from the Christmas party at Sarasota. The rest of us, gathered round the table where we had celebrated Christmas together, listened to the result.

'In our orchestra,' Artur said, 'we have many nationalities, creeds, types and temperaments. We have learnt to forget our individual likes and dislikes and our differences of temperament for the sake of the music to which we have dedicated our lives. Why could not every individual and every nation in the world learn the same secret in the service of world harmony?

'A great spiritual awakening is arising from the depths of human misery. It calls for a different way of life. It calls for a changed life for everyone. Only when every one of us and every nation learns the secret of love for all mankind will the world become a great orchestra, following the beat of the greatest conductor of all.' At the end three words were added: 'Thank you, Frank.'

What had he said? What had he meant? The millions of listeners were puzzled. Was it a twist of the tongue, a slight Polish mispronunciation for 'Thank you, friends'? Was it a Freudian slip? Or was it a very typical Rodzinski signal to all who might understand that he owed so much of what he had said and done to Frank Buchman? Artur wisely never explained.

There were years of extraordinary and unique happiness for Artur and Halina. How often I sat with them late into the night, Artur relaxing after a strenuous concert, tearing off great hunks of freshly-baked bread and pieces of cheese, reliving the concert and the many personal dramas and indeed miracles, of which life was so full. Twelve, one and two o'clock—I was sleepy, and faced an early start to the next day; Artur and Halina could sleep on. But never would I break the spell of those enchanted evenings. Bedtime at last. But not until after a last request from Halina. 'Alan, darling, please take Poodla to some trees.' Out into Central-Park with the Rodzinski poodle. It would be unthinkably dangerous now; Central Park alone at night. It could have been dangerous then. It never crossed my mind.

There were some amazing prayers before the concerts. On Thanksgiving Day, before the usual Thursday Concert but after a big Thanksgiving Day meal for all the Orchestra: 'Please, dear God, don't let them just sit there, full of turkey.' Occasional explosions, rows, family dramas. I remember coming back to their home one night to hear from the big living room, growls and shouts rising in crescendo to violent high-pitched climaxes. It was all in Polish, so I did not know

146

what was being said but, judging by *how* it was being said, mayhem was in the air. I plucked up courage to go in ready, if need be, to try to settle a war. What did I find? Artur was stretched out full length on a huge sofa. He was covered with rugs and shawls. Halina was sitting on the floor beside him. They were screaming at each other all right, but all the time Halina was peeling an orange and handing it piece by piece to Artur, who would devour it between curses and stretch out his hand for more . . . 'Get out of the house Halina, you are nothing but a priest in woman's clothes! Orange! Move, move!' Guzzle, guzzle! And then as on so many other occasions would come at last silence, the still dews of quietness, and the reconciliation, Artur sometimes on his knees before Halina, in genuine penitence. God a third party, infinitely real.

For Halina there was one thing lacking. She longed for a child. But it seemed impossible. Besides Artur would never hear of it.

The sequence of events that followed has been sensitively and beautifully described by Halina in her book, *Our Two Lives*. (Her continuing friendship has been a joy, and from her I have learnt much that is in this chapter.) It was as though God watched over every detail. Halina was in hospital, pregnant, but suffering from a tumour. Tumour and child were due to be removed together. The usual pre-operative pill had been given. She was already sinking into a deep sleep. The next thing she knew, there was Artur at her bedside with an enormous bouquet of flowers. There had been no surgery, the operation had not taken place. Driven by a strong sense of God's guidance Artur had gone to the surgeon. What would happen if the foetus were allowed to grow, if nature were allowed to take it's course? There would be no added danger. In some mysterious way the tumour might even protect and help the child. And so it was.

I was staying with the Rodzinskis when delivery time at last arrived. Halina packed up Artur that evening for a concert out of town, in Newark, New Jersey. His gun, his photographs, his elephant, his spare clothes, his scores were all in place. I went with him to the concert. Halina waved us off and then, not having said a word to Artur, she quietly took herself off to the Lenox Hill Hospital.

When we got back late from the concert and Artur discovered where she was, he tore out into the city, scouring the streets for some florist open at midnight. At last he found one in Pennsylvania Station, emptied the entire stock, and arrived at the hospital in the early hours of the morning to wake her up and decorate her room. After a few hours' sleep, he was back again to meet Dr Rodgers, the surgeon (brother of Richard Rodgers, the composer), who told him that there would have to be a Caesarean and that the operation would be at four o'clock. More frantic city wanderings. A couple of cinemas, some bars, frantic returns to the hospital to be sure all was well.

During the actual operation Artur and I paced the corridors together. It was January 23rd, 1945. 'That's lucky,' said Artur. 'The date is 1.23.45!' At last the news. A beautiful boy. Named Richard or Riki after Artur's late brother. 'Masz slicznego syna' (a beautiful boy), Artur kept whispering to himself, as the nurse led him away to see his son and Halina, slowly recovering from the anaesthetic. I went home to bed, exhausted after living through the dramas of Artur's panic, passion, and many prayers. I had experienced quite a few traumas of my own. It was not until I saw Artur next day that I learnt from him that, far from the dramas being over, last night they had only just begun.

At two in the morning Artur, restlessly unable to sleep, had a strong sense that something was wrong. At exactly the same time Dr Garbat a great friend who had assisted at the operation, woke up and, as if by a secret order, dressed and came to the hospital. He went straight to the nursery and found Riki lying motionless in a pool of blood. He had stopped breathing; the navel had burst and he was bleeding to death.

He immediately called Dr Rodgers and other help. For four hours under an oxygen tent they gave him blood, drop by drop, through the only vessel that had not collapsed, a tiny vein above his left forehead. At this point, in contrast to all the panic of the previous hours, Artur was strong and calm. When the doctor's report was still very grave, he said, 'He will live because God wanted him here.' Dr Garbat understood. 'It had to be God's doing, because it simply wasn't humanly possible.'

I was still at the house when Halina returned with her baby. And so I witnessed one of the most moving scenes in my life. That evening, shadowy, silent figures slipped in through the front door—chairs and music stands were arranged in the large living room. Other players were out in the hall. Quietly they began to play the *Siegfried Idyll*, composed by Wagner for the birth of his son. As the music mounted and fell, Halina appeared on the stairs, pale, hanging on Artur's arm. Tears poured down her cheeks as she sat, Artur beside her, and as these men poured out their best, tears were in their eyes too.

For me, that miraculous birth of Riki, the glorious consummation of Artur and Halina's love, the affection and giving of that hard-boiled bunch of musicians, Artur's pride and Halina's tears of joy, the fine baby, strong again with all the promise of a great future, the congratulations that poured in from a host of friends, special dedication pieces by Samuel Barber, Roy Harris, Stravinski, Schoenberg, and John Alden Carpenter, Artur himself conducting Haydn's Toy Symphony with the Philharmonic in honour of his little son—all this seems to me to mark the very crowning and climax of Artur and Halina's lives. The leading music critics, Olin Downes and Virgil Thomson, were united in their praise for conductor and orchestra. 'We now have an orchestra that is a joy to the ear . . . and we owe it all to Artur Rodzinski.' Only a few of us knew how behind it all, through the ups and downs, the violent flare-ups and deep reconciliations, through all the mistakes as well as the miracles, there was a sense of God at work—each day starting in quiet meditation, each crisis and decision an occasion to pray and seek God's direction. It was the one truly blissful and inspired period in the stormy history of two most loveable people.

And then, it all began to fall to pieces. Just how or why, I still do not fully understand. Arthur Judson, manager of the Philharmonic, an old enemy of Artur, had been captivated by Artur's change. 'If Rodzinski continues to work as he did this year,' he said, 'there is no reason why he should not remain with us as long as he lives.' But Arthur Judson himself had not changed. Behind an imposing desk and clouds of cigar smoke, he still wanted to be the czar of the musical world, controlling not only the business affairs of the great number of musical personalities for whom he was agent, but also their musical integrity as well. He was the manipulator, the controller, even at times the evil genius of the world he aimed to rule as king.

Conflict between Arthur the impresario and Artur the hyper-sensitive, fiercely independent artist, was indeed inevitable. How often would Artur pour out to us his suspicions and frustrations, how often he would pray and make genuine attempts, with an honest apology or a generous gesture, to make peace. Somehow the conflict would always return again. Perhaps it was part of a basic conflict between management and musician. Perhaps it had to be focused and resolved. Perhaps the tragedy of Artur's life helped to create a better balance and understanding for others in the future.

But there were other factors. The old restlessness seeped back into his life. The Stockbridge farm and country home which had supplied a balance and a relief to his hectic city life no longer satisfied him. Perhaps too, the moral standards of honesty, purity, unselfishness and love became increasingly irksome. One morning in a rage he threw his Bible to the floor and shouted, 'Toscanini and Koussevitzky live without Moral Re-Armament and look where they are now.' It was an impulsive action but it had tragic results.

During the 1946–47 Philharmonic season I, like many of Artur's MRA friends, was in Europe. The world conference centre at Caux in Switzerland, bought at great sacrifice by a large group of Swiss people, was refurbished and opened officially in the summer of 1946. I became engaged at Caux to Barbara. We were married on April 23rd 1947 in London, in St George's, Hanover Square.

It was a heady, hectic time. Europe, slowly shaking off the shackles of war; Germany groping with bare hands in the ruins and the rubble, still smelling of corpses and death;

150

thousands of refugees and displaced persons seeking somehow to build a new life; millions crying out for something new—never was the call for MRA so urgent, never was the work more effective.

It was hard to enter fully into another concert season in glittering, centrally over-heated, plushy, well-fed New York. Carnegie Hall and Park Avenue seemed a long way from the ruins of Europe. And yet how badly Artur and Halina needed their friends. There were brilliant moments. Never had Artur conducted Stravinsky's volcanic *Le Sacre du Printemps* with such pent-up, hair-raising fury, bringing the whole audience to its feet in a tremendous ovation. Even Judson sent him a note of congratulation for a 'swell job'. If only Artur could have accepted the olive branch and tried to create something with it. But there were constant disagreements; over soloists, programmes and guest conductors. There were, Artur felt, downright dirty tricks designed to humiliate him.

All the same the Philharmonic Board offered a new five-year contract with no strings attached. But there were delays, evasions, and the new contract as it finally emerged seemed to Artur to have chains rather than strings.

There was a fatal February afternoon at a meeting of the Board. Artur, whose fever and fury had been mounting and mounting, turned to Judson and his henchmen and really let fly. Everything he had suspected and mulled over, all the tricks and slights he had endured, all his frustrations and bitterness burst out in a frontal attack on Judson; he called him a dictator and, even worse, accused him of using his position to promote artists whom he personally managed and from whom he expected fees.

Of course, that was the end. Edward Ryerson, the steel magnate and Chairman of the Chicago Symphony, had been beleaguering Rodzinski with big offers to go to Chicago—'anything you want, maestro, no strings attached.'

Within a very few days he had resigned New York, getting in, he felt, before New York fired him, and he and Halina were on their way to Chicago. Headlines screamed from the newspapers, the music critics giving strong praise to his work

151

with the Philharmonic. He was on the cover of *Time Magazine*. Actually his life was in ruins.

The next winter I visited them in Chicago. Musically he had made a sensational start. His conducting of opera as well as the symphony concerts had audiences and critics in raptures. But the toll had been terrible. We found him lying in bed, like a great craggy mountain, in a darkened room. The table beside him was crowded with bottle after bottle of pills. He told us he was dying. At the same time, he was girding himself to stagger to a rehearsal for yet one more tempestuous concert. Ryerson, so friendly and flexible to start with, merely shaking hands over an unwritten gentleman's agreement, proved more dictatorial and less musical than Judson. Within a year Artur was out of Chicago. He was a sick man racked with heart pains, without a permanent job, no secure future and with a reputation for temperament and unreliability.

Again he turned to Frank Buchman and to MRA. He was given hospitality and much care in Buchman's home in Berkeley Square, while he was making his debut in London. A serious heart attack followed and the series of concerts in England had to be cancelled. He went on to Caux. But nothing was the same. Instead of the old Artur, with that open heart and winsome smile, there was a demented man, hovering on the edge of mental and physical breakdown. He would suddenly disappear from Caux and go to a clinic down the mountain. That did no good, and he would be back in Caux again.

Halina, who had joined him there, was for the first time physically afraid of her husband. There were literally fanatical, murderous elements in his furious attacks on her, blaming her for all that had gone wrong in the past, for ruining his life.

Together some of us listened to her as she poured out her terror of his threats. We felt she could be in danger of her life. And so, rightly or wrongly, we decided to get her out of harm's way. Early in the morning Halina and Riki were driven down to Geneva and put on a plane to London. When Artur awoke to find them gone, he took all the pills he could lay his hands on. Fortunately a doctor was on hand to rescue him. Next day he was off, driving to Salzburg where he had an important concert, stopping and searching for news of Halina all the way. The concert, under-rehearsed, and conducted with breakneck fury, was a disaster. I never saw Artur again.

For him there was a kind of Indian summer, first of all in Italy. He gave many electric performances of both opera and symphony. The one that meant most to him was given in the Vatican before Pope Pius XII. This, with his lifelong search for faith, brought comfort and some temporary peace to his soul. He and Halina were united again.

The condition of his heart, however, became more and more precarious. Each new concert was a kind of dice with death. The last ones of all were again in Chicago, where in the winter of 1958 he came to conduct performances of *Tristan*. The whole thing had a king of Wagnerian 'Twilight of the Gods' element about it. Tempestuous rows about travel plans from Lake Placid; a fire in the house there that might have burnt everything just before they started; violent quarrels about extra string players in the orchestra; a desperate message to Lake Placid to search for a special rosary given him in Italy—'I will not conduct without it'—more heart attacks; Halina arriving at the stage door hiding an oxygen cylinder wrapped in an old sweater, so as to help him breathe during the interval. And then finally a tremendous last performance. An ecstatic response. One newspaper: 'Maestro Rodzinski is back; we ought never again to let him leave.'

But within a few weeks he was dead. That weary, wonderful heart had broken at last. One of my most treasured photographs of Artur is of him and Halina arriving in Chicago on this last occasion. It is pouring with rain. But in spite of all the cost and the drama, there is still that smiling, gentle little-boy look on his face. Halina looks radiant beside him. That is the Artur I remember. That is the one I believe is fulfilled and satisfied in heaven.

12

Muriel Smith

When Barbara and I went to see Muriel in Richmond, Virginia, in 1983, cancer had already taken its hold, but she received us warmly in her apartment. The pictures, one or two posters, a map of the world full of little flags marking the many countries and cities where she had sung and acted—all spoke of a rich and kaleidoscopic past. She is an excellent cook and had prepared a delicious meal for us, talking, laughing and often singing as she went back and forth to the little kitchen, bringing, among other things, a delicately mysterious soup and an exotic African fruit which we had never tasted before.

Later we went to a concert of an early Stravinsky work, short and humorous, followed by a play with orchestra or, should I say, an orchestral play—the work of two brilliant contemporaries, Tom Stoppard and André Previn. Everybody enjoyed the evening but Muriel was ecstatic. She alone in the huge audience gave the performance a standing ovation. We stayed on in the theatre, re-living it all while she enlightened us about some of the mysteries of the pentatonic scale.

A couple of weeks later we returned her invitation and took her to lunch in the delightful restaurant of the Richmond Museum. She was radiant, looking beautiful, enjoying Virginia crab-cakes and talking, talking, talking.

She began with her dressing-room in the Drury Lane Theatre. She occupied that room for five consecutive years, a longer tenancy than most actors or actresses, perhaps the longest ever for anyone coming from abroad.

'The day that Mr Boxer, the chief technician of the staff, came to me and asked me how I'd like the room to be re-done was for me wonder and triumph. I had had a year there already in *South Pacific*. The wall behind me was vanilla and chocolate. The chocolate was reflected in my mirror. It was a dismal place to be—very dreary. I thought about it for a few days and then I decided. It was to be French grey and pale blue with just the right touches of gold. It was beauti-fully, lovingly done, with new closets and curtains and every-thing. It helped to give me courage when Mr Hammerstein looked in one day and, dressed in my rags as Bloody Mary in *South Pacific*, I asked him if I could audition for the part of Lady Thiang in *The King and I*, which was to follow in the theatre immediately, I got it without an audition. It was an exacting part, standing all the time, almost always motionless, usually silent, yet taking in everything. I even learnt eventually to shed real tears at every performance from one eye, in profile to the audience. The other eye didn't need any tears! I had one song alone on stage where the Lady Thiang sings out of the fullness of her heart:

> This is a man who thinks with his heart,
> His heart is not always wise.
> This is a man who stumbles and falls,
> But this is a man who tries.
> This is a man you'll forgive and forgive
> And help to protect as long as you live.
>
> The thoughtless things he'll do
> Will hurt and worry you.
> Then all at once he'll do
> Something wonderful.

'The song, *Something Wonderful*, seems to me one of Richard Rodgers' best. Almost a touch of Brahms about it. So I carried on in that lovely room for five whole years. I bought somewhere in the East End a most peculiar long glass Victorian vase with a silver top and hung it on the wall by my large mirror. I always had it in one flower of the season.

155

Only the other day I was cleaning the silver top and was surprised when I looked at the printing with my magnifying glass to find the name *Thornhill Ltd, 144 Bond Street*.'

My grandfather's shop! We had several times enjoyed and admired Muriel Smith in those musicals. We didn't know her then and never visited her dressing-room. How strange that the only product that I have seen of that Thornhill shop, which rose like a bright comet in Bond Street and then disappeared again, had been there back-stage in Drury Lane. Now it rests in our daughter Susan's home in Richmond, for Muriel gave it to her with a characteristic note: 'To all obvious purposes this piece of Victoriana seems oddly out of touch with our times, since its function is obscure (like that of some people), but I hope it will mean something to you'.

Muriel, for many years, had looked after her mother, in their apartment in Richmond until she died in her 90s. 'It wasn't easy; it's a small place and it was claustrophobic. It often drove me to a near breakdown. But I wanted to do it. After all, she looked after me in all my early years in the theatre. I was only nineteen and I became a star overnight. One day I was working in a drug store in Philadelphia to help pay my fees at the Curtis Institute; the next day I was 'discovered' by John Henry Hammond, who did so much to launch people of my race in the entertainment world. Within a few weeks I was the lead on Broadway in *Carmen Jones*. Every night in those days my mother would be at the stage door with a thermos of hot coffee, and sandwiches – and she would take me home on the subway to Harlem. I am glad I started my career that way, though I didn't always appreciate it at the time.'

As we talked, my mind went back to the summer of 1957 and that day on Mackinac Island in the Great Lakes of America. The rumble of race conflict was in the air. The fight for justice, equality and integration had begun. A black school teacher called Daisy Bates was challenging Governor Faubus of Arkansas and the whole southern white establishment in Little Rock. The Ku Klux Klan had burned fiery crosses on the Bates' lawn. There was violence and counter-violence. A passionate preacher called Martin Luther King was making his pulpit crusade. He proclaimed non-violence. His enemies and some of his followers did not agree. As we met that summer at our conference on Mackinac Island, race and reconciliation were in all our hearts. Was Little Rock a local blaze or might it become a national conflagration? A solemn heart-searching meeting was coming to an end. There was silence. Out of the audience a young black woman stepped forward. Unannounced, unaccompanied, she began to sing. It was a heart-stirring, heart-breaking spiritual. But that voice! For me it was unmistakable, unforgettable. It was Muriel Smith.

After the meeting we talked. She was on her way from making a musical in Hollywood to an appearance in Covent Garden. How she had come to Mackinac Island, why she had stopped off, I did not know. All I knew was that this was no coincidence. As a few days went by, Muriel knew it too. Little Rock was on her heart. 'If there's some way, any way, that I could use my gifts for my people, I think I would cancel all my engagements. Can you help me, can I help you, can we do something together?' Muriel was at the height of a brilliant career in theatre and films, in opera as well as in light reviews and outstanding recitals of *lieder*. Could we produce a musical dramatic work worthy of her remarkable gifts and at the same time relevant to the conflict that was on all our hearts?

It was a challenge to a playwright. Most plays begin with lonely authors, hidden away by themselves, researching their material, teasing their memories, letting loose their imaginations. Some of my favourite places for embarking on a play have been the reading room of the British Museum and the New York Library. Once it was the balcony of a villa in a Druze village in the Lebanon; sometimes sitting up in bed very early in the morning. I once had to let a key scene burst onto paper as I jolted and swayed in a New York subway train and finally came to earth on Coney Island, with the scene finished, but not the slightest realization of where I was.

The musical on which we embarked with Muriel was not like that at all. A small group of us, writers, musicians, actors

157

and others, would meet every day with Muriel and simply talk. Reminiscences, fears, hurts, prejudices, and pre-conceptions only half realized or understood, gradually came out. This was the raw material of a new musical.

This was again the point where God stepped in, as it were, and made us more than ever sure we were not dealing with coincidences. There had arrived on Mackinac Island, equally unexpectedly, another actress; a rising star of Broadway, fresh from the musical *Pajama Game*. Anne Buckles was blonde and came from the deep South. She was brilliant, racy and outspoken. Her marriage had broken up. She was a big person imprisoned in too small a life. She instantly became part of our team, Muriel's perfect foil and counter-part, becoming bit by bit her faithful friend. Together Muriel and Anne invested their personal careers to bring a uniting idea to their country.

Then we discovered our theme. Some years before at a conference of Moral Rearmament at the Shoreham Hotel in Washington, there had come one of the great pioneers of black America, Mary McLeod Bethune. She had been the seventeenth child of a family of former slaves. She was the only one of the family to be born free. She had soon taken her place alongside her brothers and sisters picking cotton in the dust of the fields which surrounded their crude wooden cabin. By the age of nine she could pick 250 pounds in a single day. She could not read or write. Then the church began to establish mission schools. Mary enrolled at the first one to open in the area of South Carolina where she lived. Each day she walked five miles to acquire learning, which she passed on to the rest of her family at night. She studied so diligently and with such faith that she became a teacher.

From that time on she burned and bled for the education of her people. With capital of $50 she opened her first school on the local rubbish dump in the town in Florida to which she had moved. She finally founded the first black college in the United States. Within ten years she had turned it into a university with 600 students. She had 'talked it up, worked it up, prayed it up.' In the end she became President Roosevelt's adviser on minority affairs.

By the time she arrived at the Shoreham Hotel she was white-haired, dignified and honoured. She spoke of the eternal struggle between the sovereignty of Almighty God and man's arrogant, rebellious will. But there was still something lacking in her life. She had been unable to give her beloved students a faith big enough to live by and to answer the divisions of our time.

After she had spoken there was a long silence. Very slowly another elderly woman rose to her feet. She was a product of the old white aristocracy of the American South. The two women stood side by side. It was the whole history of centuries, from the slave trade to Little Rock, embodied in these two women. The white woman spoke: 'All my life I have been part of a great injustice. Until today I never believed that for us to stand here, side by side, would be possible. Will you forgive me?' As they stood together you felt history was being made. Later, Mary McLeod Bethune said: 'To be part of this great uniting force of our age is the crowning experience of my life.'

Some of this may seem commonplace now. Back in the 1950s in America it was a revolution. Here was the theme of our play. It would be based on the life of Mary McLeod Bethune and it would be called *The Crowning Experience*.

From then on things moved swiftly. A large international group of more than 200 people, black and white, from Africa and Asia, Europeans and Americans, decided to stay on in Mackinac Island to produce and mount the show. Muriel and Anne's examples inspired many others. Engagements were cancelled, plans altered. Everyone gave according to their ability to make it financially possible. We needed young black children to act out Mary McLeod Bethune's first school on the city dump. Two whole families, one from Canada and one from the United States uprooted themselves and joined the company. That meant setting up a special school with trained teachers. We brought our own daughter Susan from Europe to join the children on the road. Nobody was paid anything. It was not so much to be part of a show as to help bring a spirit of healing to America, to the world.

Muriel was at the heart of the whole thing. Gradually

159

we got to know her. There were depths and mysteries and paradoxes in this remarkable woman which I certainly have not fathomed yet. Like Lady Thiang there was always that other eye which the audience does not see. We discovered first of all that she was a superb actress. How many great singers are also real actors? Not many. She was one. She was also a poet; spontaneous, immediate, unexpected. There was also what she described as the gypsy in her; another dimension, another rhythm. A passionate, perplexing, humorous, occasionally volcanic temperament that could leave you gasping.

And yet her grace and perception in some of those early rehearsals were equally remarkable. She was a seasoned professional. Many of the company were raw amateurs. Suddenly she could electrify us all: 'Stop!' came that commanding voice in the middle of a difficult scene in rehearsal. 'Stop. We can't go on. The Holy Spirit is not here.' She was right. What had been Spirit-filled had suddenly gone dead. Everyone, startled, came to a standstill. 'The Holy Spirit,' said Barbara once, 'is like an elephant. At least you know when he is there and when he is not there.' Untheological, but perhaps understandable.

On this occasion everyone had a chance to pause and recollect why we were all there. What was our aim? What was our calling? The silence went on. Somebody said a brief spontaneous prayer. The rehearsal resumed. Everything was different. It had come alive again.

Another unique element in this most unusual production was that it was all created, as it were, in public. At least once every week everyone gathered in a great hall and whatever had been written, composed, created, rehearsed, was performed without benefit of costumes or scenery for everyone to see. The play grew and took shape before all our eyes.

We had begun in late September. By Christmas, with snow thick on the ground and the lake beginning to be speckled with ice, the production was complete. Christmas was celebrated with full hearts. It seemed like a double birth for which we were giving thanks.

Then all were aboard the Mackinac ferry; props, scenery, children, teachers, parents and friends, members of the multi-national cast and crew, as we crunched and heaved our way through the rapidly hardening ice, just in time to reach the mainland before the island was cut off for the rest of the winter.

Much thought had been given as to where in America to begin. Why not begin in one of the most difficult and dangerous places of all, Atlanta, Georgia, the biggest city of the South? Many were saying that what was happening in Little Rock might be a Sunday School picnic compared to what might happen there.

In 1958, in the southern states of America, things were utterly different from what they are today. In spite of new legislation, segregation was still complete—in buses, taxis, hotels, schools, restaurants and, of course, theatres. To take a highly controversial play with a completely multi-national cast to Atlanta was a hazardous, not to say a dangerous business.

We began in the one place we could begin, the vast civic auditorium holding thousands of people, the home of bicycle races, circuses, and every form of big-scale entertainment. This was open and available for black and white alike. But how would the delicate balance of a new production, with little children and a highly explosive atmosphere, survive?

The word got around and the audience was enormous—tense, curious, and in some cases, hostile. This is where Muriel's greatness was put to its first test. Her magnificent voice filled the cavernous hall. Still more, her great heart as it were enfolded the audience. In spite of themselves they became one.

That first weekend, 11,000 people saw the play. At the end a stranger asked to speak with us. 'I came here in trepidation,' he said. 'I leave in exaltation.' He was the Jewish owner of the Tower Theatre on Peachtree Street, at that time the best theatre in town. 'I would like to have you in my theatre,' he said. And then, more hesitantly, 'I would like to do what perhaps has never been done in Atlanta before. I will open the main doors and let everyone in together, black and white alike.' Now it may seem commonplace. Then it was breathtaking. 'You can have my theatre for as long as you can fill it.'

So began a remarkable four-month run. At first people were nervous, hesitant, fearful. The local newspaper sent a reporter twenty-five times to see the play in the expectation, in the hope perhaps, that some explosive incident might take place, something to splash on the front page and so run the play out of town. They never published the real story, that not once in that long run did any kind of incident take place. The few black people who ventured to the first performances inspired others. The churches encouraged their people to go. They prayed for the cast. Once again it was Muriel's magic, with Anne Buckles' contrasting brilliance, with little children, and the Asians and Africans, that wove their spell and turned a theatre into a catalyst, a fusion.

As the curtain came down you would see a black hand and a white in a quick handshake, a momentary recognition of a new bond, a smile perhaps, and a few words of friendship and encouragement.

'Atlanta will never be the same again,' said a leading black lawyer, Colonel A T Walden. 'There is something new in the air. You can feel it in the streets, in the buses [just beginning to be integrated]. It's like the beginning of a mighty thaw. It is the herald of spring.'

So much more was to be fought for and suffered. More has to be accomplished still. Violence was still to erupt further south in Alabama and elsewhere, but it is a fact of history that no violence touched Atlanta. Andy Young, one of the black statesmen of America, is Atlanta's present mayor.

There may never be a statue of Muriel Smith in that city. Few now know what is owed to that golden voice, that big heart, those all-embracing arms, night after night in a big theatre.

'For this writing of plays is a great matter, forming as it does the minds and affections of men in such sort that whatsoever they see done on the stage they will presently be doing in earnest in the world which is but a larger stage,' wrote George Bernard Shaw. Many other forces and influences, of course, were at work. But so it happened in Atlanta.

What scarcely anyone can realize is the cost. Muriel lived during that time in Atlanta in a beautiful white home in Ponce de Leon where she could be truly private, at home among friends. Outside everything was different. We could not walk together, visit a hotel or restaurant or even shop together. I remember seeing that the New York Metropolitan Opera was coming to town. 'Wonderful!' I exclaimed impulsively over a meal, 'we must all go.' Then my stomach took a sickening lurch. There was Muriel beside me. These singers were her friends, fellow artists with whom she had performed. But Muriel could not go with us to see them. There was only one place where we could meet socially and that was the Wallahaji Hotel, a black hotel owned by Chief Aitken, a leader of his people.

Many of us stayed there. There we formed our '*Crowning Experience*' school. It was possibly the first fully-integrated school in the State of Georgia. If the Press or the powers-that-be had known of its existence, there would likely have been a riot. Susan, our ten-year-old daughter, a veteran of life on the road, loved that hotel because she enjoyed her friends and the other children. Thank God children are colour-blind. When the time came to leave and join Muriel, Anne and others in Ponce de Leon, Susan blew a rare tantrum. 'You can go,' she shouted. 'I'm staying. It's the nicest home I've ever had.'

One day the phone rang in Muriel's room. It was Sam Goldwyn in Hollywood. We happened to be in the room, and with Goldwyn's insistent crescendo we could hear most of both ends of the line. The film *Porgy and Bess* was getting under way. 'Now you come on out here,' said the insistent voice.

'Thank you, Mr Goldwyn,' said Muriel quietly, 'but I am already in a show, *The Crowning Experience*.'

'What's that? What are they paying you?'

'Nothing at all.'

'Well then, you be a good girl and come on out and we'll talk. Money's no problem.'

'Thank you, Mr Goldwyn. I realize there are very few offers or parts like that for actors of my race, but . . .'

'Well, you come out to Hollywood and see me.'

'I think you had better come and see *The Crowning Experience*.'

'OK, OK. If I come to Atlanta, will you promise to come to Hollywood?' 'I really couldnt' make that promise, Mr Goldwyn. Besides, I'm going to pray you don't make *Porgy and Bess*. I don't think right now, at this moment in America, it gives the proper image of my people.'

Things happen strangely. Two days after that conversation a fire broke out on the set of *Porgy and Bess* in the early hours of the morning. Much of the scenery was destroyed and the costumes. 'Heavens!' said Muriel with some alarm, 'I think I'd better stop praying.'

I was interested to read in Sidney Poitier's autobiography (*This Life*) how he too did not want to play in *Porgy and Bess* for the same basic reasons as Muriel. Much as everyone loved the music of Gershwin he did not like the play's inherent racial attitude. He describes how it was made clear to him in Hollywood gently and obliquely, but with as much hidden force as a steel trap: 'We just want you to understand what Mr Goldwyn's power is like in this town. He's one of the biggest, most powerful studio heads in the business, and if he chooses to, he can blackball you so you never work in a studio again as long as he is a power in the Hollywood community.' Poitier felt he must submit and play. Muriel did not. She never received an offer from a Hollywood studio again.

But that is only the beginning of the story. From Atlanta *The Crowning Experience* moved to Washington. After a run of seven weeks at the National Theatre, when 80,000 people saw it, the play and the cast returned to Mackinac Island. It had grown on the road. Peter Howard and George Fraser had added a ringing, tingling final curtain song, *The World Walked into My Heart Today*. At once came the demand for a film. There was at that time no film studio on Mackinac Island—that came later. There were, however, spacious buildings. Above all, there were people, lighting, sound,

props, builders, an enlarged and extended cast, all wholly
dedicated and convinced, all ready to give their services.

Rickard Tegström, who earlier had made superb nature
films for Walt Disney in the arctic regions of his native
Scandinavia, and after that had filmed the all-African film
Freedom, gave the best part of a year to film *The Crowning
Experience*. He was more than an artist with the camera. He
took on the role of director as well, assisted by Marion
Anderson, Cecil Broadhurst, George Fraser, William Reed,
Louis Byles of Jamaica and many others, who had played a
major part in creating the play. Phyllis Konstam played the
part of the white southern aristocrat whose dramatic speech
of apology was the climax of the story.

To describe in detail an amazing year of hard work, lessons
learned, discoveries, surprises, set-backs, mistakes and
(above all) miracles would require another chapter. The film
was made and went to the world. For Muriel it was the
beginning of a new phase in her career. She made herself
wholly available to perform in other plays and films with a
similar purpose to that of *The Crowning Experience*. Far more
even than that, she gave up her personal career for many
years of travel, speaking, singing, constant self-giving. Only
recently she again explained why she had taken this step. 'I
felt that my country and the world needed (and still needs)
the healing that could be found in facing the moral dilemma
of judging people of the human family racially, rather than
on the basis of character'. Her aim was even greater than
race reconciliation. It was nothing less than God's reign on
earth.

For a time, looking after her mother, she lived in quiet
retirement. Soon after her mother died the cancer appeared.
Her doctors took a grave view of her condition. With all this
there came another extraordinary development. Once again
she took up her career. She began singing again. She gave
major recitals in Richmond and beyond. The critics seemed
unanimous. 'Listening to Muriel Smith sing is like examining
a fine diamond,' wrote Ellen Robertson. 'Just when you think
you have heard it all, along comes another facet to dazzle
you.'

She performed on the stage as well as in concert. The National Council of Negro Women chose her to receive its highest award, with special reference to her portrayal of Mary McLeod Bethune.

The last two years living with cancer were, perhaps, the most remarkable of all. They were costly and testing years of battle and pain. Two operations with two courses of chemotherapy took their toll. But with it all came a deepening in her heart and spirit. 'No one can have a brush with death,' she said, 'without taking a fresh look at life.' She continued to look beautiful right to the end. In the year of her death she gave notable recitals, singing Vivaldi and Mozart, Brahms and Wolf and Debussy; always ending, of course, with some of her favourite spirituals.

In her final concert in the Virginia Museum of Fine Arts, she included one entitled *Prepare Me*. God indeed was preparing her. Her doctors were often amazed that she had the strength to go on. Her new quiet assurance, her generous help to others, her faith, victory over deep frustrations and bitterness, all these were the real answers to the prayers of thousands for her healing In the last words she spoke in public she said, 'I want to be filled again with love, that I may have something to give others.' This was the essence of Muriel; singer, artist, scholar, poet, but above all, friend.

13

Bishops

In my young days bishops were still very much 'my Lord'. They invariably wore gaiters, black aprons and various other special paraphernalia. They would appear from time to time at our country rectory, drink a discreet glass of sherry or port with my father as they discussed the latest ecclesiastical goings-on, make some jolly comments to us children, preach a sermon or two or conduct a confirmation, and go as mysteriously as they had come.

But my first, very own, real bishop came through a friend of mine at Repton, Alan Linton-Smith, who invited me to spend a few days with him and his folk during the holidays. I had scarcely realized at the time that his father was in fact the Bishop of Hereford, that he lived in a palace and very much in the palatial style. I can still see my arrival at the august front door as I carried my battered school suitcase, secured probably against faulty locks with a piece of rope, only to be greeted by a gentleman in black whom I first took to be the bishop but who turned out to be someone even more grand and austere, the butler.

'May I have your keys, sir?' he said to me in a highly clerical voice. Of course I had no keys and it was with a little disdain that he took my school suitcase and conveyed it to one of the spare rooms in the palace.

To my surprise, when I went up to get ready for supper that night I discovered my reach-me-down best suit laid out in state for me to put on for dinner. It should have been a black tie and dinner jacket, but I had to do the best I could.

Worse still, next morning, as I got up, all my clothes

seemed to have disappeared. There was literally nothing to put on for the episcopal breakfast table. Just as I was despairing of help, a discreet knock at the door brought my friend the butler, now also a valet, with my somewhat dubious undergarments and other clothes which had been carefully valeted, brushed, and even repaired for me to put on for the next day.

So my visit went. My friend was hospitality itself, and I am sure that the bishop, a most handsome, dignified man, and his wife, were kind, but now after all these years I have to confess my memories are not of the bishop, only of the butler.

George West

It was a good many years later, after I had myself been ordained and was a young chaplain and don in Oxford, that I had my most significant encounter with a bishop. It was at one of the Oxford Group house parties which, during the thirties, were held, summer by summer, in various colleges and to which many hundreds came from all over the world. Sitting quietly at the back of the meeting, I had seen this bishop. He was quite young, tall and handsome. His bishop's clothes had an unusual newness and gloss about them. He listened intently to all that was going on and said nothing at all.

It was after two or three days, on a lovely Oxford summer morning, that he suddenly appeared in the garden of Lady Margaret Hall and, taking me by the arm, suggested a stroll together.

'What is it?' he said abruptly.

'What is what?' I asked.

'Why, what is it that these young people have? Naturalness, unforced honesty. There is a lack of self-consciousness. It brings laughter and yet sometimes moves you pretty near to tears. What is it that they have got that I have not got?'

Later I was to become very familiar with this abruptness of speech, so characteristic of Bishop George West. He had just been consecrated as a bishop and in a few weeks' time

168

was to travel to Rangoon. He had spent the last twenty years working as a missionary in the remote jungle country of the Karen people. He had lived among them, little-known, unsung, but a devoted friend and teacher and pastor of a primitive, but shrewd and loveable jungle people, speaking their language, training them for baptism and confirmation, sometimes for the ministry. A devoted missionary and servant of Christ.

But his question rang in my ears: 'What is it? What is it these young people have got that I have not got?' After all, he was a bishop, and I a very junior priest indeed. It hardly seemed appropriate to say to him, 'Well, perhaps it is the Holy Spirit.' Or, alternatively, 'I think they have committed their whole lives to Christ, without reservation or any condition.'

You could hardly say something like that to as impressive a figure as a bishop, as you looked at his new bishop's clothes. He told me later that when he had gone to the ecclesiastical tailors for his first bishop's outfit, the attending tailor, in tones more unctious and reverent than those of any rural dean, had murmured as he took the measurements, 'A most gratifying appointment, my Lord. Such beautiful calves!'

What to answer? Finally I said, 'I could not possibly tell you, Bishop, what you might lack. But do you think if we asked God together he might be able to make it clear?' By this time we had strolled out into the Oxford parks, that most beautiful of all cricket grounds, surrounded by a tapestry of magnificent trees. We were perched in the friendly shade of one of them.

'That question of yours,' George told me later, 'put me on the spot. Could God give me the answer to my question? If I answered 'No', where did I then end up theologically? But if I answered 'Yes', where might I end up practically?'

So we sat and talked for a little, but mostly we were silent. I began to learn that George, after all those years in jungle country, among primitive people, was a shy and rather silent man, saying little until he had something worth saying, and then coming out with it abruptly, unvarnished, whether it be about cricket or his study of the Christian mystics.

As we sat there, George found the back of an envelope and scribbled down, almost absent-mindedly it seemed, a few words. He looked rather quizzically at what he had written. 'The first thing here,' he said, 'is the word "cheroot". What does that mean? There is nothing wrong with smoking.'

After quite a pause: 'My doctors have told me to give it up.'

'And have you?'

'No.'

'Why not?'

'Because I can't,' the Bishop said very simply.

He peered at the next word he had written, looking at it almost as though it were not his writing but a kind of heavenly script that had come from outside himself and was thrust into his hand. 'The next word here,' he said, 'is the word "Metropolitan". What do you think that means?'

'I don't know,' I said.

'Well, of course, that is the name of my chief. He is the Metropolitan Archbishop of India, Burma and Ceylon. He is Foss Westcott, the son of a great New Testament scholar. He consecrated me Bishop of Rangoon in Calcutta Cathedral only a few months ago. The only piece of advice he had to give me was to suggest that I might come to Oxford and take a look at the Oxford Group in action before I take up my work in Burma. You see, all my work so far has been in remote places. I have no experience of administration, elaborate ceremonial or various episcopal functions. Foss Westcott felt that here in Oxford I might learn something new about people; how to reach them, how to understand them. But what do you think this means?' he added, fingering the envelope in his hand.

'Do you get on well with him?' I said. 'Do you like him?'

'I am rather afraid of him,' said the Bishop. The Metropolitan had visited us in Oxford before. I could understand what George meant.

'I think I must go and talk to the Metropolitan,' said George. 'If we are to work together in the Far East, we must be able to be honest and frank.'

The third word which was written on that envelope was

the word 'Denmark'. Both Bishop George and I had an idea what that meant. Just recently Frank Buchman had accepted an invitation from Denmark to bring a Christian force, as large as possible, perhaps 300 or more, and introduce a nation to the Oxford Group. He had invited Bishop West to join them. Canon B H Streeter had already decided to go. Many others, from raw young undergraduates to leaders of church and state, would be with them.

'I wonder if I ought to accept the invitation and go,' he said. Then a small cloud seemed to cover his face. 'I suppose I could get away later in the summer.' Silence. Then, again abruptly, 'It's the cricket tour. I have been invited to go along. It would probably be the last chance for a very long time, perhaps the last ever.'

So our conversation ended, and we strolled back to the meetings at Lady Margaret Hall. Had God answered George's question? He certainly had lived a life full of the Holy Spirit. He certainly had given everything of worldly or material importance for his work with the Karens. There was no doubt about his sincerity and sanctity and yet, as he often said later, this marked a turning. God, as it were, had put a finger on two or three specific points. They could be either the great blocks or else beacons, not just to a new career, a new office in the church, but in reality to a whole new way of life.

And it all happened. Smoking? 'I always said,' said George, 'that I had to smoke cheroots to keep away the mosquitoes, but when the mosquitoes were far away, the smoking remained. Well, it dropped off as naturally as autumn leaves.'

Then there was the Metropolitan. With some hesitation and not a little fear, George knocked on his door there in Oxford and with his usual abruptness said, 'I want to tell you how sorry I am. I have always been afraid of you. It's marred our work together. It could spoil everything.'

Tears came into the old man's eyes. 'So many people feel that way,' he said. 'I know they do, but I don't know what to do about it. Please help me. Please let us go forward together.' It proved a lasting and unbreakable friendship.

The cricket tour was abandoned, and George did go to

Denmark. There I think he learned something new about his future role as bishop. He never saw this purely in terms of looking after a Christian minority in a foreign land. For him, he was responsible, he was a father in Christ for the whole nation, whatever their creed or outlook, for the Government and the Prime Minister as well as for the Church of the newly independent Burma. When there was to be a big memorial service in Westminster Abbey, with Earl Mountbatten present, in honour of all those who had given their lives, what Churchill called 'the great forgotten army' in Burma, George had been asked to preach. It was his wife Grace's idea that he go to Prime Minister U Nu and invite him personally to come over and attend the service in Westminster Abbey. The prime ministers of independent nations do not often make visits to foreign countries without a certain amount of protocol and invitation. Hower, U Nu had great respect for George and said he would very much like to come.

I remember when George came over for that service he spent a few weeks with Barbara and me in a flat which we had been lent in Smith Square, close to Westminster Abbey. By this time the Foreign Office had got wind of the Prime Minister of Burma's visit. They were a little perturbed as they had no official business to transact. I remember a rather worried-looking young official of the Foreign Office arriving at our flat to talk to George and explain that the Foreign Office was somewhat at sea about how to entertain their distinguished visitor.

'Well,' said George with due deliberation, 'I think Prime Minister U Nu would like to go to the zoo.' The Foreign Office official made a discreet note.

'And then?' he said.

'Then,' said George, 'I have a feeling he would enjoy a ride on the London Underground. It would be a new experience for him. And then,' he went on, 'he is very keen on the theatre. I am sure he would like a visit to Stratford-on-Avon and a chance to see a Shakespeare play. And then, most of all,' said George with a smile, 'he will want to go to visit Dr Buchman in his home in Berkeley Square.'

Notes were made and the young official left. A week or so later a much more senior and dignified Foreign Office official appeared at our flat. This time he carried a brief case with copious notes.

'We have been giving some thought,' he said a little ponderously, 'to this unexpected visit of Prime Minister U Nu. We have been wondering at the Foreign Office how best we might entertain our guest. We had the thought,' he said, brightening a little, 'that U Nu might like to go to London Zoo.'

'Excellent idea,' said George as though such a thought had never been conceived before. 'And what else are you planning?'

'Well,' said the official with even more enthusiasm, 'we wondered if he might like a ride on our Underground system. It might be for him a new experience.'

'That is very appropriate,' said George. 'Excellent.'

'And then finally,' said the official, warming to his theme, 'we know the Prime Minister is very interested in theatre, so why not take him officially to Stratford-on-Avon to see a Shakespeare play?'

'But don't forget,' George added with a slightly mischievous smile, 'to add a fourth point; a visit to Dr Buchman's home in Berkeley Square.'

Prime Minister U Nu arrived. He sat in a place of honour at the service in Westminster Abbey. He went to the zoo, and rode on the Underground. He saw a Shakespeare play, and at Frank Buchman's house in Berkeley Square he met many old friends and delivered an informal talk which did much to help unite our two countries. The whole thing proved a timely and useful experience just as Burma was emerging as a new, independent nation.

Suddenly, two days before his departure, a crisis emerged. It was discovered quite inadvertently that in his pocket Prime Minister U Nu had a speech, a somewhat long and official speech, specially composed for the occasion of his visit. He had probably envisaged himself making this speech in Westminster Abbey. For him to return to his country with the speech never delivered and never heard would have been something of a tragedy, almost an insult. George knew he must act quickly. I was there when he got on the phone to an old cricketing friend, Frank Owen, then Editor of the *Daily Mail*. 'You must help us Frank,' George said. 'Here is the Prime Minister with a speech and nowhere to deliver it.'

'Leave it to me,' said Frank Owen.

A special hall was found, announcements were splashed all over the paper, the word went out far and near, everyone gathered his friends together, a distinguished audience assembled as it were out of nowhere and the speech, a statesmanlike one, was delivered, enthusiastically received, and great satisfaction was expressed all round. Such was one facet of the work of a bishop who was also a Christian statesman.

In later years our times together were few and far between. George and Grace eventually settled down in their old age in Durham, George's own home diocese. I got up there once or twice on a visit and occasionally George and Grace would come down south, and I would see them. The depth of his prayer-life was very marked. It was he who introduced me to St John of the Cross and Mother Julian of Norwich and others of the great Christian mystics. Times of prayer and meditation with George were a choice mixture of the highly practical, often humorous, and the deeply spiritual and profound. He was also a marvellous friend. Once during a difficult time when a certain amount of disagreement had grown up between us, a sudden message came; would I go to George and would I hear his confession? I felt deeply humbled that he should turn to me for such a thing, but of course it was for my sake much more than for his own that he had chosen me.

Arvid Runestam

It was in the summer of 1946 at Caux in Switzerland, on the very eve of the first conference of Moral Re-Armament to be held in this magnificent place. Much thought and many days of preparation had gone into planning this conference. There were vital decisions to be made. How was Europe to be healed? How could Europe be healed without Germany? 'Where are the Germans?' Frank had said, as he stepped for the first time into the great hall at Caux.

Although he was faced with these momentous issues, Frank Buchman, with typical unexpectedness, had turned to Barbara and me, who had just at that very moment become engaged to be married, and said, 'You had better speak at the first meeting. Sound homes are the basis of everything.'

As he spoke we were round a small private supper table in Frank's apartment and the chief guest was Bishop Runestam of Sweden. Runestam was not only a distinguished bishop in his own right but he was also the son-in-law of Archbishop Nathan Söderblöm, one of the architects of the ecumenical movement.

'Frank,' said Bishop Runestam, 'we are expecting tomorrow several important guests from Scandinavia, including a number of churchmen. Could the meeting be about the church of the Nordic North?'

'All right,' said Frank, 'that shall be the theme.' But then looking at Barbara and me, fresh in the excitement of our engagement, he asked, 'All the same, you two had better be two of the chief speakers.'

Next morning the meeting gathered. A rather solemn delegation of Scandinavian dignitaries of church and state were present and a somewhat serious, even ponderous, atmosphere prevailed. This was to be a grand occasion, the opening of a great new centre, the start of a new era. Frank planted himself inconspicuously in a deep sofa at the very back of the hall and asked Barbara and me to sit by him.

As the meeting began, led mostly by the Scandinavians, we could hear Frank becoming more and more restive. He had an acute sense of how to capture an audience, how to make an occasion live; above all he hated boredom, the conventional, the spuriously solemn occasion.

As the meeting started I could hear him beside me erupting and bubbling inside with great annoyance and impatience. 'No national costumes,' he spluttered. 'No colour. Boring.' Then turning to me he whispered, 'You had better speak, Alan. Liven things up, for goodness' sake.'

My mind was in such a whirl after some tumultuous days leading to our engagement that I scarcely had one clear idea in my head. However, very soon Frank turned and whispered to me again, 'You speak, Alan. Speak for a long time.' My heart sank lower and lower in my boots, but messages were somehow transmitted to the leader of the meeting and almost before I knew it I was called forward to address the august assembly.

It so happened that night in Caux was to be the occasion of the very first performance on the continent of Europe of *The Forgotten Factor*, and so my best hope seemed to be to start by telling something of what the play was about and what had been done with it so far. Having got that off my chest I warmed to my subject and went on by saying, 'But now I have the pleasure of a new and far more exciting production', thinking this was my cue to introduce Barbara and announce our engagement.

'No, no!' shouted Frank from the back. 'Tell them about your other play, the one about Fredrik Ramm, the patriot and resistance fighter of Norway.'

This was quite a big subject and it took me some time before I could get around to it and tell about my second play. 'But now,' I repeated with relief, 'there is a quite new and more exciting production.'

'No! No!' said Frank, 'tell them about your third play, *The Statesman's Dream*.' It is true I had written by that time three plays, this last one a light-hearted musical fantasy that had captured and, I must say, delighted many audiences. So once again I was deep in what was becoming quite a lengthy speech.

There were no more plays so now I felt at last I could say, 'But now I would like to announce the newest . . .'

'No!' shouted Frank, 'tell about the result of the work in the coal mines of Nova Scotia.' Here I was getting more and more out of my depth, and out of breath. There was much laughter, partly at my expense, but at least the audience were wide awake.

It was not until I had covered several topics suggested impishly by Frank from the back of the hall that at long, long last I was able to announce my engagement to Barbara van Dyke, who was already pioneering wonderful things in the almost ruined kitchen of the great hotel that had been allowed to run to seed during the war.

At last my announcement was made, and then Frank brought Barbara forward on his arm, presented her to me at the front of the hall, conjured up from somewhere or someone a lovely bunch of flowers, and left us standing there before a cheering and enthusiastic assembly. So then of course we had to start again and tell some of the adventures, and indeed the difficulties, that had brought us, an Oxford Don and a young American together, in a most unexpected and delightful combination.

By the time we had finished, the opening meeting of Caux was almost over. It had been far from the momentous and dignified speeches that such an occasion had demanded, but it had been alive and fresh and, in its way, dramatic. It was very typical of the way Frank did things. How often he overturned the carefully prepared plans and programmes of the rest of us and brought in some unexpected but inspired surprise that tingled with anticipation and made people long for more.

Barbara and I were busy during the next days with couple after couple who came to us wanting not just to congratulate us but to ask questions, to talk about their own marriages and families and to form friendships which in so many cases were to last us for life.

The one who seemed most enthusiastic of all was Bishop Runestam. He took us aside and gave us his Bishop's blessing, and forever after we have always thought of him as the one who helped to hallow our engagement and whose prayers enriched our lives.

Bengt Jonzon

It was not long after Arvid Runestam's visit to Caux that an interesting chain reaction began. I received a letter from him about another Swedish bishop. 'I have persuaded a colleague and great friend of mine, Bishop Bengt Jonzon, to cancel all his immediate engagements and with his wife Eva to board a charter plane leaving Stockholm for Caux next Tuesday. I have told him that things are going on so remarkable that the Church must not be unaware of them. He has decided to come. Please look after them. They are dear friends. Bengt is a good man and a faithful bishop, but he lacks fire.'

A few days later the Jonzons arrived. I took to him right away. He reminded me of my father, tall, handsome, an athlete, a scholar, and obviously a man of deep faith and conviction. He told us about his diocese of Lulea, comprising the northernmost part of Sweden, an area about the size of the whole of England, with an immense variety of social and economic and cultural conditions; of different religious and ideological movements, with different races and languages, Swedish, Finnish, and Lappish. He described the old farms along the coast and up the big rivers, and the Lapp nomads driving their herds of reindeer (far more reindeer than there are people), the big timber industries at the river mouths, and the iron ore mines, some already long used, others recently developed. Here, far away in the midst of the silent wilderness with its few inhabitants, have been created modern settlements with all the privileges and problems of a highly technical society. Deep in the woods and the valleys there are the electrical plants where, by the damning of the rivers, the geography and the way of life of the people have been transformed. There are reindeer and railways, nomads and mines, militant trade unions, and proud, primitive minorities. The bishop would traverse his diocese by plane or train, but often by sled or on skis.

Soon he sought me out and suggested a walk. He spoke with affection of his friend Runestam. 'I've known him for years as a deep thinker and a delightful human being. But I was shaken several years ago when he told me about his meeting with the Oxford Group. He had gained something new. The innermost doubt was removed. He was free, secure, and alive. It was a grey, rainy day when we talked, but it was as if sunshine and bird-song streamed into my soul. Oh yes, I've known about this work ever since the great hero of my youth, Archbishop Soderblöm spoke to me about it just before he died in 1931, and advised me to get in touch. I have tried to act on what I heard, but life is busy, distances are great, and somehow I have never made it. So' (with a slightly wan smile) 'here I am at last.'

Without thinking I pulled out of my pocket the letter I had just received from his friend Runestam and read it to him. That is, I read it until I got to the last sentence, 'but he lacks fire'. With a stumbled 'etcetera, etcetera' I brought my reading to a close. We walked on. 'But there is one thing I have not fully understood. What in practice is this listening to God?' I remembered my first encounter with Bishop West, and suggested that the best way to find out might be to try. By this time we were sitting in a lush green meadow with the sound of cowbells higher up the slope. A silence fell. But this time it was not my friend's thoughts that concerned me most, it was my own. It was as though a voice spoke. 'You are a coward. Why don't you read the whole letter, including the last sentence?' So I did. The dignified, reserved bishop suddenly came to life. 'But that's true,' he said excitedly, 'that's why I'm here. I love my work and my people, but I lack fire. I please and encourage the faithful. I make friends with the Laplanders and try to enter into their culture and, not very successfully, to learn their language. But the tough ore miners I scarcely talk to, or their union leaders, many of whom are Communists—and nobody becomes different. Yes, my friend Arvid is right. I do lack fire. How can I find it? I would give anything to find it.'

So we were silent again. Suddenly he looked up with a somewhat mischievous smile. 'I believe I know exactly what I am meant to do. There is a Swede here in Caux. I have known him half my life, from university days. The trouble is I have never cared for him much, rather looked down on him in fact. The odd thing now is I feel clearly that he is the man I must talk to. How strange,' he said, smiling again, 'I thought we were in for a nice theological discussion, for which I was prepared. And here I am going to ask help from a man whom I've never thought very much of and really rather dislike. First of all,' he added ruefully, 'I suppose I'd better tell him about my wrong and stupid attitude over

179

so many years and ask his forgiveness.' The Bishop's step quickened and his head lifted as we approached Mountain House. I wondered what the outcome would be.

It was a few days later that the Bishop told me the answer. He had sought out his fellow Swede. The man had surprisingly grown in stature. He forgave the Bishop with a laugh. 'I can quite understand,' he said. He then answered the Bishop's question about fire: 'I can only tell you that for me and my wife quite a new life came when we decided that there should be no shadows in our marriage; that we should be completely open and honest together about the past, and also about anything and everything that we feel in the present.'

'I thought that was very nice,' said Bengt, 'but in our case not very useful. Eva and I have as warm and open a relationship as you could wish. No secrets or awkward confessions for us. But then the following morning one thing came into my mind, only that one thing again and again. It was something that had happened forty-five years ago, something I was ashamed of. I had never told it to anybody. I did not understand why I should. And I always thought there was nothing to do about it. But the inner voice was inescapable: "You have to tell it to your wife." At last I got it out. My wife smiled and said it was just the same for her, some dark remembrances from earlier days. After that we went through our lives and found many things we needed to tell each other. It was like a spring-cleaning of our relationship.'

I can only say that near the end of the Jonzons' stay at Caux, the Bishop spoke from the platform. Having mentioned discoveries in his own life he then turned to the iron ore mines around Kiruna in his diocese, and spoke of their supreme ideological importance for Europe. The Germans had had full use of them during the recent war. Who was aiming to control them now? Here, through his diocese, was the shortest way from the East to the Atlantic. Why for decades had the Communists so successfully infiltrated this area—the mines, the electric plants, the railways? What was a bishop's task in the midst of all this? To tend the faithful of course; to pursue diocesan business, with the temptation to become more and more a desk man administering an organization? Or was it to care for all the people, irrespective of whether they were churchmen or not, to get to know these union leaders, listen to them and win them; to live Christianity in its full biblical dimension, 'relating my faith, myself and all I am and have, to find and carry out what God wills for individuals, my nation and the world.' As I saw and heard Bishop Jonzon that day I knew that here was a man of fire.

When the Jonzons returned to their home and diocese their son and daughter felt instantly that their parents seemed ten years younger. And so with the diocese. With the believing Christian people, in official visits to near and remote parishes, he took the chance to help them find the full dimension of their faith. To the Laplanders he gave a new feeling of destiny and hope, while challenging the Swedes, the ordinary man and the authorities, to realize how much they had wronged these original inhabitants of the North. 'For remember,' the Bishop would say, 'it is even more calamitous to do injustice than to suffer from injustice.'

He visited the mines, sought out the union leaders, and apologized for the wrong attitude of many in the Church, himself included. 'We have fought more for existing conditions than for the dignity of man. We preached submission and patience for the oppressed when we really ought to have preached righteousness and responsibility to the possessing classes, as well as love to everybody. In Moral Rearmament I found an everyday Christianity with revolutionary implications as necessary for bishops and clergymen as for everybody else. Here is a platform with men of the labour movement where we can work together for the future of the world.'

Once on May Day he found to his surprise that he was invited as the main speaker at the great workers' demonstration in a mining town. There were red flags and brass bands with the singing of the Internationale and speeches about the downfall of capitalism. 'Naturally I did not talk politics but spoke about the problems in men's hearts that cannot be solved by political means, but which must be solved if the world is not to be overwhelmed in a catastrophe. The highest standard of living has not created a happy people in Sweden. I talked about the fathers of the church and about the new type of man needed for a new type of society. There was a tremendous response and front-page headlines in the press.'

From that moment Bishop Jonzon's long life was on the offensive, and it remained that way in his diocese and in his retirement—proclaiming the glory of the Christian life in its full dimension of personal, national and international change. The year before he died he went on a journey round the world; America, Australia, New Zealand, India, Israel, Jordan, Greece, Italy and back to Sweden.

His physical vigour was wonderfully maintained. One summer morning in 1967, in the small town of Arvika in West Sweden, he rose early and went for a brisk swim. After that he dressed and went to church. When in the service the congregation was meant to stand, he remained quietly in his pew. He had died where he would have most wanted, a simple worshipper in the church he loved so much and had fought for so humbly and yet so glowingly; truly a man of fire.

14

Three Mile Man

My sister Kitty and I 'inherited' Peter Warnett with the charming house and garden where, after a busy, travelling life, we settled in the Sussex village where I had spent my boyhood. He tended the garden for the maiden aunts who left it to us and he still came once a week to keep it tidy. For me, discovering nature with Peter began at our own front door. When we came from London we brought two handsome bushes from our Charles Street roof garden and planted them in a shady place close to the house.

'They're nice,' said Peter, 'but you won't get any berries like that. Those are *Skimmia Japonica*, but they are two females. Now I work for a lady who has got two males. We'll do a swop around and get them matched up properly.' There soon arrived a handsome male. It was not long before our remaining female broke out into sprays of glorious berries.

In our village, as in so many others, it takes a while to be accepted as being truly part of the community. John Brough, our village barber until his death, told me once that after he had been cutting hair in the village for fifteen years one of the old-timers came in for his regular trim and said, 'Well, John, how do you like it here?' John replied that he liked it very well. 'Are you thinking of staying?' asked the old-timer.

Peter has lived in Rotherfield most of his life but he still refers to himself as a 'foreigner', although he came from only six miles away. There has been no more familiar sight in Rotherfield than Peter Warnett on his bicycle, upright and sturdy, weather-worn and sun-tanned, riding for the so many thousandth time down to the village or out to the woods.

There he is on his way to tend a garden, or to repair radios and televisions in the local shop, or out in the long summer evenings to see his family of badgers, or up early to record the song of birds, or to photograph a kingfisher flying in to feed its young. He draws his pension now, and his time is his own to pursue his life's hobby rain or shine, summer or winter. He is always on the look-out for that rare flower or unfamiliar bird or butterfly, carefully noting the changes from year to year, from season to season, as the old oaks or beeches are cut down, new firs and spruce planted, as the nightingales or the corncrakes disappear, or the tree pipits or the reed-buntings come and nest in the thick new foliage.

He has the look of a man who knows just where he is going and yet he seldom seems in a hurry. There is a rhythm of the countryman in the way he manicures a hedge, or coaxes a recalcitrant mower into life. He has time to stop and chat, but his eyes and ears are ever alert.

From the drama of the sex-life of a couple of bushes came the drama of a friendship and ultimate collaboration with the 'Three Mile Man'. It began with a hot summer evening when we entertained Malcolm and a large contingent of Muggeridge grandchildren. We had a barbecue and Peter was with us to help get the charcoal going. Then we all went to see some of Peter's nature slides. Malcolm was particularly taken with the pictures and equally with the man who had taken them. 'Billy Collins,' he said, 'must see these slides. He loves nature pictures. I'll arrange it.' Collins of course are Muggeridge's publishers, and the Collins family his friends.

It was not long after that Peter and I were invited to go along with Malcolm to the beautiful Elizabethan home, not so far away, where Sir William and Lady Collins lived. Sir William, fresh from his day in London followed by a quick dip in his pool, was in good form, talking about gorillas and various other projects he had on the stocks. Lady Collins was charming and hospitable. Then abruptly, 'Well, let's see the pictures.' Somehow Peter's unpretentious home-made screen and stand and his small projector seemed hardly worthy of the occasion, but Peter in his unperturbed, natural self on all occasions, and soon the beauty of the pictures plus

184

his characteristic, colloquial descriptions won his audience, and soon there were 'oohs' and 'ahs' from all concerned.

It was while Peter was quietly packing up to go home that Sir William came up to him with genuine enthusiasm. 'Very good pictures! Very good indeed! You know I think if you were to come to Collins in London and show them to some of my people, they might be quite interested.' I was suitably excited. Not so, Peter. 'I think I'd rather not. I don't like London.'

Sir William backed away, perhaps a little taken aback himself. Soon he was with Peter again. 'Very good pictures indeed. If you don't want to come to London, perhaps you would like to lend me some of your slides and I could show them to a few people. You know I think they might be quite interested.' Peter hesitated. 'I don't think I could rightly do that,' he said slowly. 'You see I'm showing them next week to the Rotherfield Women's Institute. Then I'm booked with the local horticultural society. I really couldn't spare the slides.' In reality he was selling himself beautifully, though he did not mean it that way. I couldn't help regarding it as a triumph when Sir William sidled up to me a few minutes later, and whispered, 'Can you persuade him?' I said that I thought I could.

We departed with a warm send-off, and a promise to meet again. It was a shock and a real sorrow that three days later I read of the death of Sir William Collins. I was of course sad that an interest in Peter's work had probably gone by the board. However, when I told Peter about it, he only said, 'Well, I'm glad he saw the pictures before he died. I think he enjoyed them.'

Nothing was heard any more from Collins, until about six months later a letter came out of the blue to say that there was still interest in Warnett's pictures and could a representative come down and see them. This was arranged at the Muggeridge's home, and very soon we were in serious negotiations for a publication. I had imagined that any part that I might have in the affair would be confined to general support, with the writing possibly of a few captions. However, I soon realized they wanted a full story to go with the pictures.

My main qualification seemed to be my extreme ignorance as a naturalist, plus possibly my experience as a playwright. My job was to draw Peter out, to ask all the dumb questions and, so far as I could, to try to make Peter live as a person and to reproduce, as nearly as I could, his characteristic manner of speech, and to impart just a little of the vast store of knowledge and experience he had gained ever since he left school at the age of thirteen, as woodman, gardener, bird-watcher, self-taught photographer, natural artist and country philosopher. His knowledge was confined to the district around his home. When an enthusiastic Collins editor discoursed about the badgers of the West Country or the butterflies of the Norfolk Broads, Peter would say, 'Well, I wouldn't know anything of that would I? I've only got my old bike and my two feet. I'm just a three mile man.' 'There's your title for the book.' I said excitedly. Collins were not so sure but they came round to it in the end.

The completion of that beautifully produced book took another two years; Collins had a way of asking for more and more. For me, above all, it opened up an entirely new world. I would go with Peter on some of his walks of discovery, trying not to talk too much, because he knew that in order to discover birds and animals your ears were just as important as your eyes. I remember a golden afternoon when Peter set out specially to photograph sunbeams. The low autumn sun was shining through the turning trees, some of them still wet with heavy dew. It cast a delicate pattern of sparkle and shadow. The woods along the River Rother were unearthly quiet. All nature seemed to be still, preparing for the winter days ahead. A jay gave a single sharp cry, as we approached, to warn all and sundry of our arrival. 'We call him the watchman of the woods,' said Peter. Later the alarm note was taken up by a wren. But nothing stirred until we came to a spot where a sudden burst of song from a robin filled the air with the sheer joy of music.

That day I saw a sleeper's nest, the winter quarters of a dormouse. 'I wonder if there's anyone at home. See how dry it is in there and warm. He'll get a good sleep there and won't be disturbed among all them prickles.' That day I learnt a lot about the migration of birds, of how Peter photographs kingfishers, of how the minks get away from their mink farms, swim like anything and eat practically everything in sight. I saw something of the world of small creatures on the surface of the stream or just under the water.

Another day in the summer we would explore the old disused railway line, a wonderful reserve for birds, flowers and butterflies, with hundreds of wild roses, white on one side of the cutting and pink on the other. My nostalgia would take me back to long childhood days when we chugged up and down this very line, 'The Cuckoo Line', on outings to the sea, Sunday School picnics and the rest.

On a wet afternoon Peter and I trudged our way ankle-deep in the bog, a derelict area for me, but for Peter a wonderful spot for some of his rare finds, including a very special dragonfly, discovered and only to be found there in Sussex. 'Tell you the truth, there are people who would like to buy the bog and fence it in. Trouble is when you do that you can destroy the very things you are aiming to protect. With a fence around the bog the cattle wouldn't be able to get in and trample down the willow and suchlike. In a few years the whole place would be overgrown, and all the small rare flowers would be smothered. No, me and my mates hope they will leave the bog as it is. After all, it's probably been that way for hundreds, even thousands of years. It's too soft and wet to plough. The soil is too solid and peaty for planting. Of course there won't be too much to see this time of year, but you may as well get the feel of the place.' Peter is a great believer in leaving nature to look after herself as far as possible. Professionals running around in cars, with super-computer cameras, are not much in his line, and now he is apt to report new finds only after they have been well and truly explored by him.

A case in point are the Rotherfield badgers, with whom Peter established friendly relations for many years. Several summer evenings before dark I have been out with him to the set where he has quietly watched and waited alone or with a few well-chosen companions. The aim has never been to tame the badgers. Some people want to use badgers for their own ends—to bring them home, cage them in, or even to make sport wih them and stage fights with hunting dogs. Others, rightly or wrongly, gas them to death in their hundreds, on the suspicion that they carry TB and other diseases to cattle. 'Mind you, what I say is it was probably the cattle what gave the poor old badger the TB in the first place. Besides, when they put poison gas down there, what else are they killing?'

No, when you go out with Peter to visit the badgers, you learn to keep quiet and wait your time. You will be well advised to bring along a packet of unsalted peanuts, ready for that tense and exciting moment when the daylight has almost gone and there is framed for just a moment in one of the openings to the set a ripple of white, marked by two streaks of black. Soon there are three, then four, then five of these somewhat clumsy but surprisingly fast-moving creatures in full view.

By then you may be lying full-length on your front, the peanuts on your outstretched hand. Peter will have laid a peanut trail leading from near the set to the spot where we are stationed. Some may have been buried as deep as nine inches but the badgers quickly smell them out and dig them up. We can hear the crunch and munch of the peanuts. Then begins the most fascinating scene of all. Very gradually, following the peanut trail, the badgers come nearer and nearer. It is a kind of stately dance as the badger advances, returns and approaches again, appetite and shyness, desire and timidity conflicting with each other. Gradually peanuts overcome prudence. A surprizingly big animal pauses and crouches only an inch from your hand. The striped face and grey silvery body are iridescent in the dim light. Finally the badger comes on the final inch, places a paw on your hand, as if to hold it steady, and with a gentle snuffle eats up two or three nuts, crunching them in its sharp teeth before backing away. Soon we are feeding badgers. Fear has gone on both sides. Our food is accepted, and so are we.

But there are now scarcely any of Peter's badgers. Too many insensitive visitors have scared them away. 'But they'll be back. Whatever happens to us on this island of ours, I

think the badgers will be somewhere around. You can bet
the Rotherfield badgers will go on. I only hope there'll be
some humans around to take an interest and enjoy them as
much as we do.'

After the visits with Peter round his three-mile patch
would come long sessions at home, often with the tape-
recorder going. Some days he'd be reticent and nothing
would come. Other days he would expand with stories of his
boyhood, working with his father and brothers in the woods,
swinging a four and a half pound axe all day, or keeping up
with full-grown men on one end of a big double saw for an
hour or so without stopping. 'You learn to push down hard
on the empty saw as the others draw it back so as to slow
them down and make them tired.' Or it would be his first
experiences of poaching, and the thrashing he got from his
father. 'That's not for poaching, that's for getting caught.'
But after the war he gave up his gun and took to a camera
instead. 'I durned nearly got my whole shoulder shot right
off in Italy. When I got back home I thought about that. I
didn't like being shot at, nor do the birds and animals I
reckon. So I gave my gun away.'

But how did he become such an artist with the camera?
His first camera was bought for a couple of pounds at a
jumble sale. He used one of those metal tubes you used to
get pills in at the chemist shop to rig up a telephoto lens. 'I
got one or two slides and showed them to the local camera
club. They were good, although I say it myself. Of course
the experts ta-tahed it, called it beginner's luck. When I took
another roll, with about fifteen out of twenty good, they had
to take notice, didn't they? Later I made a bit of money
giving shows and that, and bought a proper telephoto lens.
But most of the stuff I made myself, such as a remote control
gadget so that I could stand away from the camera and
operate from there. Later still, I made a more elaborate
system for taking birds such as the kingfishers flying past at
high speed.

'I do know a little bit about electronics. In fact that was
my hobby long before I took up photography. Of course, I've
never been able to afford all the elaborate equipment that

the professionals use. After all, a gardener's job is about the worst paid going. So far as the pictures are concerned, I just aim to take as much as I can of the wildlife within a three mile radius of Rotherfield Church. Besides, I got the idea people might be interested to know how much can be seen within three miles of one Sussex village. People who travel all over the place, abroad and suchlike, often miss what's going on under their own noses.'

Peter's words remind me of Gilbert White, author of *The Natural History of Selborne*. At the beginning of his famous book are inscribed these words: 'Men that undertake only one district are much more likely to advance natural knowledge than those that grasp at more than they can possibly be acquainted with. Every kingdom should have its own monographer.'

Peter is our local naturalist and Rotherfield's monographer. He is also a friend from whom I have learnt much and gained the key to the wonders of a new world.

15

Peter and the Dragon

'Nothing secondary, nothing safe, nothing soft and nothing shoddy. The matchless genius of a God-filled nobody.'

This was the telegram sent to me by Peter Howard on my fiftieth birthday, in 1956. I was celebrating it in Norway, where they make a good deal of these landmarks and anniversaries, and I was the recipient of many kind and flattering messages considered suitable for the occasion. The one that remains with me is Peter's. It contained a glowing vision but like most of his communications, it was for me abrasive and uncomfortable. I know it was addressed to me by one who genuinely applied it to himself. 'I am just an old cup, he once said, 'and I want to convey a few drops of the water of life, in as unpolluted a form as possible, to thirsty lips and parched lives.'

As a playwright I had genuinely set out with an acute sense of being a nobody whom God had mysteriously filled. I had had a hand in several productions, raw, unstudied and yet startling in their effect on people's lives. A musical revue, *The Good Road*, written and produced in 1948 with Bunny Austin and Phyllis Konstam, had filled His Majesty's Theatre in London for a good run. One hardened old critic had written, 'There was greatness on the stage of His Majesty's Theatre.' I can still point to a number of friends who will tell you that the direction of their lives was changed by that play nearly forty years ago.

But the step from a God-filled nobody to a self-filled somebody is short and slippery. We decided to make *The Good Road* into a film. At once we were plunged into the world of Hollywood, the old pros and the young upstarts. We needed their expertise. We did not give them our faith. The result was an expensive and humiliating disaster, indeed second-rate and shoddy. We never let it see the light of day. Meanwhile I was attempting a play about corruption and subversion in Washington. Frank Buchman, whose faith in our productions may have been shaken but which never wavered, loved the first draft and encouraged us to go on. We put it on first in Caux and then in a vast theatre in Miami. The play had dramatic moments and was more ambitious than anything I had attempted before. Somewhere in the production we lost our way. A pseudo-sophistication took over from reality. We went wrong with the casting. We put our strongest, most highly-trained actor in the part of a subversive agent, and a younger lightweight actor in the part of the hero. It was the villain who won the sympathy and applause of the audience. As Jean Kerr's little son, cast in the role of Adam in the school play, remarked ruefully, 'The snake has all the lines.' The play closed in Miami and has not been seen since.

My writing seemed to have dried up. I thought of that birthday message and of the man who sent it. Peter Howard was without doubt the most versatile, forceful personality with whom I had ever worked. International sportsman: he captained England at rugby football in spite of a thin and partially deformed leg, and almost casually filled in for a friend in the British bobsleigh team that won the world championship in 1938; successful farmer in peace and war; hard-hitting, often dreaded journalist, Beaverbrook-trained in the rough, tough school of instant deadlines and no holds barred; author, with Michael Foot and Frank Owen, of a scathing exposure of the *Guilty Men* who they felt had betrayed Britain in the thirties, a fair poet, an ardent suitor, a devoted lover and husband, scourge of the self-righteous, connoisseur of scandal, lover of Britain's greatness and hater of her smallness and her shame. He seemed to drain each experience to the last drop, be it a harvest celebration on his farm or a children's party with games and practical jokes. Add to that a Damascus Road experience in the darkest days of the war, the death of his only brother at Arnhem, and his espousal of Moral Re-Armament at the cost of his job, his money and his security, and you may get a taste, but only a taste, of the man who sent me that birthday telegram.

Peter's conversion to a deep Christian faith was cast in the same mould as that of Saul of Tarsus, and like his, it embraced the world. To all this he added the role of playwright. 'I think I might have a play inside me,' he said to me one day. 'I'd like to dictate it to a secretary. Will you come and sit with me while I do it, and if you have any ideas please say so?' It was a characteristically generous gesture, and I sat with him a whole day while he dictated a complete play. This was the way he worked. He had thought about it over a long period. It was all there, and when he was ready to go the dialogue rolled out with scarcely a pause or interruption. This first play, *The Real News*, was set in a newspaper office. This was Peter's world: the overbearing boss with a smarmy assistant sucking up to him but out to get him, the jaded fashion editor, the cynical theatre critic, the idealistic cub-reporter, the politician of *Yes Minister* stamp, the copy boys scurrying back and forth to the 'stone'. To all this he added an ideological dimension, a moral and political crisis with an exciting climax. It was the first of fourteen plays that Peter was to write. As ever, he was very forthright about his motive.

'Some write for money. Some for fame. Some, though very few, for art. These reasons are not mine. My ink is sweat. I do not find dipping in that pot funny. Fame is not for me and I do not take royalties from my plays.

'I write to preach. I write for the sake of propaganda. I write with a message and for no other reason. Do not believe those who say the theatre is no place for a man with a message of some kind. Some writers give their message without knowing they do it. A man who writes as if life has no meaning is the man with a strong message. My plays are propaganda plays. I write to give people a purpose. The purpose is clear. The aim is simple. It is to encourage men to accept the growth in character that is essential if civilization is to survive. It is to help all who want peace in the world to be ready to pay the price in their own personalities. It is to end the censorship of virtue which creates vicious society. It is to enlist everybody everywhere in a revolution to remake the world.' It is, for Christians, the use of the stage to uplift the Cross and make its challenge and hope real to a perverse but fascinating generation.

The help that I gave in the writing of that first play was limited, though I felt free to throw in a few suggestions. Instead I appeared on stage as an actor, a not too convincing Foreign Secretary. 'You looked more like a Rural Dean,' was Frank Buchman's comment. Later the great German actress, Elisabeth Bergner, came to help us with our production and she sat in the audience for this play. Here was my big moment. I gave my all—more, unfortunately, than my all. Afterwards Miss Bergner came to my dressing-room. 'Alan darling,' she said in her glorious deep voice, 'you were lousy. And I loved it.' I suppose I can always quote the second half of Bergner's critique.

I again sat in on the writing of Peter's next play *The Dictator's Slippers*. It was about an ageing dictator in a totalitarian state, a prophetic play written before Stalin's death. Again I was able to make some contributions which he readily accepted. Some time later he had an idea for a play about the flaming passions aroused in the period of the Mau Mau in Kenya, to be called *The Hurricane*. It was designed especially for Muriel Smith. He generously passed the idea on to me and to a promising young writer David Allen. David and I worried-out the characters and the plot and wrote the entire first half of the play. But it was Peter who, again in a single sitting, supplied an exciting and moving second act.

Peter was a natural and gifted playwright. He longed to give more time to play-writing. Even so he reached the heights in his classic morality plays *The Ladder* and *Mr Brown Comes Down the Hill*. But that was not his priority. Once or twice he said, 'When I reach sixty I intend to leave the active work to others and to retire to my farm to write.' Would we have let him, I wonder? He gave the last ounce of his enormous strength and energy, and died while he was still in his fifties.

The Hurricane was performed in the West End and in many

parts of the world and, with *The Ladder*, formed a powerful double bill. It was our first experiment in MRA of professional and commercial theatre. Some of us earned our Equity cards, performing for the minimum legal salary of £11 a week—a sum which we promptly gave back to the production. Thus began one of my happiest and most rewarding experiences in theatre.

After a Christmas evening in 1961, with music and poetry reading, a well-known actress of great charm and outstanding gifts, Nora Swinburne, rose to her feet and said spontaneously, 'If you were able in MRA to write a play for me, I would very much like to be part of it.' I pricked up my ears and thought, 'That's an interesting proposition. Sometime I must think about that.' Peter's reaction was rather different. The very next day he said, 'I've had a few thoughts about Nora Swinburne's play.' He handed me forty pages of typescript. He must have been working all night. It was a complete first draft. 'Take it, Alan,' he said, thrusting it into my hand. 'Do what you can with it. Make it your own. I have to go to Asia' (or was it South America?) 'for three months.' His draft was full of creative ideas, rough-hewn of course, with many gaps. I took Peter at his word, worked steadily, and by the time he came back much had been altered, including a new twist in the plot. I rewrote whole pages. I felt completely free, and yet kept carefully to the basic structure and style of the play, which was based on the Hungarian revolution and the predicament of the West when challenged by the Hungarian freedom fighters to come to their aid. I handed Peter the revised script. Next day he handed it back. It was scrawled all over with notes and comments, ranging from 'Great', 'Good', to 'Boloney', 'No!! No!!!', 'Needs more', 'Give it all you've got', etc. Finally, 'Take it. Work on it further. I'm off again. We'll finish it when I get back.' So, back to the typewriter, following most of his suggestions, ignoring some, expanding others. When Peter returned he was completely satisfied, with only one exception of course. The very last lines. For the first time we actually sat down together. In an hour or two we shaped the end. Peter then went off again.

The production of this play, *Music at Midnight*, was a fine one, beautifully acted by Nora and a good cast. It had two separate seasons at the Westminster Theatre, went on tour in the North of England, and went to the United States and was well received. More interesting was the fact that the leader of the miners in a pit in Northumberland came to the play in London. The pit was threatened with closure, and a thousand families depended on it for their livelihood. The miners' leader was gripped by the philosophy of the play. Instead of maintaining a state of running warfare, he called together every element in the pit to raise production, reduce absenteeism, and improve the quality of the work. By the time *Music at Midnight* had reached the Theatre Royal in Newcastle upon Tyne he was able to invite some of the cast to the coal face on the day when production, instead of the former average of 1,700 tons a day, reached 2,500 tons. Some time later it topped 3,000 tons and the pit, instead of closing, made a profit. This was just one fruit of Peter Howard's conception of his work in the theatre.

I had a vision of further co-operation with Howard. When he came up with another play the next year, *Through the Garden Wall*, he gave it to me to read. 'I supply the trunk and the branches', he said, 'you add the foliage.' Busily I added the foliage. I positively cluttered the landscape with foliage. I lopped-off branches here and there, maybe interfering with the roots also. With some pride and self-satisfaction I passed on the results. He hated everything I had done. Not one word of mine did he use. The play was a success. From then on a period of strain and pain grew in our relationship.

More than ten years earlier I had shared a room in Rome with Peter during a long period when Frank Buchman appeared to be going out of his way to criticize and oppose him. Looking back, I can see that a man of Peter's fiery independence and burning ambition needed a drastic purge of his motives, a complete freedom from the lure and lust of people-pleasing, if he were to be ready for the kind of leadership God might require of him. Frank knew his man. He knew he had to tackle the weak points in Peter's make-up if he were to be a fully reliable man of God. He dared to risk the friendship of the man who might mean so much to the future of his work. Again and again he put Peter's loyalty to Christ to the test. 'To give and not to count the cost. To fight and not to heed the wounds. To labour and not to seek for any reward save that of knowing that we do Thy will.'

During that period in Rome I watched the struggle and the costly decision of a big man to carry the Cross, even if there were never again to be a grain of recognition, one promise of reward, one warm spark of human response, from the man whom he admired more than any other. I could not understand Peter's ordeal at that time. Yet it proved the true metal of Peter's spirit, the genuine humility at the heart of the man.

Just as suddenly as it had begun it came to an end, and Peter became, in Buchman's last years, his truest friend, most loyal helper and natural successor.

Little had I realized back in Rome that Frank Buchman's drastic tackling of Peter was to be in some measure a foreshadowing of Peter's treatment of me. Seldom a week went by without my being 'salted with the fire of discipline', as Frank sometimes described it. It might be a direct assault in private or in public. What he was getting at, I realize now, was the caution, the innate love of comfort and approval, the easy amateurism of the don, the soft underbelly of casual mediocrity in a world of harsh professionalism. Peter, in leadership, breathed the spirit of St George facing the dragon. Sword in hand he sought out dragons of callous complacency, small thinking and easy living. He attacked and attacked. To a group of complacent Christians just before Christmas he said, 'You are like a gaggle of Christmas turkeys discussing your New Year plans.' He was a slayer of dragons, with a whiff of dragon's breath in his own lungs also. I heard him challenge a group of fairly plushy Americans to refuse to pay part of their taxes so long as it was forbidden by law to teach religions in the State schools. I doubt if he expected them to risk jail, but it would not do them any harm to consider it.

Sometimes I felt he overstepped the mark. Once, in Caux,

before a group of some hundreds, he threw out a caustic comment on my character which seemed so untrue as to be intolerable. A steely resentment entered my being. Without a word to anybody I packed my things, left by a side-door, walked furiously down the steepest mountain track to Montreux and caught the train to Paris. All the way, rolling through green French countryside, my heart was numb, unfeeling, possessed with only one thought, to get out and stay out for ever.

This was the unlikely prelude to the most uncomfortable and perhaps the most stupendous night of my life. The setting was far from spiritual or inspiring. It was a sleazy Paris hotel close to the Gare de Lyon. There I lay, tossing and turning, full of rebellion and bitterness. Lovingly, gently, through a long night, Christ led me, protesting, squirming, back to the *via dolorosa*, and the way of the Cross. Supposing I was hurt. Supposing it was unfair. What was my wounded pride compared to that blood and sweat, the hammer of the nails, the taunts of the crowd? Beyond that, what of my own hatred and betrayal? That night fear left me. I was no longer a slave to what other people said or thought. On my knees beside that lumpy bed, I was emptied of self, alone with God. I was my own man. Let others say what they will, do what they will. 'What is that to thee? Follow thou Me.' I could echo the words of George Herbert:

> But as I raved and grew more fierce and wild
>> At every word,
> Methought I heard one calling, 'Child',
>> And I replied, 'My Lord'.

And then a further gift. As the wintry light of morning crept into the room, I realized something else. I cared for Peter. He was not my enemy. He was my friend who had helped to drive me towards the Cross of Christ, the most precious gift in my life. I found in my heart a longing, an eagerness to see him again. For the first time I might be able to talk with him as man to man. I had so much to learn from his fiery, uncompromising spirit. I knew some of what he had suffered. God knows, I might be able to help him.

I got to a pay phone and told him I wanted to come back. He was gracious, casual. 'Take your time, Alan. Have a good rest. Come back when you feel ready.' He understood that I needed time to simmer down, to sort things out. I stayed with some friends in Paris, slept, played classical records, and let the balm of Christ's healing enter my spirit.

Eventually I returned to Caux. By that time Peter was in America. I was disappointed, but it did not really matter. The time would come. Letters would not do the trick. We needed some kind of a confrontation; a confrontation of honesty, but also of love. I believe he longed for me to stand up to him, for some honest, heated reaction. Anything better than mealy-mouthed compliance, the mouse sniffing after the cheese of approval, the cosiness of a fellowship that was a safe conclave, rather than the free-booting comradeship of costly commitment. Better a cheerful, courageous rebel than a sullen, silent conformer. This long waiting period was not easy. Often I was tempted to doubt that night in Paris. Often I felt impatient and thought, 'Let's skip the whole thing.'

At last we met in London. Barbara and I went to see Peter together. My whole heart went out to the man. Here was someone who had dared to accept the loneliness of being 'in charge' of the work that Frank Buchman had carried to the day of his death. There was nothing soft or people-pleasing about our conversation that afternoon. We could talk openly and honestly without fear or favour. The relationship had been wrong. It had not been doing me good. Nor was it good for Peter. We had searching, caring talk between equals, equal in responsibility, equal in need. It was the kind of fearless honesty he must have longed for so much and experienced so seldom.

At the end he made an unexpected request. He asked me to travel with him and be his chaplain. Who fed his spirit? Who dealt with his personal needs? With a full heart and humbled spirit I accepted. During the next year we were often together. He talked freely. I felt the daily drain and strain on a lion heart. In the end the heart gave way. Those quiet years of writing at the farm were not to be.

But God had one further gift. During that year of travel, Peter appeared from a night journey in America with the script of a children's play. It was based on one of the stories he used to tell his children when they were little. Once more, with all the old trust and generosity, he gave it to me to work on and indeed, with Kenneth Belden, Chairman of the Trustees of the Westminster Theatre, with George Fraser's delightful score, with Bridget Espinosa's choreography and Henry Cass our Director, and the Austins' long experience, we were allowed to take it, expand it and stage it. The result was an enchanting Christmas play which ran at Christmas time for eleven consecutive years at the Westminster Theatre, and has cropped-up since all over the place in schools, on film and video and on television. Of all the riches that Peter has left behind, this simple, searching, humorous work of art and profound parable, called *Give a Dog a Bone*, is one of the best. It comes from a heart that loved children and knew how to reach their hearts. It spoke in terms that even the wise and sophisticated could understand. It is a fitting memorial to a true friend, a gallant slayer of dragons.

After finishing the first draft of this chapter, I showed it to our daughter Susan for her comments. In return she showed me three letters Peter had written to her, and which she had kept for twenty years in her Bible. They were written to a sixteen-year-old girl in the midst of the turbulence and excitement of youth in the sixties. They were written during the last six months of his life. Constant travel, unlimited demands upon him, a giant frame almost at breaking point, twenty or thirty letters often dictated on tape between 5 am and breakfast—none of this prevented his care for one teenager, just one of a host of friends, scattered thousands of miles away around the world.

Susan and we had taken a vigorous part in the last conference which Peter had architected on Mackinac Island in America. Susan had entered fully into the whole thing, so

200

much so that some of the senior ladies complained to us that she was making life a little too exciting for some of the young men! When I mentioned this to Peter he said, 'I shouldn't worry. You can thank God she's normal.' Here is his letter written to her directly after:

September 23rd, 1964: 'You were a trump all through Mackinac. You are a considerable favourite of mine and I admired greatly the way you moved among the multitude and all you did for so many people. Good luck, Yours ever, Peter.'

A few months later Susan and her friends were planning a summer camp for young people:

January 10th, 1965: 'Well done. Whether you can get young people looked after for a pound a day, I don't know. But in any case make it a mighty blow at the heart and will of the nation. See the girls live straight with the boys and vice versa. Be sure you have lots of creative action in theatre, art and lifemanship.'

January 18th, 1965: 'Greetings from good old Rio. I enjoyed seeing you in London and I salute very sincerely and whole-heartedly your battle with the youth.

'Be careful or you will outstrip that father of yours. And with his play he is running fast. Give him and your mother my love, and tell them I am thinking with tremendous hope and certainty for *Mr Wilberforce, MP*, and believe it is going to be a triumph of the British stage. Good luck, Yours ever, Peter.'

A few days later, in Peru, Peter had died.

Looking back over twenty years, I felt moved by this fresh sign of a tender heart under the often rough manner. Through the years we fought some good fights side by side. We owe him so much, and there must be so much more that we do not know. I bid him farewell with words written of St George in the sixth century: 'A good man whose deeds are known only to God.'

16

Bishop Peter

I seldom ran into the Boss or saw him after Repton days. He left Repton and became a bishop, first of Chester then of London, ending up as Archbishop of Canterbury. I remember one afternoon, some years after the war, when I had occasion to visit Lambeth Palace to deliver a note. I was received by Mrs Fisher with typical warmth and hospitality. It was during a pleasant tea that the door burst open and there, in his purple cassock, stood the Boss. He glared across the room at me and then, despite not seeing each other for years, he took me in with his gimlet eyes and in a voice of thunder shouted, 'Thornhill! What are you doing here?' It was typical of his memory for faces and names.

Soon we were having a genial conversation, though I could not help noticing a certain sharpness in his comments when I told him something of *The Forgotten Factor* and how it was being received in many countries and languages. He shot in the comment, 'That doesn't necessarily mean it is a good play.' I could almost see a school report in his handwriting.

Once, some years later, at a meeting in America of the World Council of Churches, after an early Communion service, I ran into the Boss again. I remember vividly how with his old warmth and charm he took me by the arm and strolled with me up and down a lawn, asking questions about our work. He promised that day he would come to a performance of one of our plays, which we were showing during the conference. At the last moment he cried-off, for what reason I do not know. I remember feeling at the time that might be something of a tragedy.

And so it proved. The doors of Lambeth Palace had been open to us in Moral Re-Armament during the days of Archbishop Lang and Archbishop Temple. I recall a visit to Lang before the war and the warmth of his interest as he said to me, 'You in the Oxford Group are doing what all of us in the Church are meant to be doing—changing human lives.' And then he took me into his private chapel and gave me his personal blessing. Temple in his own way gave statesmanlike help and support. But then with Archbishop Fisher everything changed.

There were, and still are, all over the land many clergy who would say that new life had come into their ministry through their touch with the Oxford Group and MRA. There are those who, like myself, would perhaps never have been ordained had it not been for a personal awakening and a fresh sense of calling. My meeting with Buchman and my ordination in Southwark Cathedral happened the same year. To me, both events were two sides of the same coin. One was incomplete without the other. I had never felt any conflict or separation between the two. Of course there has always been opposition within the Church to a fresh outburst of the Spirit expressing itself in novel ways, with disturbingly startling results, from the earliest days of Christianity to the work of the Wesleys or the Booths. We should expect it, even welcome it. 'Alan needs persecution,' were words of Buchman that I cannot forget. 'The stones of persecution are so bracing,' he would add, and he certainly experienced them himself in full measure.

All the same, as we approached the turbulent sixties, opposition to MRA in parts of the Church took on a more planned and organized form. There were many in high places who were firm in their support. But in Lambeth itself and in some quarters of the Church Assembly the doors of fellowship shut with a clang. Some of the hostile voices were mocking and shrill. Others were oblique and subtle. Both could be hurtful in their tone and discouraging in their effect, especially on some who were finding fresh faith in many lands.

I did not fully realize it at the time, but I turned away from all this, sick at heart. I felt that my old headmaster whom I had respected and admired had, as it were, kicked me out of his presence. When Bunny Austin and I had written to him asking if he would receive us informally as Old Boys of the school and give us a chance to tell him about our work and what it had meant to our lives, we got a curt little note saying he did not have time to see us and that in any case it would be a waste. 'I am sure I should never succeed in convincing you, and you would not convince me. Neither of us would change our ideas. Perhaps we had better leave things as they are.'

Archbishop Garbett of York, who had ordained me, and whom I had revered as my Father in God, delivered a particularly harsh and, to me, uncalled-for attack.

All this was a painful brush-off and indeed, looking back, I still feel such hostility towards MRA was damaging, not least for the Church of England itself. We were heading just then into the era of 'God is dead', the diluting of standards and a marked falling away of faith and conviction. Our Church would have done well through all those years with the extra backbone and conviction and militancy that it needed so badly and that MRA was there to provide. We had much to give each other, much to learn from each other. We, like all Christians, needed one another.

Something happened in my own spirit. Of course I continued wherever I could in my work as priest. I celebrated Holy Communion or preached wherever I was asked. I performed many delightful weddings and christenings, many moving funeral and memorial services for friends and fellow-workers. I took innumerable Bible studies and devotional sessions with friends and colleagues. Never did I lose my sense of commitment as a priest of the Church of England. And yet, looking back now, I realize something hard had come into my soul.

My work in the theatre was opening up and growing rapidly. I found myself more and more involved in play-writing and production, in travel through the world with plays that carried, I hope, something of the stamp of the Holy Spirit. More and more I felt that the theatre was my parish, the stage my pulpit. I knew what it was to stand on a stage as a member of Equity, an actor in the West End of London on a Saturday night, and stand in a pulpit in London on a Sunday morning, and find myself saying in rather different words the same thing on both occasions. This I believed was all part of God's plan and I do not regret it.

But the gap between our work and Lambeth was never bridged in Fisher's day and under his successor, my old study-mate Michael Ramsay, there was, on the whole, a discreet and guarded silence. It was not until Archbishop Coggan that things began to change again. Once more, old doors were opened; once more, there was communication and on several occasions Donald Coggan gave to our work and to me personally a generous and public support. He came with Mrs Coggan to my musical play about John Wesley, *Ride! Ride!* and spoke publicly about it. Stuart Blanch, then Archbishop of York, was and is a friend, and more than a friend.

New links in the Church are strengthening all the time and unite us as fellow-workers for Christ, and what applies to the Church of England applies also to the Roman Catholics and to the Free Churches.

During the time when I felt furthest from Lambeth I had the joy of visiting occasionally my cousin Derek Warlock, then personal secretary and assistant to a series of Cardinal Archbishops in Westminster, and now Archbishop of Liverpool. He was as open as Fisher was closed. He told me of his personal passion for the theatre. He also said that there had been a danger of it becoming an idol in his life and he had felt called by God to give up going to the theatre altogether. But he was eager to know all that we were doing at the Westminster. 'We pass your theatre constantly,' he said laughingly. 'We always count the coaches outside and say to ourselves, "This looks like a House Full today", or perhaps, "They're rather thin on the ground this afternoon".' At all times, in Portsmouth or in Liverpool, though we have seen each other seldom, he has held out a warmth of friendship that is more than cousinly.

Now, at Westminster Cathedral there is the closest possible co-operation and teamwork in the creation of Christian theatre. The Methodist Church played an essential part in spreading the musical, *Ride! Ride!* through the leading theatres of the North and the Midlands. From this beginning an ecumenical movement of Christian theatre is taking root and spreading; and in it MRA and the Westminster Theatre have been pioneers.

But apart from all this, something more precious and personal has come into my life during the last years. Our home in Charles Street, London, where my wife and I lived for many years as host to a community of MRA full-time workers, came to an end when leases expired. Just at the time when Barbara and I needed a home of our own, the house in Rotherfield, where my sister and I had been brought up as children, was left to both of us.

Gradually my work as a priest increased as the needs of various parishes nearby called for my services. I filled in at various churches during a period of interregnum. I was able, under a good and scholarly rector, Peter Curgenven, in Rotherfield to take a full part in the life of the parish church where my father had been rector. It was there that our daughter was married.

Several years ago in the small neighbouring hamlet of Mark Cross, the vicar died suddenly on holiday. There is a church in the heart of the village. It is simple and unpretentious, but with an air of exceptional warmth and holiness. They were suddenly without a parson and as things had lately developed in the church, it looked as if Mark Cross might not have a parson of its own again and the parish might be bereft. The vicarage close to the church was sold. I found myself stepping in occasionally to help them. I enjoyed the simple services in that church, occasionally though the congregations were very small.

We got to know one another. So there grew up, with none of the regular formalities, a kind of private arrangement between Mark Cross Parish and myself. 'I am much too old,' I told them, 'to be concerned any more with money or buildings or committees or organizations. What I would love to do is to be responsible for all the services, and then to knock on doors and get to know and care for as many people in the parish as I possibly can.'

And so the arrangement began to work. I had no title, no official licence. But I was experiencing the joy once again of looking after a parish, of taking regular services in one place, of the sense of a Christian family, of growing trust and affection between us.

As I began in those far-off days in Peckham knocking on doors, so now in the Sussex countryside I knock still and am welcomed and received with warmth, and discover spiritual adventures on every side.

All this has been made possible and enriched by our Bishop Suffragan of Lewes, Bishop Peter. Others can write of him better than I. He and his twin brother are the founders of an Anglican religious order, The Community of the Glorious Ascension. They are both monks and both bishops. Instead of the Bishop's palace of old days, Bishop Peter began his episcopate in a two-up, two-down cottage called Polecat Cottage, christened Polecat Priory. For the last twenty years he has slept on an old horse-hair mattress on the bare floor. He is up soon after four in the morning for his private devotions, followed by morning offices and meditations with his brothers in his tiny chapel, or perhaps in winter in the ice-cold village church. Later he might be receiving his clergy and official visitors to share a meal of bread and cheese, sitting perhaps on the floor.

I first met Bishop Peter at a confirmation service in another church. It so happened he had 'flu and, I am pretty sure, with it a raging temperature. Never shall I forget, however, the human touches with which every candidate as well as every clergyman or visitor was received.

He went out of his way early-on to come specially to our little Mark Cross church for a confirmation. In fact, he did not come just once, he came twice. 'I hate this idea,' he said, 'of tapping on the head people I have never met and whom I do not know. Let me come a few days in advance and meet your candidates and get to know them as people before the glorious day of their confirmation.'

Several of my first group of candidates, as I mentioned

earlier, were young would-be dancers, hoping to get into the profession. I can see Bishop Peter now, with young people clustered at his feet, talking, laughing, each utterly at home with one another while he, through all the fun and the fellowship, put before them the vision of a life dedicated to Christ.

I learnt more and more of what he does with young people. He read in his local paper of a boy, worried and frustrated by a broken home and the pressure of examinations, who had set a part of his school on fire. He was up for trial in the courts at Lewes, and because of crowded accommodation was in danger of being committed to a regular jail. Bishop Peter rushed to the court, won a hearing from the judge and from the police and offered to take on the young man in his community and be responsible in law as well as in fact for his future. Now, years later, that young man, a regular Catholic worshipper with a steady job and a fair future, considers a new dedication of his whole life to Christ. He is only one of a growing number of men and women taking up the challenge of being part of a Christian community, of a life of rigorous spiritual discipline and training in the service of Christ and the Church.

I do not see Bishop Peter very often but he has already had a very great influence on my life. The shortest of conversations with him leaves you with something to ponder. 'If you want to know about Christianity,' he would say, 'don't read theology, read Shakespeare's tragedies and the great Russian novelists. Above all, read George Herbert and the metaphysical poets.'

Once, when he was talking to a crowded meeting of mostly non-church-goers, he said something like this: 'When you think of Christianity, don't think of religion, don't even think of the church. Think of chips sizzling and bubbling in a frying pan.'

In a recent interview with Graham Turner, reported in the *Daily Telegraph*, he describes vividly our condition and longing in the Western world. 'Everything has gone stale for us,' he said. 'We have dead tastebuds. We are bored with anything that does not stimulate us more and more. Our only vision is a vision of more. I have a sense that the whole of Western Europe is struggling to slough off its old skin like a snake, and grow a new one. We are desperately longing for a new way, a new inspiration, a new vision.' He does not share in the general pessimism that is often expressed both about and within the Church of England. In his part of the diocese he is finding many fresh candidates for ordination, and is receiving into the Church many from other faiths as well as from no faith at all.

For the first time in years I have my own bishop. I would not make any serious move in my life without consulting him, and he would never fail to have the time to listen. The demands on his time are killing. I sometimes fear for his health and strength. There are times when his kindness may possibly cloud his better judgment. Yet still he will insist, 'I want to come to you at Mark Cross.' 'No,' I will say, 'we have only a few candidates for confirmation this year. We must go to one of the bigger parishes and spare you an extra visit.'

'I would come to Mark Cross,' he once said, 'if you only had one candidate.'

When I had the joy of celebrating my fifty years of ordination, Bishop Peter came specially to the church. We had an extra confirmation service and it was on that occasion that Barbara, my wife, the best Christian helper and companion imaginable, but still a loyal American Presbyterian, decided she would like to be confirmed. My newly-wed son-in-law, Rob Corcoran, thought he would follow suit, and his twin sister Anne made a third. Bishop Peter insisted on my celebrating Holy Communion that evening, and he served and assisted me. It was a day never to be forgotten.

Lately, Barbara and I asked to visit Bishop Peter once again. He has moved with his community into slightly more spacious quarters, nestled under the South Downs. He received us with leisure and humour.

I realize the danger of clinging too long to a job that I love but for which perhaps I am growing too old. There's something to be said for Studert Kennedy's remark, 'Death, that great church worker'. I wanted Peter's assurance that in my job at Mark Cross I am not standing in the way of someone younger who could do more.

'Please tell me,' I said, 'have you got someone waiting in the wings who would step in to Mark Cross if I were to bow out from the stage?'

'Alan,' said Bishop Peter with a twinkle, 'if the Archbishop of Canterbury was waiting in the wings at Mark Cross, I would say to you, "Please stay where you are. Stay as long as ever you can".'

I think it was then I realized that somewhere deep in my spirit a healing had taken place. It came about not by discussion but by fellowship with Jesus Christ at a deep level.

There are so many experiences for which to thank God. Eight o'clock Holy Communion in our little village church: a group of faithful worshippers for whom, week by week, this adds up to the most important element in their lives; the young dancers who get up early on the one rest-day of the week and walk to the church to receive the Sacrament, or perhaps a simple blessing. 'It's the peace and quiet that I like,' said one. 'It's a kind of hush with God.' Fresh outbreaks of the Spirit, often in the most unlikely places and ways; miracles known and unknown, proclaimed or quietly treasured, with repercussions in other countries or in the house next door, or the people just down the road. Sometimes, if I despair of myself or of some of the antics going on in the good old C of E, I remember the saying of an old verger who had listened to thousands of university sermons, 'Somehow I still do believe that there do be a God'.

Bishop Peter is a man of God who feels more deeply than I do the heavy weight of bureaucracy and busy-ness in the Church, who has to fight every day against all the pressures that would organize, formalize and kill the fresh promptings of the Spirit, and yet with it all can say, 'I weep as I think of that brink of destruction where all of us stand together. And at the same time I laugh with endless joy at the matchless wonders of a loving God.'

Peter has given me that official Licence! As I knelt before

him to receive it I thanked God for the friendship that came
with it.

17

The Eternal Friendship

I come finally to the realization that for me every friendship has become a three-cornered affair. Christ is the unseen Friend in every human relationship. Often not mentioned, sometimes not recognized, he is none the less there. As in Elgar's Variations there is an extra hidden melody, the Enigma, so in all the infinite variations on the theme there is the extra melody of Christ's own friendship—sometimes as enigma, but more often a living experience. It was said of the early Franciscans that every encounter on the dusty road was a spiritual adventure. In the same way Mother Teresa sees in every living person some embodiment of Christ. Of one particularly wretched, humanly revolting person, she said, 'Christ was there in very distressing disguise.'

Christ's friendship starts from the very first moment of our lives. It may be experienced and recognized very early. One morning Barbara and I were sitting up in bed, reading our Bibles, and trying to have a time of prayer and meditation, made somewhat difficult by a strenuous and rumbustious three-year-old. I suddenly said, 'Now we are going to be quiet and ask Jesus if he will speak to us.' We were quiet for quite a long time and then I said to Susan, 'Did Jesus say anything to you?' Without a moment's hesitation she replied, 'He said "Hallo".' I remember thinking at the time that if it were true that, through Jesus, the Creator of the universe, the Lord of time and space, the Architect of the atom, the Governor of the galaxies, could yet say 'Hallo' to a three-year-old, then nothing in this life, nothing in this vast universe, could ever be the same again.

That personal relationship with God, which goes back to the days when God called Abraham his friend, or Moses talked with God as a man talks with his friend, goes on to the very end of life. We can never drift so far, or fall so low, or betray so utterly, that we escape from the eternal friendship.

For me one of the most moving moments in the Gospels is in St Matthew when, in the garden of Gethsemane, Judas comes forward to betray his Master with a kiss and Jesus says to him, 'What are you doing here, friend?' I think it is the only recorded occasion in which Jesus directly addressed an individual as 'friend'.

Jesus' friendship for Judas must have gone on even beyond his betrayal. Judas might have found the way back as Peter did, through tears and forgiveness, but he went and hanged himself. Yet even after that, was Jesus making a last bid to bring him home? We repeat in the Creed that Jesus 'descended into hell.' Many interpretations have been given to this stark statement. I harbour the thought that Jesus went even to the gates of hell to make one last bid to win back Judas, this friend.

I am indebted to an Australian poet, a Rhodes scholar, and a friend of mine from Oxford days, Michael Thwaites, for introducing me to a remarkable later poem by A E Housman, entitled *Hell Gate*. It is all the more interesting because it seems so much in contrast to the pessimism of much of Housman's haunting poetry.

Hell Gate tells the story of a man being conducted across a 'sad uncoloured plain' towards the great ramparts of hell. As they get nearer to the fatal spot, he sees a tiny light passing back and forth against the towering walls. His conductor explains that the citizens of hell take turns at sentry-go. They are still on fire with hell's hatreds, and they have a kind of glow as they keep their watch, marching to and fro. It is only when the traveller arrives at the gates that he looks at the sentry.

> Then the sentry turned his head,
> Looked and knew me and was Ned.

213

There at the gates of hell stood an old friend and their friendship was strong enough to enable them both to escape. Something stirred in hell's sentry, and he dared to raise his weapon against his own masters; and soon we discover the two figures, side by side, taking the road back to life and hope:

> Silent, nothing found to say,
> We began the backward way.
> Midmost of the homeward track
> Once we listened and looked back,
> But the City, dusk and mute
> Slept, and there was no pursuit.

Christ offers us a friendship, starting from our beginning, and reaching even to the gate of hell. It is in one sense a natural, easy, enjoyable friendship. Christ was a friend of publicans and sinners. I often think that what angered the Pharisees more than anything else was not that Jesus went to the publicans and sinners to save their souls or to remove them from sin, but that he seemed to enjoy them. He felt at home at their dinner tables. He must have laughed and swopped stories and relished the chatter and the fun round Matthew's supper table. And if a woman of the streets found her way in to embarrass good people by showing her love for Christ, he could accept it naturally, not feeling ill at ease or resistant, but seeing down to the love and potentiality that lay in the heart of one of his choicest followers. He stopped under a tree to chat with a grimy little business man, and chose to spend the night at his house rather than in that of some responsible clergyman or churchwarden. There must have been times when he felt more at home in the 'pub' than in the prayer meeting, just because there was more reality, more genuine humanity in the one than in the other.

I sensed Christ's friendship towards me first as a small child with my mother. Nobody can over-estimate a childhood experience of Christ's friendship learnt from parents. I cannot go as far as Bishop Peter, who spoke on the radio recently about 'an enormous awareness of God' which he'd had from his early childhood. But I can see myself still, at not more than three or four years old, shouting with glee the words of the song 'Trust and obey, for there's no "yother" way, to be happy with Jesus, than to trust and obey.' I believed it and understood a little of what it meant.

Then, as I grew to manhood, the whole thing became real again in a new way after living in the Holy Land, which was then under British rule and, on the surface, a peaceful spot. There was scarcely a soldier in the whole land, just a handful of military police with only a baton or truncheon under their arms. I felt free to come and go where I pleased. Many a long day I spent walking, or riding a donkey, roaming the countryside round Jerusalem, a Bible in one pocket and George Adam Smith's *Historical Geography of the Holy Land* in the other.

Some people find a pilgrimage to the Holy Land a disillusionment. I remember B H Streeter saying to me once, 'I don't think my faith is robust enough to go to Jerusalem. It was hopeless at the time of Christ and it has degenerated ever since.' I can only say I could love it all. Somehow I felt closer to Christ because I was jostled and pushed by crowds, bemused with the noise of bargainers, smelling the smells that he must have smelled ... moved by human need and tragedy, the blind and the lame, the flies all over the faces of the little children, squeezed into the gutters of narrow streets by the camels and donkeys; mingling with the travellers from far countries, the merchants seeking goodly pearls; beset by the rivalry, the religious hypocrisy, the money changers offering their wares in the Church of the Holy Sepulchre. It was all his world. He knew it, and in it I began to know him too.

But he was not yet my friend. I returned from Palestine deeply disillusioned—not with Christ but with my own lack of faith, of anything relevant to deal with the troubled souls and the rising passions of the Middle East. It was at Oxford, in St Mary's Church, quite suddenly and simply, that I let Jesus become not just a friend, but my friend I had no thought at that time that I was a miserable sinner, or that I needed rescuing from Hell Gate or the Slough of Despond.

It was just the amazing discovery that Jesus was offering me everything and above all himself, his friendship for life.

The friendship with Christ that has followed, growing over the years, is almost impossible to describe with all its infinite wonder, humour, unexpectedness, paradox, mystery, its shame and its pain. It can only be lived. As with the first disciples, to begin with it was almost all sheer, inexpressible joy, every day an adventure, a new discovery. A familiar Bible verse that I had known for years suddenly lit up as though it were written brand new especially for me; there was the amazing realization that you might be able to pass on to someone else the Bread of Life that was feeding you; that miracles small or large, were as real today as in the New Testament; of walking on the water and finding that his arm did not let you down.

As with other friendships, friendship with Christ is an infinite process of discovery. For me the most precious hour of the day is the first hour of the morning. Whether it is in the cold and darkness of the winter when, huddled in a blanket, fortified by a cup of hot coffee, you face a new day; or whether amid the glory of the spring you awake to the dawn chorus of birds, and a burst of new life in nature sets your mind and senses soaring; whether you are on your knees lost in the wonder of worship, or with the Bible open to turn you back to God; whether you are racked with a sense of guilt, or kneeling at the altar to receive the Holy Sacrament, or sitting with paper and pen to note down those quiet, urgent, often elusive thoughts that the Holy Spirit gives to any honest listener; every day can begin with a fresh discovery of friendship with Christ. Lose that precious morning hour and you may have lost the day. Seize it, before phone calls and letters, newspapers and engagements come crowding in, and life that day may have a special meaning, and a genuine sense of adventure.

Lately I have been keeping a diary entitled *Discoveries*. Almost every day there is something to record; a fresh look at nature or the world, some new insight or encounter with a person, something arresting in a book or conversation, even a really good joke, an illumination pleasant or unpleasant about oneself, a spark of inspiration, a new vision of God. Every day can reveal something, if only that you are asleep, half-dead or centred on your own self. Sometimes I wake with the name of a person beating on my brain. Sure enough I may discover that person is in special need, or on the threshold of something to give. Often Christ is there with a familiar, 'Fear not. Go in peace.' Sometimes he wakes me with thunder, a stern warning or a searching summons to rise and do his bidding.

As you listen the shadow of a cross falls across the sunlit path. You encounter a different kind of friend; not just the lovable all-giving Jesus, but the revolutionary Christ, pledged to go on to the end of the line, to bring a dying world back to its senses and its true destiny. In the end friendship means identifying myself with my friend's life. Even at twelve years old Jesus knew that he 'must be about his Father's business.'

Well, if it is his business then I, as his friend, must make it my business too. There is no longer any room for an easy, in-and-out selfish companionship. It means total commitment. As he has given his life to me, now I must give my life to him. No holds barred, no private reservations, no easy options, no room for the smallest crumb of personal self-satisfaction, or the tiniest corner of a private life of my own, but everything given for ever. 'Present yourself each day,' Peter Howard would say, 'before a blazing Christ.' That for me was a new definition of friendship. I saw the shame of moral pacifism, the cowardice of compromise and the terrible cost of sin in the midst of a world torn by war, forever in the grip of the eternal struggle between the sovereignty of God and man's arrogant, rebellious will. This can result in personal decisions that are agonizingly uncomfortable at the time and far-reaching in their results. Every day I use a prayer that was taught me by Bernard Miles, the actor-manager: 'O God, please help me to help you today.'

But in the end our friendship with Christ has nothing to do with results, or activity, or what may come out of it in the way of a bonus for ourselves or for others. Our friendship with Christ exists just for its own sake, for the infinite joy of being with him, of being allowed to be part of his love for the world. That is the only motive for Christian work. He actually trusts us to be his hands, his feet, his mouth, part of his plan. Jesus chose twelve not to do this or that, but just so they might be with him.

I was ill lately, with many hours of sleeplessness at night. I made a discovery. These hours can be precious and privileged. I used them to have sing-songs in the silence of my own heart, repeating familiar hymns and poems and psalms, I literally looked forward to those times alone with him, undisturbed, not too distracted by pain.

> Yea, in the night, my soul, my daughter,
> Cry – clinging Heaven by the hems,
> And lo! Christ walking on the water
> Not of Gennesareth, but Thames!

It was in one of these nights that Jesus himself appeared to me, and spoke to me as his friend. I had at that time, quite wrongly, a sense that there was not very much more life left for me in this world. I wanted to pray to him and ask for healing. And then he said, 'Why do you want healing? You have lived well over your span of seventy years. Are you not ready for the next step?' 'Yes, I am ready.' And then very clearly he said, 'You are ready but I want you to do various things first. There are more lessons to learn, discoveries to be made, people who need you.'

And then he made his promise. 'You will have time to finish all that I have in mind for you—whether it be six days, six weeks, six months, or even six years. You will be given time and strength and the help of many. So now roll over and go to sleep. Rest in the certain knowledge that you are my friend.'